BBAC

DEATH

HARMONY
New York

DEATH

Only for Those Who
Shall Die—a Yogi's Guide to
Living, Dying, and Beyond

SADHGURU

Harmony Books
An imprint of Random House
A division of Penguin Random House LLC
1745 Broadway, New York, NY 10019
HarmonyBooks.com | RandomHouseBooks.com
penguinrandomhouse.com

Copyright © 2025 by Sadhguru

Penguin Random House values and supports copyright. Copyright fuels creativity, encourages diverse voices, promotes free speech, and creates a vibrant culture. Thank you for buying an authorized edition of this book and for complying with copyright laws by not reproducing, scanning, or distributing any part of it in any form without permission. You are supporting writers and allowing Penguin Random House to continue to publish books for every reader. Please note that no part of this book may be used or reproduced in any manner for the purpose of training artificial intelligence technologies or systems.

All rights reserved.

Harmony Books is a registered trademark, and the Circle colophon is a trademark of Penguin Random House LLC.

ISBN 978-0-593-79796-9
Ebook ISBN 978-0-593-79797-6

Printed in the United States of America on acid-free paper

2 4 6 8 9 7 5 3 1

First Edition

Book design by Debbie Glasserman

BOOK TEAM: Production editor: Kelly Chian, Cassie Gitkin • Managing editor: Allison Fox • Production manager: Kevin Garcia • Copy editor: Madeline Hopkins • Proofreaders: Deborah Bader, Jane Hardick, Russell Powers, Jinah Yoon, Megha Jain

CONTENTS

Foreword Death Blow vii

PART I: LIFE AND DEATH IN ONE BREATH

CHAPTER 1 What Is Death? 3

CHAPTER 2 The Process of Death 22

CHAPTER 3 The Quality of Death 56

CHAPTER 4 Can Death Be Hacked? 90

CHAPTER 5 Mahasamadhi 113

PART II: THE GRACEFULNESS OF DEATH

CHAPTER 6 Preparing for a Good Death 135

CHAPTER 7 Assistance for the Dying 180

CHAPTER 8 Assistance for the Disembodied 215

CHAPTER 9 Of Grief and Mourning 253

PART III: LIFE AFTER DEATH

CHAPTER 10 The Life of a Ghost 283

CHAPTER 11 The Riddle of Reincarnation 309

CHAPTER 12 Final Round 352

Glossary 363

About the Author 371

FOREWORD

DEATH BLOW

We all want to live well and, when it is time, die well too. This is the essence of most human aspirations. Within this, much, if not most, of human endeavor is dedicated to living well, and the outcome reflects it. Humans have achieved much in terms of living well. We have managed to acquire more comfort and convenience than any previous generation. However, when it comes to dying well, it cannot be said that we die better than our ancestors in any way. Many factors explain why humans have been successful at living better but not dying better—the most significant of them being the disparity between the way we treat life and death in our societies.

Everywhere in the world, life is mostly considered a success that is to be sung about and celebrated, but death is considered a failure that is to be shunned and mourned. Oddly enough, in the construed dichotomy of life and death, it is "life" that is a four-letter word, not "death." Yet, in the world, it is death that gets the bad press. The mere utterance of the word "death" can hush dinner conversations. Children are taught never to utter the word at home lest the God of death might feel invited and choose to visit. On the other hand, the adults are on a quest to invent overly sanitized euphemisms that try to mask the bluntness of the event with vanity.

It is said that humans do not know much about death because they do not know much about life in the first place. Death is a brief occurrence at the end of a long life. But even after having lived a full lifetime, people are clueless regarding simple questions about life—like, where did we come from and where are we going. So confusion about death is understandable. However, it must be acknowledged that in recent times, humankind has indeed traveled far from its simplistic understanding that "Life is God's gift and death is His wrath."

Traditionally, it was only religion that people looked to for the unraveling of this mystery. Adjudication of matters related to death and dying was mostly in the hands of shamans and priests of various kinds. It's only in the past couple hundred years, when a slew of medical discoveries began making a considerable impact upon health and mortality on a global scale, that people began turning to modern science for answers on death and dying as well. The success of modern science in dealing with matters of death and dying can be seen in the phenomenal improvement in just two of the key global health parameters—life expectancy and infant mortality. No better testimony to the success of modern medicine is needed than the burgeoning global population of more than eight billion people on the planet. With this development, modern medicine has firmly dislodged everything else as the final adjudicator of all matters of life and death.

Modern science, characterized by objectivity and universality, has now enabled people to look at death in ways that were not possible before. However, the blazing trail left behind by modern science is not without its blind spots, dangers, and destruction. One major outcome of death being handled by modern science is what has come to be called the "medicalization" of death. Death, especially in the more advanced countries, is no longer looked at as a natural phenomenon but as a medical event, with even ordinary life events and conditions being treated as risks and diseases. Death being preceded by excessive and often aggressive medical interventions has become the new norm.

Moreover, humans have never been comfortable with their mortal nature. So the success of medical science has only breathed fresh life into the historic quest for immortality. Riding on the shoulders of modern science, people have now begun to speculate whether deathlessness is not in fact the norm and death an aberration. It has emboldened people to wonder if death is not just one more disease that needs to be conquered—something that our super sleuths in white coats will surely do within our lifetime. Our growing capability to interfere with the fundamental life process has undoubtedly increased our propensity to overdo it.

One reason why scientists appear akin to the six blind men studying an elephant—getting parts right while missing the whole—is their keyhole vision of life. Death—just as life—can be understood as having three components. There is a biological part, a psychological part, and a metaphysical part that together cause the biology and the psychology to happen. In recent times, our understanding of the biology of death has greatly increased. Today, we have a much better understanding of the point where, biologically, life ends and death begins. In terms of psychology too, much progress has been made. What makes a person? Is it nature or nurture? What is the role of each? These aspects too are much better understood. But the more profound questions of why death or life happens, and how, are still largely unanswered.

Unfortunately, today's science has access to the being only from the point where the body begins to the point where it ends. Science does not even acknowledge the possibility that something could precede life or succeed death. The hypothesis that life is just a chance occurrence in this vast Universe of infinite permutations and combinations of factors is riddled with many holes. The simple fact that an unseen force abruptly turns on the biology for a period of time, and then turns it off equally abruptly, begs a deeper investigation even by the standards of science. Although science stops where the body drops, the religions of the world are full of speculation as to what happens after that, leaving one lost somewhere in the no-man's-land in between. It is in such times that the presence of a yogi or a mystic like Sadhguru—who draws primarily from an inner experience rather than tradition or scriptures or academic learning—becomes invaluable.

Sadhguru is a modern mystic and a yogi who has touched and transformed the lives of millions of people around the world with his unique insight into life and the tools of self-transformation. One afternoon, almost four decades ago, Sadhguru, then a young man at his "cocky best," had a deep spiritual experience that changed his worldview and life entirely. "Suddenly, what I had thought all my life was me was all around—my inside had become the outside. I did not know which was me and which was not me." It also made him deeply ecstatic. Over the next few months, the experience became more stabilized and a living reality. This spiritual realization also brought back a flood of memories of his past lives and a deep understanding of the process of life and death. This experience inspired Sadhguru to set out with a plan to teach the whole world to live as joyfully and ecstatically as he does.

Over the past four decades, this plan has turned into a global movement aimed at self-transformation. But looking back it is unclear at what point Sadhguru, who has long been considered a foremost authority on joyful living, began to be regarded as an authority on death as well. Was it when he began recounting clearly his past lives? Or was it twenty-five years ago, when he articulated for the first time the purpose of his current life—to consecrate the Dhyanalinga, the dream of many accomplished yogis, which was entrusted to him by his Guru three lifetimes ago? Or was it when several people around him were able to spontaneously recollect their associations with him in their past lives? It is not very clear when, but soon people began to turn to Sadhguru on matters of death and dying as well.

However, Sadhguru has not always been the most communicative about death. In fact, one would think he was being evasive. Too many people who thought they could extract the deepest secrets of life through a single innocuous question—"What happens after death, Sadhguru?"—have been disappointed. To their dismay, they were usually teased by responses like, "Some things are known only by experience!" Others who wanted to know how to communicate with the dead were told to worry about communicating with the living first. People who asked about the existence of souls were told they had two of them—one under each foot. Yet all his teachings and practices have not been without a tinge, or more, of death.

Sadhguru is probably the only person on the planet who would, in a deadpan tone, talk about death to a hall full of people first thing in the morning during certain residential programs. He would then lead them through a guided meditation on experiencing death firsthand. He is probably the only one who would teach the "Way of Effortless Living" by initiating people into a deathlike experience of meditation, to be practiced twice a day. He is the ambitious person who sets out to teach everyone in the world the ways to live joyously but, on finding that he is falling short, pragmatically embarks on teaching them methods to die peacefully at least. He is also the person who assures people, "If you have been initiated by me, or have made the mistake of sitting in front of me totally, even for one moment, there is no rebirth for you." And the list goes on.

Once when we were filming Sadhguru for a DVD, somebody asked him, "Why is it that in most Eastern traditions a very high level of sanctity is accorded to the moment of death? Why is it that the moment of death is granted a sort of quasi-spiritual status?" Speaking outside his usual script of deterrence, Sadhguru said that if the moment of death is handled properly—if there is proper preparation, proper guidance, and perhaps some outside help as well—then, in spiritual terms, even that which probably did not happen in life could happen in death. This was a revelation to me. I had never heard anyone speak of death as a spiritual possibility.

Some discussion followed this, but since it was mostly outside the scope of the video being filmed, Sadhguru did not elaborate further. I was very intrigued. Did Sadhguru just say that there is a big spiritual possibility hiding in plain sight in that much-feared, much-abhorred aspect of life—death? Is there a huge free ride waiting to be taken at the moment of death, and we're oblivious to it? If so, why haven't we heard of this before? Why is it not being spoken about more? Why are we not alerting people to it? Could Sadhguru offer the necessary guidance for the preparation, could he give the required "help"? Of course, he could. But would he? Could he be coaxed into opening another front in his engagement with the world? Sadhguru was certainly willing, but the task of compiling this book was not as easy as I had imagined. I had assumed it would be a simple task because, after all, if one knew something, how difficult would articulating it be? Well, that turned out to be somewhat naïve on my part, because explanations can only traverse from the known to the unknown, and in this case the gap turned out to be rather formidable.

The grand phenomenon of life cannot be confined to the period between birth and death, as seen by modern science. It goes back all the way to the beginning of Creation and extends all the way to wherever the Creation is heading. Hence, any understanding of death that does not take this fact into account is bound to be incomplete and incorrect. In the first part of the book, "Life and Death in One Breath," Sadhguru describes the essential mechanism of life and death using several approaches. He describes the Yogic understanding and further simplifies this using the example of the familiar soap bubble. Taking the discourse beyond the usual boundaries, Sadhguru traces the origins of life from the beginning of Creation to the cycle of birth and death that we all undergo. He also talks about the different kinds of deaths and what choices we have in death. He concludes the first part by describing the highest form of death—the dissolution of the Self—which is the goal of all spiritual seekers.

In addition to explaining the underlying mechanics of birth and death, one of the objectives of the book is also to help one achieve a "good" death. In the second part of the book, "The Gracefulness of Death," Sadhguru clarifies what a "good" death is and what preparations we can make for it. Moreover, when a person is dying, he is in the most vulnerable situation, unable to help himself. Sadhguru explains what assistance one can provide in such situations and the difference that can make for the dying person. He talks about how the person's journey after death could be assisted by doing some simple acts. He also shares some precious insights into grief and how we can deal with it in a meaningful manner.

The afterlife is not strictly a part of the process of death and dying, but a by-product of it. In the third part of the book, "Life after Death," Sadhguru offers us insights into this much misunderstood and maligned aspect of life. Here, Sadhguru talks about ghosts and spirits, their origins and their lives, what they can and cannot do to us, and how we can protect ourselves. He also talks about the process of reincarnation, what passes on from one birth to another and what is lost. He also examines whether our previous lives are of any relevance to our present lives at all. In this context,

Sadhguru talks about his own past lives and answers the question people frequently ask him: Will he be coming back?

The book is in no way complete in presenting all that we seek to know about death and dying. Nor is it the sum total of all that Sadhguru has to offer. But we hope it will be an active force to dispel the gamut of misconceptions about death in the world. The most significant aspect of the book, however, is how the tools offered by Sadhguru and his presence in our midst can help us make our own deaths more graceful and spiritually significant. In all the ensuing chatter about death and dying, it is hoped that this primary purpose of the book is not lost on the reader.

SWAMI NISARGA

PART I

LIFE AND DEATH IN ONE BREATH

DEATH

Life and death live in me at once
Never held one above the other
When one stands far, life I offer
In closeness, only death I deal
In death of the limited
Will the deathless be
How to tell the fools
Of my taintless evil.

CHAPTER 1

What Is Death?

> Death is the most fundamental question. Yet, people can ignore it, avoid it, and just live on in their ignorance simply because all kinds of idiotic stories have been spread in the world in the name of religion.

DEATH: THE MOST FUNDAMENTAL QUESTION

Do you know you will die one day? Oh, I bless you with a long life, but anyway, you will die one day. We cannot be sure about other things in your life. We don't know if you will get married or not, or if you will get a job or not, if you will be successful or not, but this one thing is guaranteed in your life: You will go straight to your grave! One of the biggest human follies is to engage with death in the third person, as though it is an abstract event that happens to other people, not us. Do you know that about one hundred and sixty thousand people who were alive in the world yesterday are not there today? Each second, two people die in the world. And one day, it is going to happen to you and me too. It does not take enormous research or intelligence or even education to know this. This knowledge is built into every human being. Yet, we think we have an unlimited lease on life. This situation is best expressed in the Hindu epic Mahabharata.

The five Pandava princes, who are the protagonists, are lost in the forest. Severely starved and parched, they scour the nearby hills for water and food. They spot a lake, and as they try to drink from it, they are confronted by a *yaksha* (a celestial being) in the form of a white crane who insists they answer his questions first. Refusing to be stopped by a mere bird, one by one they try to drink from the lake and drop dead. Only Yudhishthira, the eldest of them, is left. Always the humble and righteous one, Yudhishthira ignores his thirst and engages with the yaksha, who fires a volley of questions about life at him. One of those questions being, "What is the biggest wonder of life?" Without hesitation, Yudhishthira famously answers, "Hundreds and thousands of living beings meet death at every moment, yet the foolish man thinks himself deathless and does not prepare for death. This is the biggest wonder of life." The yaksha is pleased with this answer, so he allows him to drink from the lake and also restores the lives of his dead brothers. This happened five thousand years ago, but the human psyche regarding death has changed very little since then.

Death is a very fundamental question. Actually, death is closer to us than the statistics we read about it. Each moment, death is happening in us at the organ and cellular levels. This is how, with just one look at your insides, your doctor knows how old you are. In fact, death began in us even before we were born. Only if you are ignorant and unaware does it seem like death will come to you someday later. If you are aware, you will see that both life and death are happening every moment. If you breathe just a little more consciously, you will notice that with every inhalation there is life, with every exhalation there is death. Upon birth, the first thing that a child does is inhale, take in a gasp of air. And the last thing that you will do in your life is an exhalation. You exhale now, and if you do not take the next inhalation, you will be dead. If you do not get this, just do an exhalation, hold your nose, and do not do the next inhalation. Within a few moments, every cell in your body will start screaming for life. Life and death are happening all the time. They exist together, inseparably, in the same breath. This relationship goes even beyond the breath. Breath is only a supporting actor; the real process is that of the life energy, or *prana,* that controls physical existence. With certain mastery over prana, one can exist beyond breath for substantial amounts of time. Breath is a bit more immediate in its requirement, but in the same category as food and water.

Death is such a fundamental concept, because if one small thing happens, you can be gone tomorrow morning. Forget about tomorrow morning—one small thing now and you could be off the next moment. If you were like any other creature, maybe you would be unable to think about all this, but once one is endowed with human intelligence, how can you just ignore such a significant aspect of your life? How can you avoid it and live on as if you were going to be here forever? How is it that after living here for millions of years, human beings still don't know a damn thing about death? Well, they know nothing about life either. You know all about the trappings of life, but what do you know about life as such?

Fundamentally, this situation has come about because you have lost perspective as to who you are in this Universe. If this solar system, in which we are, evaporates tomorrow morning, no one will even notice it in this Cosmos. It is that small, just a speck. In this speck of a solar system, Planet Earth is a micro speck. In that micro speck, the city you live in is a super-micro speck. In that, you are a big man. This is a serious problem. When you have completely lost perspective as to who you are, how do you think you will grasp anything about the nature of life or death?

One reason people can ignore death and continue to live on in their ignorance is simply that society and the religions of the world have spread all kinds of idiotic stories about life and death. They created some silly, childish explanations for everything. "How was I born?" "The stork brought you." "Where am I going to go?" "To heaven." This explanation is very simple but absurd. At least they could have chosen a more efficient mode of transport than a stork. Storks migrate only in a particular season, so all the children should have been born in that season alone, not during other times! Moreover, if people are so sure that they are going to heaven after they die, I ask them, "Why are you delaying your departure, then? Why not go right now?" All these silly stories have snuffed out the basic human curiosity about life and death. Otherwise, sheer curiosity—if not the pain and suffering of life—would have strongly propelled many people to seek answers to this fundamental question.

Mortal Nature

People always think that reminding themselves of God will make them spiritual. Not at all. If you keep thinking of or believing in God, you will not do your job properly, but you think you will produce good results. You will not study for your exam and yet think you will be first in class because of your prayer. Such people become more brazen than others about life because now they have God's support. Always, people who believed that God is with them have done the most violent things on the planet. "God is with me" gives you a new confidence, which is very dangerous. If you think of God this way, you will not become spiritual—you could actually become very brazen and stupid.

Once it happened: There were two young boys—very energetic boys—in a neighborhood. Usually, when young boys are very energetic, they are in constant trouble. The same happened with these boys also. Their parents were very embarrassed by them because the entire community was discussing their children. So, not knowing what to do, they decided to take them to the local parish priest to correct them. Because the boys would be too strong to handle together, the parents decided to take them to the priest separately. They took the younger boy first, made him sit down in the priest's office, and left. The priest walked in with his long robes and walked up and down the room a few times with a grave face. The boy sat there, his eyeballs doing a ping-pong act.

As he walked up and down, the priest worked out a strategy. He thought, "If I remind this boy that God is within him, all his mischief will go." So he dramatically stopped mid-stride and, with a booming voice, asked the boy, "Where is God?" The boy looked bewildered. He started looking all around because he thought God must be somewhere in the priest's office. The priest saw that the boy was not getting the point. Thinking that he should give him a little clue that God is within him, the priest leaned on the table and, pointing at the little boy, boomed again, "Where is God?" The boy appeared even more bewildered and looked under the table. The priest saw that the boy was still not getting it. So, he walked around, came close to him, and, tapping on the little boy's chest, boomed again, "Where is God?" The boy now got up and bolted out of the room. He ran to where his elder brother was and said, "We are in real trouble." The elder brother asked, "Why? What happened?" He said, "They have lost their God and they think we did it."

Thinking about God, you will believe that you can do idiotic things in your life, and with a prayer everything will be fixed. This is not becoming spiritual. When you become conscious that you will also die, only then will you turn spiritual. Only when this awareness of mortality seeps into you, will you turn inward. The moment you address the mortal nature of who you are, you will also want to know what the source of this life is. You will develop the longing to know what this is all about and what is beyond this thing. It will become a natural quest. That is the spiritual process.

No one would seek spirituality if they did not know that they would die. When you are young, you think you are immortal. Slowly, as you get older, at least your body definitely reminds you that you are mortal. And when you are faced with death or the death of someone dear to you, you will surely begin to wonder what all this is about. If you are aware of the mortal nature of your life, where is the time to get angry with someone or to quarrel with someone or to do anything stupid in life? Once you come to terms with death, and you are conscious that you will die, you will want to make every moment of your life as beautiful as possible. Those who are constantly aware of the mortal and fragile nature of existence do not want to miss even a single moment; they will naturally be aware. They cannot take anything for granted; they will live very purposefully. Only people who believe they are immortal can fight and fight to death.

The Hindu civilization, the oldest civilization on the planet, has always nurtured a deep awareness of our mortal nature. In Hindu tradition, cremation grounds are always held to be very sacred. When someone dies, even if it is someone that you do not know, it hits you somewhere. In any genuine spiritual practice, there is always the smell of death. If you go deep enough into it, it will remind you that you are mortal. Whatever *sadhana** we have been teaching, whether it is *Shoonya* or *Shakti Chalana* or *Shambhavi Mahamudra*—even more so with *Samyama*†—essentially, there is a tinge of death in it. If there is no tinge of death in it, there is no

---
* Spiritual practices.
† Some of the various practices and programs offered by Sadhguru under the banner Isha Yoga.

spirituality; it is just entertainment. If someone taught you a superficial la-la practice, it might make you feel good, but there is nothing more to it.

Traditionally, every yogi started their spiritual pursuit in the cremation grounds. In fact, many Masters have used this as a spiritual process. Gautama the Buddha made it compulsory for his monks. Before he initiated anyone who came to him, he asked them to go and sit in the busiest cremation ground for three months, just watching the corpses burn. Even today, if you go to Manikarnika Ghat* in Varanasi, a minimum of a half dozen bodies will be burning there at any given time. And it is handled like a normal business, very casually. These days, there is not enough time for them to fully burn the body, because even before one body is fully burned, the next body has already come. So they throw this half-burned body into the river. It is actually very good for you to see that this is how people are going to treat you also one day.

When I was young, I had no knowledge of all this. But from the age of eight to seventeen, I happened to spend an enormous amount of time in the cremation grounds. It simply intrigued me. Everyone talked about so many eerie things happening there; I had heard stories that spirits hang upside down from trees. I wanted to see these things for myself. So I spent many days and nights in the cremation grounds. There was one very close to our home and another in the foothills of Chamundi Hills. The one at Chamundi Hills was very busy. Anytime you went there, there would be at least four or five bodies burning. Whenever I went trekking, I spent the nights there because the hill would be cold, but here there was a fire burning all the time. So I would sit by the fire and simply watch the burning.

---

* One of the spots on the banks of the Ganga River, known for its round-the-clock cremation of dead bodies.

There was also a lot of drama that used to happen around the pyre. Usually, when people come with a body to the cremation ground, they are all crying like they have lost everything in life. Then they set fire to the body. They stay there for half an hour or forty-five minutes and then they leave. The fire is still burning, but they leave. Probably they have other business to attend to, but I would sit there, watching. If you have carefully observed a body being burned on a pyre, the first thing that burns up is the neck because it is narrow. When this happens, unless they have made a large and proper arrangement of firewood, the half-burned head invariably rolls off the pyre like a soccer ball. It looks a little eerie—a head rolling off the pyre! Probably because firewood is expensive, or because most people do not have sufficient experience in arranging a proper pyre, this used to happen often. It would happen after three and a half to four hours of burning. By that time, no relatives would be present, so I would be the one to pick up the head and put it back on the pyre.

I spent many days and nights in the cremation grounds just sitting and looking and helping these bodies burn fully. It set forth a completely different kind of process in me. I know you would want to avoid this, but it is good to sit down and watch the bodies burning continuously. Living in the comfort of your house, it is very easy to think you are immortal. But when a body is burning in front of you, it is not very difficult to see that this could be you tomorrow. Mentally and emotionally, you may have different reactions, but the most important thing is that your body perceives life in its own way. The sight of another body burning deeply unsettles it. It raises a different kind of awareness and sense within you. Many things that you have imagined about yourself will all get burned in the cremation ground if you sit there and keep watching what happens.

When you are watching the bodies burn, you should not think about it. Simply look at it; just look at it and look at it and look at it. After some time, you will see, it is just you. It is not any different. It is your own body. Once you can replace that body with yours and still sit there, there is a deep acceptance of death. This is not a psychological process. When your very body perceives the fragility of its existence, there is a very profound relief and acceptance. Once there is a deep acceptance of death, then life will happen to you in enormous proportions. It is only because you tried to keep death away that life has also stayed away from you. This is why almost every yogi spent a significant amount of time in the cremation grounds at some point or the other in their life.

Exploring Death

An incident occurred when I was still in school that made me deeply intrigued by death. I was thirteen at that time. I was a fairly unusual child in school, but, usually, no one dared to tease me because I would beat them up. But there was this girl named Sucharita, who was a little crazy, and for some reason, she would go on teasing me, "Jaggi* the Great! Jaggi the Great!" I was irritated, but I ignored it. Once, after a school vacation, she did not come back to school. Every day, when her name was called during attendance, some of us would squeak out a female voice and try to answer her attendance for fun. This happened for a few days. Then this girl's brother, who was junior to us by two years in the same school, told us that his sister had died of pneumonia during the vacation. That really freaked me out. Not because someone had died, but because someone who was alive and here with us had vanished just like that.

---

* The name Sadhguru was known by in his childhood.

I became deeply intrigued by this. This girl was my age, doing many things in class, and she was suddenly gone. They said she was dead, but I wanted to know where she could have gone. Until then, to me, it was only old people who died. But being of my age group, the girl had brought death to my doorstep. Now it was no longer a curiosity question, but a very existential one. I wanted to know where the hell people go when they die and what happens after death. I had already asked these questions to many people even before this incident occurred. I had also spent a lot of time in the cremation grounds in the town, but still I did not know what happened after death. So, I thought I would undertake a journey to death myself and see what happened.

My father was a physician, so he had a medicine cabinet at home. I knew there were lots of medicines in it. Among them, I found a bottle of Gardenal. It is a kind of barbiturate that can put you to sleep. The bottle was supposed to contain a hundred tablets, but when I took them out and counted, there were only ninety-eight. Someone had opened it and used up two. I thought ninety-eight tablets should be a dose strong enough to cause death. Next, I went through my cupboard. I had some money and lots of personal property like marbles, catapults, and a few pet birds, which are of great value for a young boy. I decided to give them all away because I was going to die anyway. Some things I gave to my brother, the rest I distributed among my close friends. I told them I was leaving. They all thought it was a big joke. Then one day I decided that I would do it that night. I did not eat my dinner that night because I knew if there was food in the stomach these things might not work very well. I told my family I was not hungry and went to the terrace with the tablets. I popped in all the ninety-eight pills and just went to sleep, hoping that I would know where all the dead people go.

In the morning, they did everything to wake me up, but I would not wake up. Usually, it was a little hard to wake me up in the mornings, but this time I just did not wake up at all. Then my father saw that I was limp. Everyone became terrified and took me to a hospital. They did a stomach pump, put me on oxygen, and all that, but I did not wake up. For three days, I was lifeless and in a deep sleep. On the third day, I slowly came awake. Still lying down on the bed, I slowly opened my eyes. The first thing I saw were the rafters in the ceiling above the bed. Immediately, I recognized where I was. I had seen those rafters many times before when I had visited my father at the railway hospital, where he worked. There I was, lying in a bed in his hospital with all kinds of tubes sticking out of me. It was very frustrating, because I had gone through all this trouble hoping to see where one goes after death, and all I see are the damn rafters at the railway hospital!

That was a desperate attempt to know what happens after death, but I had learned nothing about it. The only consolation was that I learned that this was not the way to know. Later, I managed to bully my friends into returning most of the stuff I had distributed to them, and life carried on! Many years later, when I was a young man living life at my cocky best, a deep experience came unasked that changed my perspective about life and death completely.

One warm September afternoon, I was just sitting alone on a rock in Chamundi Hills. I had my eyes open—not even closed—when something began to happen to me. Suddenly, what I had thought all my life was me was all around—my inside had become the outside. I did not know which was me and which was not me. The air that I was breathing, the rock on which I was sitting, the atmosphere around me—everything had become me. It was crazy because what was happening was indescribable. What was me had become so enormous, it was everywhere. I thought this lasted a few minutes, but when I came back to my normal senses, the sun had set and it was dark. My eyes were open. I was fully aware, but what I had considered as myself until that moment had disappeared. From the time I was eight years of age, I had not shed a single tear. But now, as I was sitting, tears were flowing to the point where my shirt was wet. I have always been peaceful and happy—that has never been an issue. But here I was, drenched with a completely new kind of blissfulness. It was about seven-thirty in the evening. About four and a half hours had passed like this.

When I went back home, this sort of experience became recurring. It became more and more frequent. For a period of time, it was a bit of a war between a phenomenal experience with a flood of memory and my "super impressive" intellect. The intellect struggled; it would not give in. The only thing that my mind could tell me was that I was losing my balance. But the experience was so beautiful that I did not want to lose that either. It was absolutely fantastic, but at the same time, somewhere I was thinking this could be some kind of madness going on because it was too good to be real.

Questions about death did not even come into the picture because life was happening in such proportions. But this experience made me realize that people don't die. They may disappear from your perception, but they don't die. They live on. I was flooded with lifetimes of memories and experiences that made me realize that the past few lifetimes for me were about the same work, in the same place, and to some extent with the same people! It is this understanding of life (and death) that has shaped my life since then. In a way, death is a fiction created by ignorant people. Death is the creation of the unaware, because if you are aware, it is life—life and life alone, moving from one dimension of existence to another.

Is Death a Calamity?

People think that death is a tragedy. It is not. People living their entire lives without experiencing life is a tragedy. If you die, there is really no tragedy. That is the end of whatever problems you are experiencing in life. But if you are alive and not experiencing life in its totality, that is a true tragedy. This is expressed very beautifully in a Sanskrit verse that says: *Jananam Sukhadam Maranam Karunam*. *Jananam* means birth or life. It says life is a pleasure or joy. This is so. If you learn to handle your body and mind properly, your experience of life will be a pleasure or joy. But *maranam*, or death, is *karunam*, or compassion. Death is compassion because it relieves you.

Right now, people have a distorted orientation of life. They don't want to die. They don't realize that if you were ever condemned to become immortal, or if death were taken away from you, it would be the most horrible thing to happen to you. However beautiful your life becomes, if death comes at the right time to you, you are very fortunate. If it comes late, if life stretches itself beyond a certain point, that will be the worst kind of suffering. Then you will find that when death comes, it will be a great relief. Life needs a certain amount of tension to keep it going, but in death there is relaxation. In fact, death is the highest relaxation. However, if you also know the relaxation of death when you are alive, then life becomes an utterly effortless process.

If we look at life and death as a happening in terms of your experience, your inhalation is life and your exhalation is death. You can experiment with this: Take one big inhalation and see how your body and your mind are. Now do one big exhalation and see how your body and mind are. Which do you find is more relaxing? In fact, whenever tension builds up in you, the natural mechanism in the body wants to exhale. This is what you call a sigh. It relaxes you a little bit. Life needs a certain tension. Otherwise, you cannot keep it going. Death is utter relaxation. This is how it would have naturally been if your mind had not banished death as evil.

If your traditions and cultures had not taught you that death is evil or a calamity that should be avoided, believe me, you would breathe in a completely different way. If you observe people around you right now, you will see that for almost 99 percent of the people their exhalation is never complete. Their mind has rejected death, so their exhalation will not happen totally. They will inhale, but exhalation does not happen totally. This is one of the reasons why, over time, you build up so much tension within the system that it is reaching a breaking point—both mentally and physiologically.

The greatest calamity of the human mind is that it is against death. The moment you reject death, you also reject life. You think life is right and death is wrong. It is not so. Life is what it is only because death is. A river always happens between two banks. But you are standing on the right bank and say, "I don't like the left bank, it should disappear." If the left bank disappears, the river also will disappear, and the right bank also will disappear. If the right bank has to be there, the left bank also has to be there. Could there be light without darkness? One who does not embrace death will not know life at all. If you sit here saying, "I don't want to die, I don't want to die, I don't want to die," all that will happen is you will not live. You will anyway die, but by denying death, you will not live well until then either. If you are afraid of death, you will only avoid life; you cannot avoid death.

Even now, in some cultures, death is held as something that is to be celebrated, not mourned. After all, from somewhere you got released into this planet within this atmospheric space. Within that, however large a space you occupy, it is still a small prison. But death is an endless possibility. So there must be much more joy, much more of a sense of excitement about this than birth. For someone who is aware of this possibility, there is no such thing as life and death. Life is death, and death is life; they are not different.

Death is in fact life in a very intense form. People who have experienced moments of great danger in their life clearly know this. It once happened: Two old men met in a tiny little town in Indiana, U.S.A., in a local bar. And both of them were sitting grumpily at two different tables and drinking. Then one guy looked at the other and saw a birthmark on the other person's temple. So he walked up to him and said, "Hey, is that you, Joshua?"

"Yeah, who are you?"

"Don't you recognize me? I am Mark. We were in the war together."

He said, "Oh my God!" and they lit up suddenly. They were together in World War II and it had been fifty years since then.

So they sat down at one table and started drinking, talking, and eating. They had seen about forty minutes of action in those treacherous European trenches of World War II. Forty minutes of blitz. They talked about those forty minutes in so many vivid ways for more than two hours. After they were done with all this talk, one guy asked the other, "What have you been doing since then?" He said, "Ah, I have just been a salesman." Forty minutes of war, they spoke of for two hours with great excitement but fifty years of life after that were summed up as, "I've just been a salesman"! That is how it happens.

Moments of danger are moments when you experience both life and death together at the same time. These are the moments you realize that life and death are here at the same time. They are not two separate things. They are one inside the other. Life is all packed like this. The Creation and the Creator, life and death—are all packed one inside the other. It takes attention—a lot of attention—to see it. Otherwise, one just lives on the surface, half alive. If you don't know life and death at the same time, you will know only one half of life. Being half alive is a torture always.

If you want to live a full life, you should look at your mortal nature every day, not only when you are beyond a certain age. Every day of your life, you need to be aware that you are mortal. It is not that I want to die today, but if I do, it is all right with me. I will do everything to protect myself, to nurture myself, to take care of myself, but if I have to die today, it is okay with me. Only then can I step out and live. Otherwise, I cannot live.

Stop Inviting Death

If avoiding death is avoiding life, dodging life is inviting death. For most people, if life becomes unpleasant or burdensome, then, knowingly or unknowingly, they start dodging life. Once you start dodging life, you are invariably inviting death. There is no better method in the world to dodge life than to invite death. Either you do it consciously or you do it unconsciously. One major contribution to the multiple complex ailments that you see on the planet these days is that people are trying to dodge life and, in the process, are inviting death. The body is only cooperating with this. The body is just fulfilling your desire to invite death. Ask, and it shall happen!

People are trying to avoid life because they think it is unsafe. You should know that the only safe place on the planet is your grave. Nothing happens there. There is no safety in life itself. Like I said earlier, tomorrow morning you may be dead, no matter how much security you create for yourself. I am not wishing you this, but it does not matter how healthy you are, how well you are right now, tomorrow you may be dead. It is a real possibility. So there is no such thing as security in this life. The moment you start seeking security, naturally you become death-oriented. Unknowingly, you will seek death.

In India, it is a tradition that whenever you see a sage or a saint you should not miss the opportunity to get their blessings. So many times, people come to me and say, "Sadhguru, please bless me that nothing should happen to me." Really, what kind of a blessing is this? My blessing is let everything happen to you. Let everything that is life happen to you. Have you come here to avoid life or to experience life? If you want to avoid life, I can give you much simpler methods than Inner Engineering.* If you want to avoid life, all it takes is a few feet of rope to hang yourself from the ceiling. And it is not expensive either! I am talking of efficiency; when alive, to try to avoid life is very negative. Our aliveness is a very brief happening but we shall be dead for a very long time. So taking one's life should not be an option. This happens by mistaking the psychological drama for the existential life.

The moment you think of security, you are assisting death. I want you to know: Death does not need your assistance. Death is super-efficient. On the other hand, life needs your assistance. If you notice, whatever you do with life, no matter how much you do with life, there is still something more you can do with it. Life needs all your attention and efforts. Death does not need your support. It will anyway happen and it will happen with absolute efficiency. There is no failure here, as all shall pass.

People think nothing new should happen to them, but they want an exciting life. How is this possible? This is a no-win situation you are creating for yourself. What can happen to you at the most? At most, you will die. There is nothing more that can happen to you. And whatever happens in your life, you did not come here with an

---

* Referring to the spiritual program taught by Sadhguru.

investment. You came empty-handed. You cannot lose in this life. See how wonderful it is! Whatever happens, you are still on the profit side, so what are you complaining about?

This happened about ten years ago. At that time, the stock market in India was going down. Some people in Mumbai brought a man to meet me. It seems he was initially worth about three hundred million dollars. Then he took a beating in the stock market. In about eight months' time, he had only about thirty million dollars. Now the man was broken, depressed, and wanting to commit suicide. He was in a bad state, so they wanted me to help him. I thought this was funny because, for many Indians, thirty million dollars is more than heaven. If you give an option between heaven and thirty million dollars, they will choose the money. But this man is depressed and wants to commit suicide because he has only thirty million dollars! This is not just about him; you are doing this to yourself all the time too!

Let new things happen to you. If you create this kind of nothing-should-happen-to-me situation within yourself, you will become stagnant. Stagnation is death. If life does not move on, if new possibilities don't arise within you, you are living dead. This is the reason that even when nothing has gone wrong with people's lives, you can see so many long faces on the street. For most of them, life has worked out far better than they ever imagined. Materially, we are all living much better than our fathers and grandfathers did. But still there are these long faces on the street. This is happening not because something has gone wrong. This is because of stagnation. You cannot live with stagnation because that is like living death.

If you are alive, it is wonderful. If you are dead, we are not bothered about you. There are too many dead people walking, which is why there is such misery on the planet. They were all bright and alive at one time; now, slowly, they are half into the grave. Yes, with time the physical body will deplete. That is why if only psychological and physiological processes are in your experience, it is only natural that with the passage of time, you will deplete. As you can exercise your body and mind, and consequently notice a distinct difference in how they function, you can also exercise your energies—this exercising of your life energies, in yoga, we call *kriya*s. If this fundamental life energy is in your experience, and you do the right things about the life process, then the question of depletion with age will be only about your body and mind. As a life, you will become greatly enhanced.

CHAPTER 2

The Process of Death

What you are calling as life, right now, is like soap bubbles being blown. The entire Yogic process or the entire spiritual process is to wear this bubble thin, so that one day when it bursts, there is absolutely nothing left and it moves from the bondage of existence to the freedom of non-existence, or *Nirvana*.

WHAT MAKES US TICK

If you want to understand fundamentally how life and death work, you need to understand how Creation works and the role played by the various memories that are present in Creation. When I say memory, it is not only what you remember. Memory runs much deeper in its many layers. According to the Yogic system, memory is basically an accumulation of impressions. Further, there are fundamentally eight types of these memories in Creation. The most fundamental of these memories is *Elemental Memory*. According to the Yogic system, the first step from the unmanifest to manifest is the formation of *Pancha Bhootas*, or the five elements. These elements are *prithvi* (earth), *jal* (water), *agni* (fire), *vayu* (air), and *aakash* (ether). The names represent a particular quality and not the substance itself. These elements have different characteristics and are manifest in all aspects of Creation and are the most fundamental basis of all Creation.

Of these, Elemental Memory is the memory that decides how

these five elements interact and play out in life. The next layer of Creation is the material substance that the Universe is made of. The rules of how they play out are contained in what we can call *Atomic Memory*. Today, every child is taught atomic theory in school. The word "atom" comes from the Greek word *atomos*, meaning indivisible. When modern science discovered the atom, it was believed that atoms were indivisible and the most fundamental building blocks of the Universe. Today, of course, we know that it is not so. More than two dozen subatomic particles have since been discovered and more are possible. Atomic Memory relates to how subatomic particles, atoms, and, in turn, molecules of various physical substances are made and how they behave. Elemental Memory and Atomic Memory together constitute what can be called *Inanimate Memory*. This memory governs the inanimate aspect of life. The other types of memory relate to animate life and can be called *Animate Memory*.

Of these, the most fundamental layer of memory is *Evolutionary Memory*, which relates to how the evolution of life has taken place. This is instrumental in you having two eyes, two hands, taking the shape of the human form and not any other creature, and so on. Upon this layer is *Genetic Memory*, which comes from the genetic material passed on by your parents that makes you the unique human being that you are among all the other humans. This memory decides the color of your skin, the shape of your nose, and other such things. The next layer of memory is *Karmic Memory*, which is an accumulation of all the impressions that you have gathered, not just since birth but all through your previous lives, and the process of evolution. This will play out in your life in so many ways beyond one's understanding.

The next three layers of memory are impressions or accumulations related to your mind or the mental body. There is a large body of memory that you are completely unconscious about, which we can call *Unconscious Memory*. Then there is another body of memory that is just beneath the *Conscious Memory* that we can call *Subconscious Memory*. And, finally, there is Conscious Memory itself, which you can recollect and articulate. All these eight types of memory will play out in your day-to-day life according to the impressions accumulated and the situations you are faced with. Broadly speaking, these are the layers of memories that make you the life you are.

Now, there are many ways to look at the essential nature of life. One of them is that there are two seeds that make our lives. One is the seed planted by our parents, which gave us a body, and the other is the seed planted by the Creator, which gave us the life within. These are two different types of seeds or, in other words, two different dimensions of Nature. The first is programmed for certainty, while the second is programmed for possibility. The body is physical and there is a sense of certainty of its existence. The life that you are beyond the physical is a debate for most people; most are uncertain of the nature of their existence.

The seed of physicality that was transmitted by our parents has a certain set of rules, traits, and compulsions of its own. This aspect of Nature only tries to survive. The survival process includes procreation. It always tries to avoid everything that threatens its survival. Now, our parents gave us just a seed and that became the body. But what the Source of Creation gave us was not a seed in that sense. It gave itself. This is the reason that all the possibilities that the Source of Creation holds are kind of encapsulated in us. Whether that possibility is realized in an individual life or not is questionable, but the possibility is always there.

With these two seeds, when a human being is born a certain software is set within. This software is a combination of time, energy, and the information that he or she carries with them from previous lives. These three together will determine various aspects of one's life. Depending upon the information that is carried, energy is allotted for different aspects of life, which we will look at in a bit. In India, this information that is carried forth is referred to as *karma*. Of the entire memory, or the entire lot of karma, that one has, Evolutionary Memory is only significant for the structure of who one is. Let us leave it aside. But if all Genetic Memory and the Karmic, Unconscious, and Subconscious Memories that you have flooded into your Conscious Memory right now—you could not deal with it. It would become too overwhelming. So out of this entire load, Nature has a way of apportioning a portion for you to handle or wear off in this birth in the form of different kinds of activity.

Traditionally, in Hindu culture, the whole stock of Karmic Memory a person has is called *Sanchita Karma*. You can say Sanchita Karma is the entire warehouse of karma that a person carries. Out of this stock, a certain portion is allocated to be handled in a particular lifetime. This is known as *Prarabdha Karma*, or the karma that is allocated for that lifetime, which has some extra urgency to it and expresses a little more compulsion than the rest of the heap. This is Nature's way of handling something that is extremely complex in simple intermediate steps. So at birth, Prarabdha Karma creates an orientation and Sanchita Karma creates an unconscious tendency toward various things. However, how much karma you perform daily and with how much awareness either releases you from your Prarabdha Karma and Sanchita Karma or it enhances the same. In a nutshell, these factors are what determine how and for how long a person will live.

In the natural course of life, even if one lives simply in unawareness, Prarabdha Karma will somehow get worked out. With a little suffering here and a little well-being there, a little pain here and a little pleasure there, one will work out one's Prarabdha Karma. They just need to learn how not to create new karma in this life, that is all. So the next time when another set of Prarabdha Karma is allocated, that also will get worked out. This will repeat lifetime after lifetime. Now, Prarabdha Karma does not per se determine the outside situation, but since your inner arrangements always find expression outside, it affects your outside situation as well. So in India, whenever one saw someone suffering, they would say, "*Aiyyo,*[*] *prarabdha!*" It used to be a common refrain because the suffering is mostly coming from within. In most cases, suffering is a consequence of *how* one carries their memory and not necessarily the content. Hence, the need to fix the *context* of one's life through spiritual processes and not so much the content.

If you want to see how different people come with different karmic baggage, you should observe infants. How much hand and leg movement one child does is very different from how much another child of the same age does. This is not because of the differences in parents. In fact, how much one baby kicks around in a mother's belly is very different from how much another baby of the same mother kicks around. Usually, it has very little to do with the parents. In fact, if you observe, a lot of lethargic parents suffer super-active children. This is not because of the attitudes and psychological limitations of the children either. That develops afterward. This is because each "being" comes with a certain level of energy allotted to activity at birth itself.

Now, even within the allocation of energy to each person at birth, it is further divided into various aspects. Let us say, according to your karmic structure, you came with 1,000 units of energy when you were born. Of this, 250 units may be allotted for physical activity, and within that 100 units for involuntary activity and 150 units for external voluntary activity. Out of the rest, 300 units could be for mental activity and another 200 for emotional activity, and so on. This allocation will depend on what kind of software

---

[*] Common southern Indian cry of distress.

you have. This is why you will see each individual has a certain level of energy for different aspects of life. In children who have not yet been through much influence, this is very distinctly visible. You can see it in adults too, but in adults this could also be ascribed to many influences in one's life.

Now, the way the allocated energies are expended within you has serious implications for your life and death. In today's world, because of the impact of technology, the energy allocated to physical activity is mostly unused in people. If you were on this planet two hundred years ago, the level of physical activity that you would be performing naturally to fulfill your day-to-day requirements would be at least twenty times higher than what it is right now. In the tribal village near the Isha Yoga Center, no one has any sleep disorder. They put in so much physical activity that by the time they go to bed, they are ready to die. If they just put their heads down on the pillow, they will fall asleep.

If you happen to travel on Indian roads, it is common to see laborers traveling on top of loaded trucks. They would have loaded some stones or bricks or some other material into the vehicle and they would also be traveling in it to unload at the destination. Usually, you will see them fast asleep, lying on bricks or stones or some other coarse material in the moving truck, even under the hot sun. This is because the level of their physical activity is such that they have used up all their allotted energy. Now, if you initiate them into meditation, they will easily meditate. You will see that it is the educated people who cannot sleep or meditate or sit in one place because they are not using up their allotted physical energy. When they don't use it up, they cannot sit in one place. Right now, you see a huge surge in activities like trekking, cycling, and running. This is not only for fitness. Most realize that by just being in a demanding activity, they sleep, think, and act better. Their enthusiasm and energy for relationships and work are enhanced. In a way, in their consciousness, they have managed to put their concerns about the body aside.

This is why, once you are on the spiritual path, we want you to exhaust your energies allocated for physical activity very fast. Let us say, you have 500 units of energy allotted for your physical activity. We want to finish it off in ten years so that after that, if you sit, the body will simply sit. It has no need to move. Without any physical urge to move, it will simply settle down. Most people cannot meditate without sufficient physical activity. So, when we allocate work to people at the Isha Yoga Center, we do it with a lot of care. Some people work four hours a day, some six hours a day, some ten hours a day, some fourteen hours a day, while there are some who work eighteen to twenty hours a day. The idea is to expend their physical energy.

However, if you are full-time on a spiritual path, if you are a *brahmachari*, we not only want you to empty your Prarabdha Karma, we want you to expend the Sanchita Karma, or the entire stock, too. The idea of being on a spiritual path is to put life on fast-forward. We don't want you to take ten lifetimes to handle this warehouse of memory. We want you to finish it now. So we try to open up other dimensions of memory in you. The reason why so much discipline was always brought into Yogic practices is that even when things that would otherwise overwhelm you come up, you should be able to handle them. If you open up things for which one is not ready, karma can just smother you completely.

Once you are full-time on a spiritual path, we give you sadhana to handle this. Now you are willing to walk into trouble. You are not dodging trouble anymore. People want to avoid whatever is unpleasant in their lives because they cannot handle it. Only once we know you can handle your Prarabdha Karma well, then we can open up the entire warehouse of memory. This is also the reason why, when a person walks the spiritual path, if they don't handle the situation properly, they will suffer much more than other people. While others handle only what is allotted to them, this person tries to take up the whole stock.

Some people who are at the Yoga Center have gone through these phases: When they came, we gave them lots of activity. They went through it for a certain period and then slumped. They could not do anything for some time. They thought they were physically sick. They went to various doctors, though I told them, "Don't go to any doctor, just relax for some time. Something else will happen." And after some time, once again they are swept away by activity because we open up another room in the warehouse for them. What they should have done in their next life, they do it now. Actually, there are many more aspects to this—I am putting it in an overly simplistic manner. The main aim is that we want them to finish it all now.

This is also the reason why many spiritual systems in the East always had grammar and mathematics attached to them. Yogis want to develop their bodies and their minds because if they are born again, they don't want to be born with small amounts of Prarabdha Karma and go on for many lifetimes. They don't want to postpone it; they want to fast-forward everything. They want to enhance their mental capabilities, so that even if they are not able to end it this time around, because they left with very great physical and mental capabilities, when they come next time, they will get a bigger software. They will get more Prarabdha Karma. So along with the spiritual process, people took to grammar, music, astronomy, and mathematics, because they want to use their intelligence in every way.

Now, along with the memory and energy, there is a third dimension—time—that determines the duration and nature of one's life and death. Both life and death happen within the ambit of time. Time ticks away incessantly. You can neither slow it down nor hasten it. You can conserve your energy, you can throw it around, you can develop it, you can make it phenomenally big or insipid, but time, it just keeps slipping away. It has its own intelligence, and it flows according to certain parameters of karmic information and the energy allotment that is available in one's system. So, can we not do anything about it? We can, but that is a much more elusive dimension of life than the other two. The other two are much easier to manage and manifest in one's life. Generating energy and using it the way you want, not allowing your tendencies to determine the nature of your thought, emotion, and activity, is far easier than taking charge of time. Even Adiyogi[*] took charge of time only when he was in certain states. When he was in such states where he took charge of time, we refer to him as Kalabhairava.[†]

One who has mastery over one's information, or mastery over the tendencies caused by the information, has mastery over the quality of one's life. He or she can determine whether the self becomes pleasant or unpleasant. One who has mastery over one's energies will determine the nature of one's activity and how one lives. They have absolute mastery over their life, but not over their death. But one who has mastery over time will determine the nature of one's life and death. They can determine whether they want to live or die. This is how the three dimensions that constitute your life are connected to your death.

A Bubble of Life and Death

People think in terms of life and death as a binary situation. You are either alive or dead. You are either walking and talking or you

---

[*] The first yogi, one of the many epithets of Shiva.
[†] A fierce form of Shiva, where he has mastery over time.

are dead and gone. This is a very superficial and simplistic way to understand life and death. In fact, it is incorrect.

Generally, the human perception of aliveness has always been that something must bleed, otherwise it is not alive. Not anymore. Slowly, as science is advancing, our perception of what is alive and what is not is changing. Now we know that not just the plants and animals but even the rock and the soil are alive. The air is alive, the water is alive, the soil that you walk upon is alive, and the very cosmic space is alive. Today, science proclaims that water has its own memory and intelligence. Someday, when science goes far enough, we will find that there is nothing in the Cosmos that is not alive. The important question is: Are you alive enough to perceive it?

For me, even a rock is very alive. It has its own energy and I see that it gathers its own memory over a period of time. It lives with it. It is only based on this, that a Dhyanalinga* is consecrated. It is only based on this that every Hindu deity exists. If we give this combination of energy and memory a certain amount of vibrancy of energy, it will slowly gather an intelligence of its own. Once it has a combination of all these three, it can have intent. Once it has an intent and the necessary energy to back it, it is capable of action. This is how life is.

Right now, our idea of death is like this: When people say something has died, it only means that something just relapsed from a dynamic to a more inert form of Existence. We recognize life as a certain level of dynamism, intent, and capability of action in a human being. If this dynamism sinks below a certain level, then we say they are dead because, as far as our perception and our practical purposes are concerned, the things that we expect from a human being are no longer possible for them anymore. He or she may rot,

---

* A powerful energy form consecrated by Sadhguru at the Isha Yoga Center in Coimbatore, India.

become maggots, become manure, and then a mango or a coconut. All of these are life, but still we don't consider them alive because they are not able to find expression as we expect of a human being.

Essentially, there is a scale of dynamism from zero to infinity. (Actually, there is no zero, that is the whole problem!) Let us say, Shiva—that which is not—is zero, and what we consider as Divine is the highest level of dynamism. There are many levels of dynamism even among human beings. For example, let us say someone has Alzheimer's disease. They don't remember a thing, but this does not mean there is no memory in them. It is very much there, but the dynamism of the memory is gone. It has become inert. But if the memory goes away completely, your body also will fall apart right away because what you call "this body" is held together just by memory.

Right now, if a man eats a mango, it becomes a man. If a woman eats a mango, the same mango becomes a woman. You give the same mango to a cow, it goes inside a cow and becomes a cow. Is this the smartness of the mango? No. There is such a strong memory structure in you that whatever you put in, the memory will make sure it becomes you, not some other person. This is why if you eat a mango, one part of it becomes your skin in the same skin tone as yours; your skin does not turn yellow because the mango you ate was yellow.

Moreover, biologically also, a certain level of dynamism of memory is needed to bind all organs, cells, and atoms together to our intention of living. Right now, you have trillions of cells in your body that are functioning the way you want because there is a strong intent that is holding them together. But if you lose this intent, which is your ability to make all these atoms and cells function the way you want, we say you have died. The deterioration of the body begins to happen. The organism goes through certain disorganization, but it becomes a part of a larger organism of the planet, Universe, or Cosmos. As an organism ages, it loses its intent. If you lose your intent, then, gradually, action goes first, then your Conscious Memory will begin withdrawing and along with that your energies will follow.

The air is alive, a rock is alive, a tree is alive, an animal is alive, a bird is alive, and a human being is also alive. It is just that they have different levels of intent, different levels of intelligence, and, above all, different dimensions of memory.* That is all. The volume of Conscious Memory that you are capable of determines your capability of intent. From an amoeba to a human being, it is only a question of complexity. Every creature has intent, but it is largely unconscious intent. Only with the human being is there conscious intent. That is what sets us apart. Right now, my unconscious intent may be that I want to eat. But my conscious intent is to write this book, which no other creature really thinks of. For them, whatever is their unconscious intent is also largely their intent. Maybe dogs and a few other animals are capable of conscious intent in a small way, but, beyond that, everything is unconscious intent. But if a human being is willing, we can develop a large conscious intent from the banks of memory we have on various levels because there is such a huge foundation for this life.

If you want an analogy, consider this: In a way, what you refer to as life, right now, is like soap bubbles being blown. A rock, a plant, and a human being are all like soap bubbles of different kinds. The layer covering the soap bubble is the complex amalgamation of memory—various kinds of memory. In that sense, the nine avatars† that they talk about in the Hindu tradition are just different levels

---

* The word "memory" in this discussion is used not just in a neurological sense. Any trace of influence from the past that is retained is being referred to as memory.
† The incarnations taken by the Divine, according to Hindu scriptures.

of Evolutionary, Genetic, Karmic, Unconscious, Subconscious, and Conscious Memory.

The difference between a "human bubble"* and a "rock bubble" is just this: A rock bubble is mostly physical, with a thicker covering and less air inside, because all that is there is physical matter. It is only its physical integrity due to Inanimate Memory that holds it together, not so much a conscious web. You can break it with a hammer and it will be gone. But if you break a human bubble with a hammer, only the body will break. The web of Karmic Memory contained within is such that it will always find another way to create another bubble or physical form. The entire Yogic process or the entire spiritual process is to wear this bubble thin so that one day when it bursts, there is absolutely nothing left. It then moves from the bondage of existence to the freedom of non-existence, or Nirvana.

What I am saying might disappoint a lot of people because what I am telling you, in other words, is that there is no such thing as an encapsulated life. This whole thing about the soul, the "being," and other fancy things are all made up to give solace to people. If you tell them there is no substance within them like that, they will become terrified. So what about the person or the personality? There is no such thing as "this person" either. It is only a web of memory that creates an illusion of "this person." This is why when a person's memory is removed or dislodged in some way, like in Alzheimer's disease or something else, their personality is one thing that dies immediately. Suddenly, they are not the same person anymore. But still they have their own traits. It is like a scorpion has its traits that are very different from a grasshopper's. Similarly, people who have lost their memory will have different traits but no personality. If the Conscious, Subconscious, and Unconscious Memories are gone, if

---

* Life energy that has taken on a certain form; e.g., human or rock.

they are either dislocated or maybe wiped out, the Genetic Memory will come into play. If the Genetic Memory is wiped out, then the Evolutionary Memory will play. Even then, life is not completely gone because it has not completely dissolved.

If you take out the memory altogether, if you pull the plug on it, it collapses completely and then the bubble cannot hold the air. Here, what you refer to as air is the fundamental life energy. You can call it consciousness. Consciousness is a quality, not a substance. It is the nature of the Cosmos. You just blew a bubble and caught some amount of it. What we are trying to do with conscious living or with sadhana is catch as much air as possible so that you are one big bubble, and the wall of the karmic bubble becomes very thin. You don't want to be a tiny little bubble—you want to become one big bubble because dissolution is an imminent possibility for a sufficiently big bubble.

With sadhana, you blow a huge bubble. You want to blow this in such a way that it will never again exist anywhere as the same memory form. For this, you have to grow it really big. Essentially, enlarging a bubble means making the wall thinner and thinner. With sadhana, you wear it out from the inside. You stretch it. You stretch it so much that it will burst one day. You make it so big, where the memory stretches itself so thin, that when it is broken it is really gone. Suppose, somehow—either due to life experience or intelligence or wisdom or whatever—someone blew a big bubble, and it cannot be ignored anymore. The moment such a life rolls out of the mother's womb, it will depict certain extraordinary qualities, simply because it is a big bubble. A hundred other bubbles may be floating about, but everyone will look at that one. Such a life may spend at least eleven to twenty-four days longer in gestation in the mother's womb. As an infant, some qualities it may exhibit include steadier vision, almost adult-like. In terms of limb movement, its actions will be more purposeful, and it will roll over from supine to prone position much earlier than other children. In speech, its utterances will be free of lisp and noticeably clearer. This is what we call an evolved "being."

It does not matter whether one becomes a spiritual teacher or simply walks on the street—wherever the person is, people cannot ignore that being because there is a certain level of activity and intent.

Now, using this analogy, what happens when someone dies? Your physical self is largely an accumulation of Genetic Memory and Evolutionary Memory. The other dimensions of memory are not in it so much. It is the energy body which holds that memory, largely. So when death occurs, whatever memory you gathered on the surface—the Genetic, Evolutionary, and other Memories—is gone but the deeper layer of Karmic Memory remains intact. Therefore, it seems to be almost eternal in your experience. It is in this context people say that the soul is eternal. It is not eternal, but in your experience, if something goes beyond your body, you call it eternal. In that sense, this long-term memory within you, which will carry on through death, which will determine the nature of your future life and experience, is eternal.

Of the eight types of memory that you carry, all the seven types of memory will go when you fall dead. Evolutionary Memory, which is instrumental in you taking the shape of the human form, is gone. Genetic Memory, which decides the color of your skin, the shape of your nose, and such things, is also gone. The Conscious, Subconscious, and Unconscious Memories are also gone. Once you become disembodied, it is largely only the Karmic Memory which holds you together. In the process of death or disembodiment and the continuation of the life process, we must understand that only one memory—the Karmic Memory—remains. Within this, you may categorize something as Sanchita Karma and something else as

Prarabdha Karma, but, essentially, it is karma which remains. One way to handle this bubble is to capture a larger piece of life when the bubble is being formed. Now, even if you did not do anything much about dismantling your karma, the karmic wall becomes very thin simply because the volume of life energy is high.

The other way is to wear down the karmic wall. Very few people with properly intact karmic substance know how to just open the karmic wall and leave one fine day. The rest have to wear it down. The reason why an enormous amount of activity is generally prescribed on the spiritual path is that if you cannot blow your bubble thin from within, you try to wear it out from outside. Either way, you try to make the walls as thin as possible. The reason they said you should go and sit in a sacred place like the Dhyanalinga or some other energetic place or that you should go on *yatras*, and so on, is to fix your karmic body. The karmic body is subject to influences because this whole thing has happened because of the accumulation of influences. So you can undo the karmic body by the right kind of influences, or by being in the right spaces, in communion with the right kind of people and the right kind of atmosphere.

This is the idea behind structuring spiritual life in a certain way so that one is constantly active, but it is not about oneself. The moment I make my life all about me, karma will grow; immediately, the karmic wall will gather substance. Its walls will become thicker and thicker. The moment it is about me, I will have a strong sense of likes and dislikes—I can do that, I cannot do that; I can talk to this person, I cannot talk to that person; I want to love this person, I want to hate that person, and so on. These kinds of things will become a natural part of me the moment it is about me.

So the whole spiritual path in Hindu culture has been designed in such a way that the karmic wall does not gather substance. At the same time, you go on enhancing the volume of life that you gather. It does not matter how much brains you have, it does not matter how much knowledge you have, the significance of your life is always determined by the volume of life you captured. So the idea is to increase the real substance of life so that the cover or package becomes irrelevant. When it becomes irrelevant, it will dissolve. When it dissolves, this substance that was captured, which does not belong to you and which is anyway there everywhere, you become part of it.

When you have a thick wall, you are like a golf ball, because only a little bit of life is there; the rest is all karma. Now, if something pushes you a little, you will bounce all over the place. But if you have become a big bubble, if something pushes it, it will just glide, that is all. It is not going to hit this wall and that wall and go all over the place. This is the way life is happening to people: People who are very enslaved to their karmic structure, if you just pat them on the shoulder, they will bounce all over the place. But somebody who has grown in a certain way, whatever hits them, even if a bus hits them, they don't go all over the place. They will just glide away.

See, not everybody who takes to a spiritual process, or sadhana, is going to burst into Enlightenment. But why they are living like that is because they are wearing down their karmic bodies. When the time comes, if the bubble becomes incompetent to house Genetic Memory and Evolutionary Memory, then it cannot retake another body. Embodiment is not possible; it is over. All of it may not be gone, but the ability of the bubble to come back is over.

If you burst the bubble completely, it is possible to completely eject out of this cycle. Then we would not call it death. It is the ultimate end of life. To do this, if it was a big bubble, you simply touch it and it would be completely gone. It does not need much action. Simply of its own nature, it can burst. Even with a soap bubble, if you try to poke it when it is small, it will only stick to your hand. It will not blow up. It will take a lot more action to burst it, but big bubbles just burst upon contact or on their own. This is why many spiritual paths try to do just this: They try to blow the life bubble bigger and bigger with each lifetime so that one day it will burst on its own. But even when the bubble is small and the walls are thick, if people acquire the necessary wisdom and the intention, or if they are on to very powerful spiritual processes, they can crush it in the present lifetime itself. They don't have to wait for lifetimes to grow it very big.

Understanding Life and Death

If you want to understand what happens during death, you must have some understanding of the mechanics of how a human being is built. In Yoga, we look at everything—the entire organism—as the body. This body is a composition of five sheaths. These five sheaths, or *koshas*, as they are known, are *Annamaya Kosha, Manomaya Kosha, Pranamaya Kosha, Vignanamaya Kosha,* and *Anandamaya Kosha.* Each sheath has a distinct purpose and properties.

The outermost periphery, or outermost sheath, of a human being is the physical body. It is called the Annamaya Kosha. *Anna* means food, so we call this the "food body." When you were born, you were just six or seven pounds in weight. Now you are about twenty times more. All that came only from the food and nourishment you ingested. So what you call the "body" is just an accumulated heap of food. That is how it gets its name.

The second layer is the Manomaya Kosha. *Mana* means the mind. This is the mental body. It comprises your thoughts, emotions, and all the mental processes, both conscious and unconscious. Today, doctors talk a great deal about the psychosomatic nature of many ailments. This means that what happens in the mind affects what happens in the body. Every fluctuation on the level of the mind has a chemical reaction in the body, and every chemical reaction in the body in turn generates a fluctuation on the level of the mind. When you say "the mind," people generally think it is located in one place. It is not so. The mind is not in any one place. There is an entire anatomy of the mind. There is memory and intelligence in every cell in the body. There is a whole body of mind, which we call Manomaya Kosha. This is the entire mental body.

The physical and mental bodies are like your hardware and software. Hardware and software cannot do anything unless you plug into quality power. So there is a third layer of the self, called the Pranamaya Kosha. Prana is life energy. This is the energy body which powers and drives the Annamaya Kosha and the Manomaya Kosha.

All these three—the physical body, the mental body, and the energy body—are physical in nature. It is easy to understand that the Annamaya Kosha is physical because you can see it and feel it. But the Manomaya Kosha and the Pranamaya Kosha are also physical in nature. It is like this: You can very clearly see that a lightbulb is physical, but the electricity that runs through it is also physical. So is the light that emanates from the bulb. All three are physical. Similarly, the physical body is grossly physical, the mental body is a little subtler, while the energy body is even more subtle but still of the physical realm. These are the only three dimensions of the self you are aware of right now. These three physical dimensions of life all carry the imprints of karma, or Karmic Memory. Karma is imprinted on the body, on the mind, and on the energy. It is this karmic structure that holds the being together.

The fourth layer of the self is called the Vignanamaya Kosha. *Gnana* means knowledge. *Vishesh gnana,* or *vignana,* means extraordinary knowledge or knowledge of that which is beyond the sense perceptions. This is the etheric body. It is a transitory body—a transition from the physical to the non-physical. It is neither physical nor non-physical. It is like a link between the two. It is not in your current level of experience because your experience is limited to the five sense organs and these organs cannot perceive the non-physical. If you learn to find conscious access to this dimension, there will be a quantum leap in your ability to know the cosmic phenomenon.

The fifth sheath is known as the Anandamaya Kosha. *Ananda* means bliss. It has nothing to do with the physical realms of life. Only the physical can be here and there. Anything that is non-physical is neither here nor there. It is everything and nothing. So the deepest core is that dimension which is beyond the physical. It is nothingness. When I say "nothing," you should put a hyphen between "no" and "thing"—no-thing. It is not a thing, it is not physical. It is beyond the physical nature. It cannot be described or even defined. So Yoga talks about it only in terms of experience. When we are in touch with that aspect beyond the physical, we become blissful. So Anandamaya Kosha is called the "bliss body." But it is not that a bubble of bliss lies within your physical structure. There is no such thing. It is just that when you access this indefinable dimension, it produces an overwhelming experience of bliss. It has no form of its own.

When someone dies, only their outermost sheaths—the Annamaya Kosha and the conscious parts of the Manomaya Kosha—are lost. But one is not completely dead. The rest of the structure is still intact; it will seek another womb and manifest itself once again in the physical plane. This is why death is not dissolution—you will pop back in no time. But if the energy body, the mental body, and the physical body are taken away, the bliss body will become a part of the Cosmos. Only if the energy body, the mental body, and the physical body are in place can they hold the bliss body in place. When they are no more, the bliss body is also no more. Now they are completely no more. This is the whole story of life, death, and dissolution.

PANCHA PRANAS: THE FIVE VITAL ENERGIES

If you want to further understand how the separation of the physical body happens at death, you need to have some understanding of the Pranamaya Kosha, or the vital energies that govern life. In Yoga, we call this prana. It manifests itself in five basic dimensions. These are called *Pancha Vayus*, or *Pancha Pranas*. There are other forms to it, but it is too complicated to explain here. So we will just look at these five dimensions.

These Pancha Pranas are in charge of various activities or processes in your body. The first one is *Samat Prana*, or *Samana Vayu*. This Samana Vayu is in charge of maintaining the temperature of your body. By activating the Samana Vayu, you can activate your energies in such a way that you become less and less available to the external elements in Nature. If you have traveled in certain parts of the Himalayas, especially if you have gone to places like Gomukh or Tapovan, you will see some sadhus* living there in the extreme cold, in bare-minimum clothing. These are glacial, subzero-temperature areas, but these sadhus can be found walking around barefoot. This is because, by doing certain kriyas or mastering certain mantras, you can activate the Samana Vayu and create a *kavacha*, or a shield, around yourself. You can create a cocoon of your own energy whereby the external elements don't bother you so much. This is not only about the cold; even the heat will not disturb you. It is like you have an

---

* A holy person or ascetic.

internal air-conditioning where neither the heat nor the cold disturb you so much.

Generating heat in the body is one aspect of Samana Vayu, but it is also very healing in nature. If your Samana Vayu is high, your very presence becomes healing for others. Samana Vayu is also in charge of your digestive process. If your Samana Vayu is high, you will notice that, whatever you eat, your stomach will become empty in about an hour and a half. Your stomach should always be empty because both your physiology and your mind function at their best only when the stomach is empty. So yogis always want to keep their stomachs empty. An empty stomach does not mean you starve yourself. You just burn up the food as quickly as possible.

Samana Vayu is also related to the sun, the basic source of energy and temperature. The sun is the heating source of the planet and the body. Samana Vayu is important because one's life and its span are related to the cycles of the sun. Through the sun, Planet Earth has also become a source of warmth—or a minor sun—by itself. So establishing a deep connection with the planet will lead to an ageless sort of existence in terms of energy and vitality. With this, a yogi can transcend the solar cycles* and be released from their grip. He can become independent of the physical source of life in the solar system. Such a yogi's life and death will be most interesting to witness, as, without any transcendental quality, he will manage death with the ease of a breath.

The next aspect of prana is called *Prana Vayu*, which is in charge of your respiratory process and your thought process. If you carefully observe, for every kind of thought that you get, your breath will change in a subtle way. You sit here and think about the ocean,

---

* A solar cycle in the human system is 4,356 days or approximately twelve years. This cycle has a strong bearing upon what happens in one's life during that time.

you will observe that your breath will be one way. You think about the mountains, it will be another way. You think about a tiger, it will be yet another way. The reason why thought and respiration are so directly connected is simply because both these are handled by the same energy, known as Prana Vayu. Prana Vayu is related to the Earth. It is earthy in nature. Earth is the only planet in the solar system to have a breathable atmosphere and therefore the possibility of respiration. So this is the only planet where there is an active intellect or thought process.

The next aspect of the prana is called *Udana Vayu*. *Udana* means to fly. You may weigh 150 or 170 pounds on the scale, but you don't feel the 150 or 170 pounds on you because Udana Vayu creates buoyancy and makes you less susceptible to gravity. There are Yogic practices to activate this. There were whole schools of Udana Vayu in China, where those who gained mastery over this prana could float around a little bit. You might have seen this in the movies, where it is a little exaggerated. But the body becomes lighter because of a more buoyant force in the body.

For a martial arts fighter, to be buoyant is important. There have been many cases where certain ballet dancers, footballers, and martial arts experts have executed what all physicists believe is simply impossible, by leaping to incredible heights. They have defied gravity simply by creating more buoyancy within the body. If you have complete mastery over udana, they say you can even fly. But more important, if you activate your udana, you become less and less available to gravity. On the weighing scale, you are still the same, but in your experience you will feel as if the body has become so light. You don't have to carry it. It is like it is floating around. This is another way of making you less attached to your body.

Udana Vayu is also in charge of your ability to communicate. Now, if your Udana Vayu is active, your ability to communicate with people will come naturally to you. Udana Vayu is related to the moon. The cycles of the moon are intimately connected especially with the female body. Only because our mothers' bodies were in sync with the cycles of the moon were we born. The moon, being the manager of the feminine dimension of life on the planet and the platform upon which life is built, becomes the determining factor as to when the body can truly come to an end. Once Udana Vayu has left, the very platform that provided the needed foundation for life to build itself upon is not there. Hence, from this point on, seeking the next womb begins in earnest.

The next aspect of prana is called *Apana Vayu*. Apana Vayu is in charge of your excretory system and the sensory function. Only when the excretory system is efficient at the cellular level will you have the necessary sensitivity for sensory perception. And hence such importance is being given to the purificatory aspect in Yoga.

When I say "excretion," I mean not just the outcome of digestion, but excretion on the cellular level that needs to happen. Every moment, the cells are pushing out impurities. This excretory system will be efficient only when the stomach is empty. When there is food in the stomach and digestion is in progress, the excretory system slows down. So if excretion does not happen properly, the body becomes impure. When the body becomes impure, lethargy and other kinds of dullness will settle. Once this inertia manifests in the body, it will slowly be transmitted to the mind also. So Apana Vayu cleanses the system in a big way.

The next aspect of prana is called *Vyana Vayu*. Vyana Vayu is that which knits all these billions of cells into one organism. There have been some instances of certain yogis whose bodies did not show any signs of decay for months after their death, even though no preservation was attempted. This is particularly common among Tibetan monks. This is possible because when they die, they leave a certain amount of Vyana Prana in the body, which preserves it for a long time.

You may have heard of transmigration, where people leave their bodies and enter another body. If one has mastery over one's *vyana*, one can leave one's body at will. Now, this leaving of the body is not the pinnacle of Yoga; it is a simple aspect of Yoga. If you activate Vyana Vayu in your body, you slowly become loose inside your body. Now, the question of getting identified with the body does not arise within you. This gives you a completely different sense of freedom in your life because maintaining the awareness that "I am not the body" comes naturally to you. This is like if your clothes are very tight-fitting; slowly, you will tend to think that is you. But if you wear loose clothes, you are more conscious that these are clothes, not you.

Now, another aspect of Vyana Vayu is that it is also in charge of your ability to move, or your locomotion. You will see that your ability to walk will come naturally to you when your Vyana Vayu is high, even if you are not a seasoned walker. Vyana Vayu is a very important aspect of spiritual growth. It also enhances your intuitive nature.

There are many more aspects to pranas, or *vayus*, but, fundamentally, this is how they affect the physical body. A basic understanding of the pranas is necessary to understand how death happens because, at the moment of death, each of these pranas recedes differently and affects the dead differently. The process of death or the process of disembodiment extends well beyond the point where the breath has stopped.

THE SEQUENCE OF DEATH

Definitions are central to the progress of modern science. To study anything, they must be able to define it first. But when it comes to defining death, modern science ties itself into knots. The best definition they have for death is "the absence of life." But then again they have no definition for life either. Defining death or being able to determine the point of death correctly are necessities because of the social, medical, and legal aspects of life and death.

In the olden days, they said if the breath has stopped, the person has died. But then some people who were declared "dead" by this definition came back to life and a whole lot of chaos ensued. So they went a step further and said if the pulse stops, i.e., the heart stops, then it is death. But again, people came back to life even after their breath and heart had stopped. Today, they have a battery of terms—clinical death, brain death, somatic death, heart-lung failure, whole-brain death, higher brain death, and so on—to hide their inability to precisely define death. This problem is essentially because they are only looking at the manifestations of the process of death and not the cause, which is the exiting of the Pancha Pranas from the physical body.

This happened many years ago. A research institute invited me because they wanted to check my gamma waves. Apparently, these are patterns of neural oscillations in the brain that show a correlation with mental activity. At that time, I did not know what these gamma waves were or if I even had them in my brain. I don't usually put myself through these indignities, but that day, due to an obligation, I gave in.

They connected me to fourteen electrodes and asked me to meditate. I said, "I don't know how to meditate."

They were a little taken aback. They said, "But you teach everyone meditation."

"Yes, I do. But I teach meditation to people because they don't know how to sit still." In reality, there is no such thing as meditation. There is only stillness—many levels of stillness. Because it is very difficult to teach people stillness, the term "meditation" is used as an intermediary. So I said, "If you want, I will sit still. Totally still, on all levels." Then they said, "Okay, sit still; we will check that." So I sat down.

After about fifteen minutes, they started hitting me on my knees with some metallic object. Then they tried my ankles and then they moved to my elbows—you know, that funny place where it hurts the most. I thought, "This must be a part of their experiment," and kept quiet. But it became very persistent and painful. Then I slowly opened my eyes and asked, "Did I do something wrong?" All of them gave me a weird look. I said, "Why are you looking at me like this?" They said, "Our monitors have gone flat. According to our machines, you were dead." I said, "That is a great diagnosis!" Then they came up with a second opinion. They said, "You are either dead or you are brain-dead."

I said, "I will take the first one. 'I am dead' is okay with me. But don't call me brain-dead, that is insulting." This is what happens if you let machines decide death. Your breath stopping, your heart stopping, or your brain going flat on the monitors is not death. It is death only when the Pancha Pranas exit the physical body completely.

When the breath stops, or when what we call death occurs, the withdrawal of the pranas happens over a period of time. All the pranas do not exit the body at the same time. There is a definite pattern in which they exit. This can be observed in some simple ways. For example, harvesting of organs can be done for a duration of a few hours after the breath stops, depending on the organ. It is also well-documented that if you keep a dead body for more than two to three days, you will notice that the hair will grow. If it was a man and he used to shave, you can see this from the facial hair. The nails will also grow. Therefore, in countries where they preserve the dead bodies for a longer time, the undertakers clip the nails and shave the beard. Current medical opinion is that this is because the skin has dried or shrunk. Those factors may contribute, especially in a young person with a level of vitality of life energies, but it is mainly because hair and nails are special in a way because there is no sensation in those parts of the body even when you are alive. There is no sensation in these parts because there is no Prana Vayu in them even during life, but the other vayus are present there. So immediately after death, when Prana Vayu has exited the body, these parts of the body are not affected much. This is why you will observe some minimal growth there until the other pranas exit the body.

The process of withdrawal of the pranas spans a period of time, so there is a window of opportunity for outside interventions and manipulations that can sometimes "revive" the dead person. It is only because of this that it is possible to assist the dead in their journey after death or allow for processes like transmigration. We will be looking at this in more detail in chapter 4.

An overview of the withdrawal process can be summarized as follows:

SAMANA VAYU	Once the breath stops, the slow process of the five pranas exiting the body will begin. Of these, Samana Vayu is in charge of maintaining the temperature of the body. The first thing that happens after death is that the body starts cooling down. Since the differential between the atmospheric temperature and the body temperature is significant, the Samana Vayu exits much faster than Prana Vayu. Within twenty-one to twenty-four minutes of the breath stopping, Samana Vayu exits the body completely.

PRANA VAYU

Once the breath stops, Prana Vayu also starts exiting the body. This means the respiratory action and thought process will begin to recede along with the withdrawal of Prana Vayu. Prana Vayu exits the body completely within forty-eight to ninety minutes after the breath stops, depending upon the nature of death. If it is a natural death out of old age, it should be over within sixty-four minutes. But if it is a young and vibrant body, then it can be prolonged for up to ninety minutes. Till this time, the respiratory and thought process is on; if not in the usual sense, in a vague manner. This is why cremation should be deferred for an hour and a half, at least.

If you keep the body of the person whose breath has stopped on earth or open soil, there is a possibility of revival with a little intervention from the outside. If other aspects of the system are conducive, then the soil and elements can reignite the needed energy to revive life. This is why, in the olden days, dying people were placed on the ground outside the house, in hopes of revival. But, today, with the body being laid on a cot or a concrete floor, the chances of revival are very remote.

UDANA VAYU	Between six and twelve hours after the breath stops, Udana Vayu exits. Once Udana Vayu goes away, then the buoyancy in the body is also gone. Suddenly, the body becomes heavy. The weight does not increase, but you can feel the weight much more simply because Udana Vayu is gone. This is why people feel a big difference between carrying a live person and a dead person.
APANA VAYU	Somewhere between eight and eighteen hours after the breath has stopped, Apana Vayu exits the body. Once Apana Vayu starts receding in a major way, then the sensory aspect of the body is gone. Even after someone's breath is gone and they are declared dead, they can still feel sensations. There have been any number of cases where people get terrified because a dead body moves a little bit. There could be mild twitching in the body because the sensory activity is still on.

VYANA VAYU	Vyana Vayu, which is the preservative nature of prana, is the slowest to exit. It will continue to do so for eleven to fourteen days if the death is because of old age and life became feeble. If the death was because of an accident when the life was still vibrant, unless the body is totally crushed, the reverberations of this life will continue for somewhere between forty-eight and ninety days.
	For that period, certain processes will continue and there will still be some element of life. During that time, there are things you can do to assist that life. This is the opportunity that death rituals in the Hindu culture attempt to make use of.

So with this understanding, how would you define death? Fundamentally, what we call death is a certain line, or a certain stage, in the process of disembodiment. In that context, it is appropriate that in the English language you don't *diagnose* someone as dead, you *declare* them dead. You declare someone dead when he or she does not respond to your stimulus or when you do not have access to them anymore.

An ordinary person may feel that someone is dead if they do not respond to their voice and other kinds of physical probing. But a medical professional would not accept this. They have a more sophisticated understanding of life and also have subtler tools and probes. They know that with suitable interventions the life can be revived, and the person can be brought back into the body. But if the process of disembodiment has crossed a certain stage, then one will not be responsive to these medical stimuli either. Such a person would be declared medically dead, but this would still not be considered spiritual death in the Yogic tradition.

A person well versed in Yoga and Tantra has an even finer understanding of life. They have much subtler tools and techniques to access that life and possibly restore it. So they would still not declare them spiritually dead. However, if the process of disembodiment has progressed beyond a certain point, then even they cannot restore life into the body. Now, for all practical purposes, that person is completely gone—they cannot be brought back at all. One can only assist their further journey,* that is all.

So the answer to the question "When is a person dead?" depends largely upon what the purpose of the declaration is and what capability one has to interact with life at the different stages of disembodiment. The more capable you are, the more leeway you will have in the situation.

Chakras: The Gateways of Exit

The pranic system in the body comprises various energy channels and their points of intersection, known as *chakras*. There are a total of 114 such chakras, 112 of them in the body and 2 outside the body. The chakras within the body are classified into seven main categories of sixteen each. In life, the levels of activation of these chakras greatly determine the quality of life led by the person. Correspondingly, how energy moves through these chakras in death determines the quality of the death too. So, each death is characterized not just by how the pranas have exited the body but also through which chakra or chakras they exited. Adept yogis are able to plan these things in advance and work toward which chakra they want the pranas to exit the body from.

---

* See chapter 8, "Assistance for the Disembodied."

Even if you are liberated within yourself, even if you have attained a certain state within you, you still need a lot of skill to leave the physical body consciously. You need to know the science of how life and the body got connected and what you need to do to disentangle it. Otherwise, you will not be able to leave the body consciously. People who are on the Yogic path can simply sit in the open and leave—just like dropping one's clothes and walking away—because they know the science of how to leave the body. Depending upon how much skill and freedom with which someone left the body and through which chakra they left the body, the situation around each death will be different. For the sake of simplicity, we talk mostly of only the seven main chakras in the body.* Each is given a name and has certain qualities.

For a person whose experience of life is very gross or basal, or if someone leaves in fear—which happens to a lot of people—they end up leaving through the *Muladhara Chakra*, located at the perineum. This is why you will see that at the time of death, many people will pass urine and feces with a certain force. This is not because of incontinence, as people think, but because the prana has left through the Muladhara Chakra. This is not a good way to die. If we are not able to leave the body at will, at least we should be able to welcome death and allow it to happen rather than resist it and struggle with fear. Generally, if one leaves through the Muladhara Chakra, it is considered a very base exit. But in rare cases, one who consciously exits through the Muladhara Chakra can come back with enormous occult powers.

One who exits through the *Swadhishthana Chakra*, located in and above the genital organ, can be reborn with extraordinary creative prowess. One who exits through the *Manipura Chakra*, located just below the navel, can be capable of a very organized sense of action.

---

* The seven main energy centers in the body, according to the Yogic sciences.

One may become a great businessperson or a great general—essentially, a genius of organization—in his or her next life. One who exits through the *Anahata Chakra*, where the rib cage meets, can become a prodigy in music or the arts. One may also become a very sensitive poet or a devotee who can inspire many. The Anahata Chakra also has the possibility of finding access to all the other dimensions, so one could be a potential polymath.

For someone to exit through the *Vishuddhi Chakra*, situated at the pit of the throat, is very rare. But if that happens, one will possess an incredible perception of this world and the beyond. Such a person will also exist in an absolute sense of dispassion and fearless involvement in all aspects of life. A phenomenal sense of clarity will be predominant in them. Though the *Agna Chakra*, located between the eyebrows, is of a higher order, it is more common for people to exit through the Agna Chakra than the Vishuddhi Chakra.

A person who is fully conscious will leave through their *Sahasrara Chakra*, from the top of their head. That is the best way to leave. Normally the prana just leaves, but sometimes it actually leaves a physical hole there at the moment of death. If you know, the bit of the skull at the top of the head is not yet formed in infants for quite some time. That spot is called the *brahmarandhra*. For some people, when they leave the body, an actual hole will be found there. When one leaves through their Sahasrara Chakra, it means that they were fully conscious.

If you want that moment of death to happen in full awareness, you have to live a life of awareness. Otherwise, at that moment, there is no way you are going to be aware. One who is conscious can leave whichever way they want, but one who is unconscious simply goes in a fixed way—because their life was a bondage, so death is also a bondage. If at the moment of death, a person can be 100 percent aware, that person will not have to go through rebirth. They will not take another body—they are released.

CHAPTER 3

The Quality of Death

No two people in the world live their lives the same way. Similarly, no two people die the same way. People may die in the same situation, of the same cause, but still they don't die the same way.

TYPES OF DEATHS

Now, are there some deaths that are good and some others that are bad? You must know that no two people in the world live their lives the same way. They may be siblings, living in the same house and doing the same things, but even then their experience of life will not be the same. Similarly, no two people die the same way. People may die in the same situation, of the same cause, but still they don't die the same way. Right now, if the sky falls upon us and all of us get crushed under it and die, still, we will not die the same way.

It once happened: A rich man built a big house for his family. It has been a tradition in India that when you build a new house, you want to welcome some sage or saint or yogi to your home. They don't do it anymore because today there is too much housing and not enough yogis. So this man invited a yogi to his house. They welcomed him like a king and did *Pada Pooja** and many other poojas.

---

* Literally, worshipping the feet of someone. Traditionally, this is the highest kind of worship for a person you revere.

Then they served him a great meal. Then when the time came to leave, the husband and wife bowed down to him, asking for a blessing, as per the tradition. The yogi raised his hand and said, "First, may your father die, then you die, and then your children die." Hearing this, the man became furious. He said, "What nonsense! We invited you to our new house, treated you like a king, fed you well, and you say that first my father should die, then I should die, then my children should die? What is this rubbish?"

The yogi was shocked. "Why, did I say something wrong? Is it not good if your father dies first, then you die, and then your children die? That means life will be in its natural cycle. Before your father dies, if you die, that is not good. Before you die, if your children die, that is not good at all. So first your father must die, then you must die, then your children must die."

In recent times, there has been growing awareness about the quality of death, and just as there is a Quality of Life Index, people have created a Quality of Death Index too. Furthermore, as people create "life goals" for themselves, there is growing awareness that one should set "death goals" as well. This is a welcome change; however, they are working with a very superficial understanding of the quality of death, as such. People think that if one is free of pain and suffering, if one does not struggle with it, if one does not die suddenly, and if one does not die alone but instead is surrounded by loved ones while dying, then it is a good death. On the other hand, they think if someone dies suddenly or violently, then it is a bad death. These considerations are very medical and social. Existentially, they are not very significant.

In India, deaths were classified taking into account deeper and existential factors as to how the death occurred. This is important because it has a considerable impact on what happens after death and what kind of assistance can be provided to the person who has died. Traditionally, in India, people classified deaths as only two kinds—timely death (*Su-mrutyu*) and untimely death (*Akaal Mrutyu*). If a yogi left his or her body consciously at the age of thirty, we don't say it is untimely. It is timely for them because they decide the time.

We call a death untimely when someone has intent to live—that is, they still have Prarabdha Karma to work out—but suddenly something strikes them down and they die. Their body collapsed when the intent was on full scale—this is an untimely death. If intent itself has gone away, it is not untimely; it is very timely for that life. Chronological age, whether you are thirty-five or sixty-five or ninety-five years old, is not the point. The criterion is that the intent is gone. Then, in terms of life, it is a timely death. I cannot give you an accurate percentage, but I think we can easily say that more than 80 percent of the people do not die a natural death or a timely death anymore. Their death is unnatural or untimely because they die while their intent is still on. This is unfortunate, and it has a bearing upon how the death happens and what happens after that.

In a natural or timely death, Prarabdha Karma, or the information that runs the life, runs out and life becomes feeble. When the information runs out, life peters out slowly and this is not torturous. This is very beautiful. When your Prarabdha Karma runs out, even if you lived a bad life, the last few moments will become very peaceful, wonderful, and perceptive. Suddenly, you will see such people become so wise. They are not attached to anything around them; they show an extraordinary sense of maturity—something they failed to show throughout their life. This is because it is a natural death. Natural death is not a bad death. It is a good thing for you and a good thing for those you are leaving behind because you are not being forced out of your body. For this to happen, you need to empty your Prarabdha Karma before your body wears out.

How rapidly you empty your Prarabdha Karma depends on how quickly you move from one aspect of life to another. If you are eighty and still think like a teenager wanting to romance someone, your Prarabdha Karma will not run out. If, at eighty, you are not rid of what you should have done at sixteen or eighteen and you still want to go sit on the street side and watch women walking by, then your Prarabdha Karma will not run out. Now, it will not matter if you live to be a hundred, you will still die an unnatural death because the body will run out, but the Prarabdha Karma will not. When death is close to you, everything that you know as yourself is going to end. It is not just a psychological process. The life within you knows it is going to exit its abode, and it will flutter rather than have a smooth transition. If a person dies naturally, he or she clearly knows that they are going to die, and you will see they will display extraordinary wisdom. That possibility is being completely obliterated in the so-called modern society because you have not come to terms with death. Almost everyone is trying to be immortal at any cost, and they will die a bad death because of that. You can die well only if you accept your mortality.

There is another kind of death, called *Iccha Mrutyu* (loosely translated as "death by choice"), which, in a sense, is not death, but actually the transcendence of the cycle of birth and death. This can happen when a person is into spiritual sadhana and has achieved such a mastery over their energies that they are able to untangle their life energies from the physical body without damaging it. The person has understood where the keys to his or her karmic structure are and is able to dismantle it completely. Such a person becomes truly no more. This is considered the highest kind of death. This is also referred to as Mahasamadhi in the Hindu tradition and Mahaparinirvana in the Buddhist tradition. In English, we simply call it Liberation, meaning one has become free from the very process of life, birth, and death. One has become free from the basic structures of body and mind or free from the karmic structure which holds these things together. To use the earlier analogy, one has burst the bubble completely. This is the ultimate goal for every spiritual seeker.

Predictions of Death

One of the most common questions people have for astrologers and fortune tellers is: "How long will I live?" "When will I die?" If life follows a certain rationale, then is it possible to determine when it will end as well? More precisely, we saw how it is karma, the software of life, that determines the span and the nature of life. So is it possible to somehow read this and be able to predict death?

Now, just as karma is impressed upon your physical body and mental body, it is also impressed upon your energy body. As the allotted karma, or Prarabdha Karma, is reaching completion, the pranic body's ability to hold on to the physical body recedes. Life, as you know it, which is physical, will begin to lose its vibrancy. At the same time, the subtle body gathers more vibrancy because the physical body is losing its grip on the subtle. This is the reason why you might have noticed that sometimes even a person who has lived a crude or gross life seems to carry an ethereal peace about them during the last few days preceding their death. Such a person, you will see, suddenly becomes wise. This usually happens for people whose awareness becomes acute. However, if someone is dying a natural death, then with a little bit of awareness—at least six to eight months in advance—one can clearly see it coming. Actually, many people unknowingly start talking about it. They start making strange statements and behaving strangely. This is not out of psychological degeneration; unconsciously they blurt out this and that. Later on, after they are dead, people look back and say that he or she had said this or did something which was indicative that they were aware of their impending death. An uncle of mine even knew the exact date and time of his death.

Death is not something that will happen suddenly; it builds up over time. Many a time, the body is setting forth the process. The person may not be fully conscious of it—the mind may not be alert enough to grasp it, but the body speaks it in many ways. Apparently, there have been some studies examining the blood work of people who were killed violently—through crimes or accidents. Their blood tests were done on a whim or just by chance, or for some other reason, a little prior to their death—no one knew they were going to die, but by chance, they got it done. And those reports were found to be completely haywire. They spoke a different language altogether. I don't know how far this is true, but this sort of thing is quite possible because the results may have nothing to do with physiological problems. As the body approaches its end, the entire body starts speaking the language of death at that time.

So is it possible to predict death? Yes, it is possible, but it is very limited and highly exaggerated. If I see a coconut tree, looking at the age and the health of the coconut tree, I can say when it will first bear flower, when it will bear fruit. I can also foretell approximately when it will die. I can tell you all this right now, but in between now and that time, if you chop the coconut tree down, the prediction becomes false. This is true for human beings too. Whatever the horoscopes say, someone can die just like that. A whole lot of people in the world died yesterday in an accident or from disease or some such thing. Do you think all their horoscopes said they were going to die yesterday? No. They all said "long life," but they died at twenty-five.

You may have heard of this: Traditionally, in India, before one marries off their child to someone, they always scrutinize the horoscopes of the two people. They do this because they want to make sure that the temperaments of the two people are compatible. They also want to make sure that their children have a long and prosperous life. Yet, it has happened many times that even after all this, the man who married their daughter died in a few days. Of course, if they were able to know that he was going to die in three days, they would never have gotten their girl married to him. This is not to say that there is no basis to these calculations. It is just that these calculations are very limited in scope and their significance is exaggerated.

One's death is usually set in relation to one's solar cycles, which are approximately twelve years each. In other words, the phase or segment of the solar cycle in which you will die is largely set. The day and time are not very relevant because it need not necessarily happen exactly like that. You can take a few more breaths, or some medic may pump something into you, and you may live a little longer. All these things can happen. But if you have the necessary perception and look at a person, it could be easily determined which segment of the solar cycle he or she will go in. It has happened that it looks like the person is going to die by such and such time, even their medical parameters indicate death, but still I have said they are not going to die now. That is because they are in the wrong segment of their solar cycle to die. Even in their designated segment, if they pass just that ailment or situation, they may not die because the death may get pushed for some more rounds.

There are many Indian historical stories where people have chosen a certain time to go. Not just very accomplished yogis; even kings and others have chosen when to die. I am sure everyone has heard of Bhishma,* of course. He was completely shot up with ar-

---

* A great warrior and grandfather figure in the epic Mahabharata.

rows during the Mahabharata war. (That he was lying on a bed of arrows is a more poetic expression of the fact that he had many arrow wounds.) Yet he hung around until that time because his segment had not come. He wished to die in Uttarayana* because he wanted to leave in a certain solar segment.

Predictions are basically about estimating the probability of an event occurring, based on certain things which could turn out to be accurate. Right now, I can look at the sky and say whether it will rain today or not. I have been right 90 percent of the time but sometimes I was wrong. It is the same thing with life. There is no perfect estimate, but the more knowledgeable you are, the more accurate your estimates can be. Predicting death is also like this.

This is like if you look at the speed, the angle, the ambient conditions, and all that, you can with some certainty say where a projectile will land. Rockets, missiles, artillery fire, or a golf ball are all worked upon by adjusting the angle and the speed of the projectile. Similarly, reading your energy, how you are working out your Prarabdha Karma and various other aspects of you, we can say, "Okay, this is how the trajectory of life will be." Based on this, in this culture, it was common for someone who was well versed in these things to look at someone and say death is nearing for this person. So they would say, "You better go to Kashi† now." But some people went to Kashi and ended up living there for twenty or thirty years. That has also happened.

With elaborate calculations, one can say this is how many years your body will last. But in between, if you start doing Inner Engineering, you can surprise the guy making the prediction, because those practices can change the trajectory of your life and he was

---

* The six-month period from the winter solstice in December to the summer solstice in June.
† Another name for Varanasi—one of the oldest and most sacred pilgrimage towns in India, where people traditionally went to attain a good death.

unable to factor that. This is why, traditionally, astrologers said, "If you are on the spiritual path, we will not make a prediction for you." Because with spiritual practices you are tampering with these calculations. You may die sooner or much later. All the other things he said also may happen or may not happen.

Predictions may be accurate or off the mark, but when death is imminent it can be perceived in different ways. If you are around animals, you will see that certain animals can sense death. Dogs, cats, cobras, and many other carnivorous animals can also smell death because, in a way, death has a smell. All the subtler aspects of the physical have their own smells. All carnivores have a special sense of smell because their entire survival process is in their nostrils. They have hearing and vision too, but these are not as keen as their sense of smell. If they want to know something, they don't look—they just smell it out. So because they have such a keen sense of smell, most carnivorous animals know the onset of death. They can even smell death in advance. Not months ahead, but within forty-eight days it can definitely be sensed. Human beings can know it too. For example, with the kind of diet our brahmacharis eat, very easily one can develop a keen sense of smell for these sorts of things.

Once the vayus* start exiting, there is a certain smell to them. This is something even modern science is finding out. They have found that humans have a unique "death smell," which can be used to train dogs to find human cadavers. They have isolated some eight key chemical compounds that make up the human scent of death. They say humans share this with pigs, for whatever reasons!

You can even smell a ghost because a ghost is just a subtle physical form that can be smelled. All dogs can do this. When there is

---

* See the section "The Sequence of Death" in chapter 2.

a ghost, they start barking because they can smell the ghost. They cannot see it, but they can smell it, so they get confused. They go and sit in one corner, put their tails between their legs, and bark. They can see that nothing is happening around them, but there is some activity going on, which makes them very nervous.

Yet smell is not the only indicator of death. You can even see death coming. This happened with one of our residents at the Yoga Center. Just before a large event in Erode one day, I was talking to three or four of our teachers about the arrangements for the event. This resident, who was also a teacher, was standing there. His wife was also a teacher, and she was there too. I looked at him and I did not do anything. I simply ignored him. Now, I never ever look at a person and ignore that person. That is not in me at all. Whoever they are, at least I will nod or do *namaskaram* or smile at them. I will definitely acknowledge their presence in some way. Always. So, after the event, suddenly this incident came to my mind. "Why did I do this? I did not acknowledge him." I thought, "Why?" Then the next evening, I asked, "Where is he?" They said, "He has gone to the Himalayas." I let it pass; I did not pay attention. You know, in our lives, there is no time to dwell upon anything, given the pace at which events happen at Isha. If there was a little time to dwell upon it, it would have been different. I thought about this and I left it. Three days later, he drowned in a stream in the Himalayas.

When he was in front of me, there was a certain lack of presence that was so glaring that I did not respond to him physically standing in front of me. When there is an imminent death, the defined boundaries of the body will be somewhat diffused, which will dilute one's physical presence in our vision. The experience of the physical is essentially because of its defined boundaries; when that is diffused, our visual experience is lowered. If I had not been so focused on going onstage for the event, if I had paid a little attention, I would have just told him. And normally—at least it was so at that time—if someone wanted to go to the Himalayas or such places, they would always tell me and go. But these people—the resident, his wife, and a few other people—decided to go without telling me. His death happened accidentally, but if it had not happened that way, it would have happened some other way. He was heading for it, and it was so visible, but I did not pay enough attention at that time.

So then are there signs that a common man can observe to be able to predict one's death? Yes, definitely. The transition from life to death is a transition from a certain level of dynamism to a certain level of inertia. When this happens, there are things you can certainly notice within yourself. There are sure signs which can tell you, but it is such a complex process that it can always go wrong. Another reason why this is difficult is that people are no longer sensitive to what their bodies express on a daily basis. The body keeps changing all the time—even on a day-to-day basis, even within the day, the body is changing. With everything, we have become modern, meaning we have become all about information and not attention, so we don't know a thing about these aspects. Picking up information from outside is only socially relevant, not life-relevant. In the modern age, we know everything without knowing a thing. Most people don't even know when it is a full moon or a new moon without looking at the calendar. But the body clearly reads these things. If you are able to read these expressions, you will definitely know where the body is heading.

Some very simple signs are very noticeable in the sense organs. For example, a person for whom this transition toward death has begun will not be able to look at the tip of their nose. Even a person with a short nose can still look at the tip of their nose in normal conditions, but when the process of death has started, your eyeballs will not focus. For those who are practicing *Bhrumadhya Sadhana*,* they will suddenly see that the eyeballs will wander like they are loose. They cannot go there. With breath also, it is very noticeable. When you breathe, if you observe carefully, you will see that once the process of death is near, the breath will not go into the lower lobe of the lung. You will breathe mainly from the middle and upper lobes. It is to help the organs shut down one by one. But maybe you are an asthmatic or someone who breathes like that most of the time, so you don't have to think, "I am going to die."

If you are very conscious of the different *agnis*[†] in the body, you will notice when certain dimensions of fire are gone. Once they are gone, you know it is only a question of a limited amount of time. Foreseeing death up to four to six months is very much a possibility. So at that time, if you become meditative, you will go peacefully and joyfully, and the shutting down will happen well. Otherwise, if you fight it and do this and that, you will leave in ugly ways; it may become painful and disturbed.

I can say a few more things about it, but we must understand the consequence of what we say. People will not keep this to themselves. They will look at someone, and if their beard looks a little yellowish, they will make a prediction that this person will die in three days because someone told them it is a sign. They will not keep quiet about it. They will tell this person and everyone around him that he is going to die in three days. They will even gather around him just to watch the prediction come true. Just the level of confusion and nonsense they will create will be huge. And if this person does not die, they may think they have to help him! I am not saying there is no relevance at all to knowing when one will die. We

---

* A particular practice taught to brahmacharis, where the eyeballs are focused between the eyebrows.
† Refers to the five fundamental fires in the body according to Yogic tradition.

could also help people a little more with this. But there is no saying how people will use or misuse these things or confuse themselves completely. Above all, if they notice some signs in themselves—right or wrong—they might think they are going to die in three days. And instead of becoming more peaceful and calm, they will become fearful. All this is possible.

This is why it is said that you must be ready for death every moment of your life. You should live your life in such a way that if you were to drop dead the next moment, you still have ended it reasonably well. You trying to deal with death at the last moment is not the way. Moreover, if you understand that you are mortal, you are always conscious of your mortal nature and you will notice it. When it is time, you will know how to sit in a conducive posture and in a space to transition in the best way possible.

Negative Energies

Using negative energies to cause harm to someone else is a very ancient practice in the world. In India, they made a whole science of it. Of the four *Veda*s,* the *Atharvana Veda* is all about occult practices. It also talks extensively about how to use the energies to your advantage and to someone else's detriment. It explains how if someone who has mastery over this wants to use it, extreme suffering and even death can be caused. There is no doubt about it. One simple way people try to hurt others is through a curse. Now, what is a curse? It is a certain level of black, negative thought that is directed toward you. Because of this, you become sick. When this happens, if you don't find a good doctor, you can become mentally unstable or even die. In the olden days, most people who became mentally unstable would die in a very short time because they would do

---

* The four most sacred Hindu scriptures.

something which would kill them. Either that or they would not eat and just run themselves down. Only a certain kind of people who were in a state of peaceful madness or pleasant madness would last long.

It is possible for a curse to even kill the person who curses. If they don't know how to let out the poison they generate, it could kill them. Or it could kill someone else. Right now, let us say, someone wants to curse you to death. They have generated a certain amount of blackness in their minds and let it out, but you happen to be a little away, or in some way, you are not available to this. Another person who happens to be close by may receive the curse and be affected. This is like how every time you fire a gun, it is not necessary you hit the target; you may hit some bystander. In fact, it is a bystander that gets hit most of the time.

Some people suffer unexplained levels of tragedies or disturbance after they visited a certain place. Everything goes wrong in their life. Then, suddenly, they recover one day and become okay. It is very dangerous to say these things because then people will start imagining things and create a lot of drama about it. But at the same time it is very much possible that other influences that they are not conscious of have touched them.

Today, you need not be too worried about people trying to harm you because there are not too many people who can do occult or black arts. Even if there are people who claim to do these things, they are of doubtful capabilities. In the past, everyone had a family witch doctor just as they had a family doctor or lawyer. This used to be so in southern India and to some extent in the north also—they would not do anything without consulting them. That tradition has more or less died out completely.

What we see of these things today is mostly exaggerated fear and little understanding of the tradition. Human imagination has no control and, unfortunately, there are many charlatans who are using fear as the key. If there is fear, negative impact will keep happening, because fear itself is black art. Otherwise, why would people get scared in a horror movie? They scream, they hold hands in fear, some even get up and run away, when we all know it is only light falling from the projector. If you simply keep your hand across the projector, the ghost is finished. Everyone knows this. Still, all the drama keeps happening. People are not acting scared; it is actually happening to them. So, in many instances, fear itself can work like black art—you don't have to do more.

Essentially, the entire Atharvana Veda is about how to use your energies to create well-being or destroy one's life. These arts are like double-edged swords; you can swing it both ways. Manifesting or avoiding illness, death, or disaster is also possible. If one wants to be able to kill someone, it is not that simple. It takes a lot to actually cause death to someone unless they manage to put something in the food. I don't mean a chemical poison; there are certain energetically charged forms that could be put in the food, which would enter the system. Depending upon how vulnerable you are to these things, accordingly, at that pace and intensity, these things would grow within you. As it grows in the system, it slowly destroys everything about the person. It can eventually cause death. But to be able to do this, one would need access to the person's food. Without that, causing death to someone would take a lot. I think there are only a handful of people in the world today who could do that—as acquiring such capabilities will demand extreme striving and risk to their own well-being and life. This, fortunately, is a deterrent. Most of these people are using the psychology of fear to make things happen, but they can certainly cause a lot of disturbance. Beyond psychological factors, they can cause havoc in the energy system and in turn in the body.

In terms of disturbance, it is relatively easier to disturb people mentally. This is so especially for women. A woman has a greater biological responsibility of bearing a child and keeping the race going, so she goes through phases in her physiology, which makes her vulnerable at certain times.

In terms of harm, harming the body is not so easy to do. The body is an organism which is reinventing itself every day in so many ways. When I say reinventing itself, let us say, you eat one kilogram of food. Of this kilogram of food, at least three to four hundred grams become the body. So a certain reinvention and recycling is happening in the body. Because it is reinventing itself every day in a certain way, the body has protection of its own. If you want to do something to the body, let us say, cause some ailment to the person, it will take much more capability to do that than to psychologically freak someone out. The content of the mind keeps spinning on old things, so psychologically freaking someone out is the easiest thing to do.

Of the five elements that make our body, water, because of its liquid nature, is the easiest to influence. In the science of *bhoota shuddhi*,* thought, emotion, and blood are all under the management of the water element. Considering their vulnerability, it is natural for evil intentions to aim toward the water element in our system. If someone wants to do something physiologically, the easiest thing to affect is the blood. When someone is under some kind of negative energies or that kind of influence, their blood work will go crazy. This is always the sign. This is not in any way connected with any of the organ functions. Every day, it will manifest differently because blood is the flowing part of who you are. After the mind, blood is the most susceptible thing. The next thing that can be affected is your liver or your kidneys because, once again, certain things flow through these. But if someone wants to cause a heart attack to a person, that is very difficult, because the heart just pumps—there is

---

* Cleansing of the five elements in the system. A fundamental form of Yoga.

no chemical process. Sometimes, there are certain types of people who manage to cause neurological disorders also. But by and large, these are the main kinds of harm they can cause to a person.

In the twenty-first century, it is very hard to believe that such things are possible, but unfortunately they do exist. Most people do believe that with prayer, love, best wishes, and good intent, you can cause well-being and create a positive impact on people around you. If you can have a positive impact, the negative impact is also always a possibility. Above all, it is vulnerability of fear that generally does a large part of the work. If one, either through devotion or meditativeness, comes to a sense of fearlessness, that is the simplest way of being above such base arts.

How to Get Rid of Negative Impact

If one is already suffering from the ill effects of the black arts, what is the best way to rid oneself of these effects? There are many ways to sort out these situations; some simple ways are to spend time in nature without people's influence on you, sitting under a tree and allowing sunlight to fall upon your spine especially when it is below an angle of 30 degrees with the horizon after sunrise or before sunset. If you are able to be in a powerful shrine, it will make a huge difference. Dhyanalinga is an example of a space like this that thousands of people have benefited from.

A human mind is a structure with a million rooms. When one accidentally breaks into a new segment of one's mind, what they know or do not know and their basic character may change; sometimes even new languages may surface. And this could be easily misunderstood as being possessed by a new force. Those who think they are possessed by some beings or who are impacted by the occult and such problems can make use of Dhyanalinga, by sitting within the 15-degree angle in front of the Dhyanalinga or behind it. That space has been specially created to remove these influences. They can also sit in the Linga Bhairavi and perform certain beneficial rituals, and it will be over.

If there is strong sadhana, one does not have to worry about all these things. For such a person, these things don't matter. But for those constantly influenced by what is around them, periodic purifications are needed. Otherwise, slowly, inertia will set in. These are not big things, but these small things can slow people down. This is happening to people all the time. You might have picked it up in so many places without knowing. It can come from the food that you eat, the places that you walk into, or the air that you breathe. It could even be just the atmospheres or certain spaces that you came in contact with, and so on. It can make life difficult because, now, certain inertia has set in. It is extra weight, that is all. But if you have just a little extra load, you will see that everything suddenly becomes much more effortful. For example, it is well known today that some minute parasites can get on the backs of honeybees, causing them to travel much shorter distances, and reducing the quantity and quality of their honey. Such things are always happening to people because of the places and people they came in touch with, and life becomes effortful and less productive. So it is always best to do some sort of periodic cleansing.

Traditionally, there were systems in this society for periodic cleansing. This is also the significance of people taking a dip in the river in all the holy places in India. You go and dip yourself three times in the river—in flowing water—and it becomes a significant cleansing. This is one reason why people bathed in rivers. It is a simple way to cleanse yourself from these influences. Of course, today, you cannot dip yourself in a river because flowing rivers are so few, and even those are highly polluted. But if there is a clean flowing river, and if you bathe every day in the river, that is a simple way of washing off everything. It is *klesha nashana*,* where, instead of fire, you use flowing water to cleanse. A shower is not very effective for this because, in most places, the shower does not have that much volume of water to make a difference. Pouring bucketfuls of water upon yourself is much better. There are powerfully consecrated water bodies in the East, like the Teerthakund, where being in that water can make a huge difference. Rain is also good klesha nashana. Rainwater can do wonders to one's energy. These are simple ways by which one can protect oneself from the little bits of negative influences that one may have gathered unconsciously.

SUICIDE: A PERSPECTIVE

Suicide is one classification of death that has become a growing epidemic of our times, even though our generation of people have more comfort and convenience than any other in the history of humankind. Today, there are many studies that suggest a large percentage of the population has contemplated suicide at least once in their lives. Among these, a significant percentage of people have attempted suicide at least once. Currently, in the United States, more people kill themselves every year than those who get killed by homicide and war put together. And more people die of suicide than road accidents in recent times. This is an indicator of things going seriously wrong with humanity. So is there any reason or cause for so many people to feel suicidal? Well, there is really no good or bad reason to commit suicide. They just need a reason, that is all. And you can make any reason a good enough one if you want to. If you want, today, from morning till evening, you can find a hundred reasons as to why you should not live. As for me, I am

---

* A personal aura cleansing ritual offered by Isha Yoga Center.

always searching for a reason to live.* Otherwise, I have no reason. So it is not a question of higher or lower reason; it is just that people find a reason, something that pushes them sufficiently to do that.

For a majority of people, they feel suicidal because life isn't happening the way they want. Except for medical reasons, the rest is largely because of unrealistic expectations. You are just a tiny speck in this Creation. If you look at yourself in the context of Creation as a whole, you are nothing. If you understand that you are nothing, you will be only too glad that things are happening to whatever extent they are. You will be too glad that when you are a bloody nothing—when you don't know one thing from another, when you are sitting on this planet, in the middle of nowhere, in this vast existence—at least you are breathing, your heart is beating, you are living, and everything is working out well. You don't know anything, nor can you control it, nor can you manage it, but still it is happening well. So if you understand the real context of life, you would only be too glad to be alive.

It once happened: A salesman decided to venture into a new housing development. He thought no other salesmen would have gone there because it was a new development. He wanted to be the first one, the early bird. So he knocked at the very first house that he saw there. A lady came and opened the door. Without giving her a chance to speak, he slipped into her house, took a lot of cow dung from his bag, and threw it all over the new carpet. He said, "See, I have a wonder vacuum cleaner. Watch this, I will clean this carpet without leaving the slightest odor. If I don't do it, I will eat every piece of this dung myself." The lady asked, "Would you like some tomato sauce to go with it, because we still do not have electricity

---

* Referring to Sadhguru's own peculiar predicament, where, having already dismantled his karmic structure, he has to strive to keep his body.

in the house." If you feel you have a bad deal in life, and you should commit suicide because of it, what you really need is a little bit of tomato sauce. Eating just dung, you feel like dying. With tomato sauce, it tastes a little better, and then you suddenly want to live. There are many people for whom life is not happening the way they want it to, but they don't turn suicidal because they have hope that tomorrow things will be better. The poor man on the street buys a lottery ticket, so he has to live for a month at least, until the results are out. He has the hope that when he wins the lottery, he will live like a king. After the results are out, there is the next lottery for him. This is how he keeps going. He does not turn suicidal. But for the rich man, the lottery has already happened, and he knows it does not make too much of a difference. There is a deep sense of hopelessness. It is not that you have to consciously seek suicide. You will become death-oriented because the experience of life has become unpleasant. It is only natural that you will try to dodge anything that is unpleasant. This is why, unless you make your experience of life very sweet, you will naturally become death-oriented, not life-oriented.

Fundamentally, people want to commit suicide because in some way they don't know how to handle life. It is like you want to find a permanent solution to a temporary situation in life. That is all it is. Either they don't know how to handle their emotions, thoughts, physical ailment, financial or family situation—there is something they don't know how to handle. When you are trapped in that situation, it may look like it is the end of the world in your understanding. Essentially, you do not know how to handle a specific aspect of your life. So you think the best thing is to end life. It is ignorance, ignorance about the nature of life.

In my perception, I would say a small amount of people are committing suicide because of incurable diseases that they don't know how to handle. It is so painful and horrible that they feel it is better to die. Another small percentage are committing suicide because they are trapped in horrible situations—they are in a war zone, or in the hands of an enemy, or somewhere else where they are being super-exploited and have no way to get away from it. There may be another group who are committing suicide for financial reasons because they feel trapped in a society that is ruled by money. They may have a family and end up without any money, and they just don't know what to do with themselves. They will end up on the street and have a horrible life. They cannot think of themselves being like a homeless man out there begging for food and living; they just cannot imagine the indignity of that. So they commit suicide.

So about 20 percent of the people committing suicide need to be treated compassionately because life has been cruel to them in some way. These are people who are being tortured by the world. The world is not compassionate to them, and they get trapped in certain kinds of debilitating situations. Unfortunately, they decide to take their own lives, because, if they live, it is worse. For these people, it is the world that needs to be fixed. A lot of fixing is needed in the world because sometimes people do terrible things to one another.

There is also a small percentage of people who want to end their life just like that, not for any reason. They have nothing else to do today, so they want to end it. Trust me, there are people like that! I am talking about a life that just wants to end. They have no suffering, no depression, nothing. Simply, they feel like dying today. This is another kind.

Then there are those on the spiritual path who think they should end it. When someone is spiritually evolving, a moment like this comes because your intellect is not able to grasp the profoundness of the experience that is happening to you. So, today, let us say, you sat down in meditation and felt like you were totally bodiless. Then the first thing your mind says is, "Maybe I am ready to leave." It will try to interpret it as, "It is enough; everything has happened." Really! There are people at the Yoga Center who keep writing to me every six months, saying, "I think I am just ready to leave." But when I ask them not to eat one meal, they struggle with even that!

These people must understand that their interpretation of what is happening is completely wrong because they don't have an intellect capable of grasping what the hell is happening within them. For every little experience beyond the body, your mind or intellect may start saying, "Oh, I am ready to die." No, you are not ready to die. It is just that with any dimension of experience beyond physicality, you think it is death. You don't understand there is a whole dimension of Existence, which is beyond the body, which is for the living—not for the dead. Unfortunately, most people enter that realm only with death; that is a different matter. But the nature of the intellect is such: "Okay, if this is not life, what else is it? This must be death." So these people think they should die.

People who are on the spiritual path who feel, every now and then, that their time has come, need firm guidance. This is why spiritual processes were always conducted tightly under the supervision of a Guru. Your spiritual process is not yours; it is his. This looks scary in the twenty-first century, but that much discipline needs to be maintained in spiritual seekers so that there is no question of you jumping into something because of the wrong conclusions you make in the process of your evolution. You should know that if life is not making enough sense to you, it is obvious that you don't have enough sense. Instead of seeing that "I lack sense," you are projecting that life does not make sense.

Of the remaining people, there are those who kill themselves because they have a predisposition toward suicide. They want to terminate life even if there are no external stimuli for doing so. If you notice, there is always a small percentage of people who are suicidal no matter what you do. No matter how you counsel them or what treatment you give, they will keep going back to being suicidal over and over again. For some reason, in these people, their karmic software has developed a glitch, and it keeps attempting to shut down again and again. These are a different kind. For the rest of the people, their urge to commit suicide is fundamentally rooted in ignorance.

Usually, people who are struggling hard in difficult situations will never commit suicide. Even though a thousand things don't happen the way they want, they will work harder, but they will not commit suicide. But people who sit in one place and think life is not happening the way they want will commit suicide because they are dwelling on that. Only if your engagement with the world is very minimal, then 90 percent of things may happen your way, while 10 percent may not. But if your engagement is extensive or global, 90 percent may not happen the way you want. Many things in my life are not happening the way I want. The moment you set this condition that life around me should happen the way I think it should happen, you are setting up a crippling process—you will try to do less and less in the world, because the more you attempt, the fewer number of things happen your way. It is this crippling process that makes you feel cornered and less alive as time goes by, because you have set an impossible condition for your life. You have started inviting death even when you are alive. Death does not need invitation; it anyway comes. You are committing suicide in installments, becoming less and less alive. If you sit alone in a room and go on thinking about how many things are not happening your way, you will feel like ending your life. That is how it is. Today, if life is not going the way you want it to go, you want to end your life. But if things get a little better tomorrow morning, you will start making plans for the future. By tomorrow, if something is going right, you want to live, and you want to live long enough to have your third baby. You even want to have grandchildren. But when everything looks bleak, you think of suicide. This is a self-destructive game that you are playing in your mind; there is no existential basis to it.

Succor for the Suicidal

If you honestly look at it, in the grand scale of things, you are really of no consequence in this Existence. Whether a thousand bubbles are floating in the air or nine hundred and ninety-nine, what is the big difference? How many human beings like you and me have come and gone? But some people think they have a God-given purpose and God made them especially for something. Now, when things don't happen that way, they will freak out because they have such grand ideas about themselves, they have become too important in their own thought process. Once you have become too important in your own thought process, you will be like a tyrant, super confident and bombastic. A diffident person will sit there and grow miserable for the same reason. So between the two of them, who is more stupid? I think the miserable one is more stupid. But a tyrant can cause more pain. The miserable will cause pain to themselves, but the bombastic one will cause pain to everyone else. Well, I'm not chastising you for your stupidity, as the word "stupid" simply means to be amazed or stunned. When one is stunned by the drama that is happening in their psychological space, the phenomenal value of the life process will be lost upon them. So don't be stupefied by your own psychological drama.

Most people who want to commit suicide do it not because the world is torturing them; it is because they are torturing themselves through their own thoughts and emotions. They drive themselves to this point, simply because they have not made an attempt to know anything about the fundamental nature of their own existence and the mechanics of life that they are. Silly little thoughts and emotions that they created become an entire Universe. When their Universe begins to collapse, they think they must end their life. This is simply because there is no *Asatoma Sadgamaya** in them. They are *asatoma;* they have decided to live in darkness. Whatever you give them—it does not matter what—they will turn that into darkness, into a problem. You give them a spiritual process, they will make that also into a problem. Get them married, they will make that into a problem; get them divorced, they will make that into a problem. Get them educated, they will make that into a problem. Leave them uneducated, they will make that into a problem. Poverty, riches, wealth, and everything they will make it into a problem because they are in ignorance. That is all.

Ignorance in this context does not mean you don't know nuclear science. Ignorance in this context means you don't know a damn thing about the nature of your life, and you aren't interested in exploring it. You are busy with your own thoughts and emotions, with your own silly little things that you are creating around yourself. You are living in your own Universe. You must understand that there is no such thing as *your* Universe. Your Universe is an illusion. So this is why I bless everybody that the sooner you are disillusioned, the better it is for you. People say, "Oh, I was disillusioned," as if it is a tragedy. No, it is a great possibility. With disillusionment, all your illusions got destroyed. Isn't it fantastic? Another positive word for disillusionment is Enlightenment. Enlightenment is when all illusions collapse. Right now, you selectively keep some illusions and some you let collapse. If everything collapses, you are Enlightened. If you learn how to handle your disillusionment joyfully, then there will be no suicidal thoughts.

---

* A part of an ancient Sanskrit invocation that means "Let us move from untruth to Truth."

Certain people threatening to commit suicide are doing it only to get attention. Sometimes, it goes bad—they only tried to create some trouble for everybody, but it went bad. It is a terrible thing. It is also true that what people go through just before committing suicide is worse than the death that follows. So if somebody wants to commit suicide, they need empathy. But it is also very important that the necessary understanding and life sense is brought to them because suicidal tendencies should not become an enduring prospect. For every little bit of difficulty that someone faces, he or she should not think it is the most difficult situation and want to go. It is best that people understand this: You did not create life, so you have no business to end it either—whether it is yours or someone else's. It is as simple as that. There are life situations; some are beautiful, some are horrible. Still, it does not give you the right to take a life because you are incapable of creating one. People who want to commit suicide need empathy, but mostly they need a little treatment and above all, life sense.

Once it happened: A young boy and girl in a local college fell in love. They had really become very passionate and intense. Then, of course, coming from traditional families, the parents got in the way because of caste distinctions. They said, "No way. Over our dead bodies." Usually, this is a common proclamation that parents make. It is just a threat; they will not die. If the families do not oppose, most love affairs will fall apart. But the moment they resist it, it becomes like a cause. It is like the couple are fighting an injustice and people will rally behind them. So it went on and a big social scandal happened. When this happened, the lovers thought all this trouble was because of themselves, so they decided that they would end their lives. So they went up the Velliangiri Mountains.

On top of these mountains, there is a place where you can leave your body. From there, you have a clear seven- to eight-hundred-foot drop that will give you a free fall without touching anything before you are splattered on the rocks. Some people have discarded their bodies consciously;* others fall and do it. So the boy and girl reached the top and stood there, hand in hand. They were just about to jump, when the girl said, "Raju, I am so scared. You jump first." (Somehow the name of the idiot in all the romantic movies is always Raju!) The boy was in full form, so he said, "Come, hold my hand and jump." She said, "No, you do it first, then I will come. I will be right behind you." The boy had seen too many Hindi movies, and he jumped. The girl stood at the edge of the cliff and screamed, "Oh, Raju, I love you." Then she started thinking very pragmatically. "Now, Raju is gone. My love is gone. All of the problem is gone. When the problem itself is over, why waste one more life?" So she walked down, and because she could not go back home, she came and settled down at the Isha Yoga Center. For many people who are on the verge of committing suicide, just one moment of distraction is all it takes to prevent it. Most people who managed to overcome that one moment went on to live for a long time.

Those who really want to commit suicide generally become quiet. In Yogic traditions, they say: If a person sits alone in a room in the dark, without lighting a lamp or turning on the light, this means that either they are going to commit suicide or they are going to become a yogi. Both are connected. "I became a yogi" means, in a way, consciously, I killed myself. Even the man who commits suicide has no intention of killing the body. He wants to kill himself. Because he does not know how to do it, because he thinks that the body is him, he hangs the body. Otherwise, he would have just hanged his persona. So if somebody sits alone, without light, with eyes open, you know they are heading for suicide most of the time. If it is in the world at large, maybe 1 percent of the time, but if it is in the Yoga Center, we would say, 10 percent of the time they are

---

* See the section "My Past Lifetimes" in chapter 11.

heading toward something else which is a bigger possibility. They may be just practicing Samyama!*

Now, what can be done for people who chronically feel suicidal? Western science tends to look at suicidal tendencies only from the angle of psychology and physiology. Though their interventions are getting better, they are inherently limited to these two domains. In Yoga, the physiology and the psychology are only consequences of something deeper. Treating the consequences alone is like treating the symptoms and not the ailment. In Yoga, a suicidal tendency is considered the result of an aberration or distortion at the energy level of the person. For such people, only if you are able to bring a certain amount of vitality and exuberance to their energies will they be able to come out of that state. There are tools and methods to do this, and it is possible to pull most people out of it. Time, energy, and organization are the only barriers to this.

If bringing about exuberance in their energies is not immediately possible, the next best thing you can do is to become exuberant yourself. Is it not true that if you are feeling a little low sitting in a dreary office and you go into a beautiful garden, everything becomes wonderful and you are suddenly lifted up? So please be the flower for them. With some fragrance and beauty, even those who are feeling depressed or miserable will rise a little bit. Depression, grief, and joy are all infectious. You have to make up your mind as to what you want to infect the world with. If you are exuberant and they are in your company, it can make a big difference. But today all you are willing to dedicate is a phone line. It may also help to an extent.

As I already said, you did not create this life. So you should not talk about ending it unless your identity as a separate being or a separate person has disappeared and you and the Source of Creation are the same. If you come to that point of evolution, then you

---

* A spiritual practice taught by Sadhguru that involves gazing at something for long durations of time.

can throw away your body consciously. You are allowed to do it. But you are not allowed to do it by damaging the body or by hanging from a tree. Once you are dead, we don't mind burying you under the tree, but hanging from a tree is neither good for you, nor for the tree. Moreover, whether life has been a good deal or a bad deal, if you have a larger purpose, everything is a stepping stone for your ultimate well-being.

Life is precious to everyone. It is naturally so. But if someone has gone beyond that and tried to take their own life—if they are still alive, I would say an absolute no to suicide, but if it has already happened, we should respect their decision; there is no need to be judgmental about that. In spite of life being the most precious thing, if someone has taken the extreme step of taking their own life, it does not matter how silly it looks to you and me. We should respect their decision because that is how it is. But for those of us who are alive, we have no business to take our own life or another life.

In terms of the karmic structure, in terms of the spiritual evolution of a being, suicide is 100 percent unjustified—no question about it. You have to see every situation as a possibility to move toward freedom rather than getting entangled. If you use every situation as a stepping stone, then there is no question of suicide. If a spiritual process becomes active in societies, suicide can almost disappear completely, except in cases of pathological derangement, meaning certain compulsive tendencies have built so deeply into their system that it is beyond their personal will. They might do something because what they do is not in their control.

THE CONSEQUENCES OF SUICIDE

For a person to die of suicide is a terrible way to go. But in terms of life, is there a difference in what happens to them after that? You must know, in terms of life, whether it is suicide or natural death or accident or whatever, it does not matter how you broke your body. Whether one broke one's body by eating badly, or whether one smoked and smoked, or drank and drank, or fell in love with someone and broke their own heart, or simply shot oneself—for the Existence, it does not matter how it happened. They broke their body while the Prarabdha Karma was still on. That is all that life cares about.

However, it matters how one worked toward it. Let us say, someone smoked happily by choice and died. Someone else had some financial problem and became utterly miserable about it, and broke their heart and died. Here, the two deaths are very different things. The smoker is better off because he worked himself to it joyfully, while the other person did so miserably. Society will not like it that a smoker, drinker, or drug addict can be in a better state when he dies than someone who is toiling endlessly. But that can happen because how one worked toward it is important. The existential has no moral compass. It is about life and the ingredients of life, not about social or psychological judgments. Socially, you may think that being above ten other people is a great thing, but this life does not think like that. Are you making a pleasant experience of it for yourself, or an unpleasant experience—this is all that life cares about and the consequences come accordingly.

You need to understand that either with suicide or with another kind of death, you are killing only the physical body. You can kill only the physical body, but with that you are putting an end only to the Annamaya Kosha and the conscious parts of the Manomaya Kosha, that is all. You cannot end it completely. For that, you have to dissolve the subtler portions of the body, which needs something else altogether. Now, if you kill the physical body, the rest of the body, which is still intact, will try to find one more physical body. It will have its own scope and limitations—accordingly, it will choose the new body. It may immediately choose, or it may choose after ten years, or it may choose after a hundred years. The duration depends on certain factors. Till certain things are over, it will hang around; it cannot seek another body. It hangs around here and there not because you died of suicide or accidental death or heart attack, but because your allotted karma had not been finished before death.

Suppose your suicide is timed such that your Prarabdha Karma is almost over; then it is as good as a natural death. If you look at it on that level, as far as this body is concerned, whether someone kills you or you kill yourself, or if you overate and had a heart attack, or whatever—it does not matter. If you don't live properly, you will get a disease and die. So would you call this a suicide? Society calls it suicidal. When someone is smoking away to glory, they say it is "suicidal," but not a suicide. But if you jump off the mountain or if you hang yourself, only then we call it a suicide. But these are mere societal, technical, and legal terms. In terms of life, did you exhaust your Prarabdha Karma or not? This is the only factor that matters and determines what happens after that.

This happened about thirty years ago. At that time, I had a coconut and mango plantation, which I had set up from scratch, in a very remote place. There was a very beautiful lake in front of my farm. Things were going well. There were no proper buildings there, so I used to pitch a tent and stay in it whenever I went to the farm. It was nice this way; I liked it. Those were my motorcycle days. Sometimes, I had some help who would cook something for me; other times I used to ride down about three miles to a little restaurant in the nearest village and eat something. One morning, I was riding down and, very close to the restaurant, I saw a group of people had gathered around a well. I stopped to inquire what was happening. They said a woman had jumped into the well and killed herself around three-thirty or four in the morning.

I sat there on my motorcycle, thinking a little bit about what could have happened in her mind for her to walk out of her house at that time, in the dark, and jump into the well. She must have struggled with what would happen to her young children. Whatever suffering she was going through, it must have been a great struggle to come to that decision. I am sure she would have definitely been terrified about jumping into the well. But still she went ahead and did it, probably hitting the walls on the side or falling into the water and drowning slowly. We don't know which way it happened.

No one had ventured into the well to get her body out, so I volunteered. I went down the well with a rope for about eighty-five or ninety feet and saw her body floating about three feet below the water. She was a very young woman, maybe in her late twenties. Getting her out was not much effort: All I had to do was tie the rope to her body and come up. The villagers hauled her out.

Later on, I went on to my breakfast. From an early age, the moments when I munched on my food have always been moments of enormous depth for me. Here something else is happening—the food that you are eating is slowly becoming a part of yourself. Something that was not you is becoming you. Something which was in the ground somewhere else, in the market, in the vessel, on the stove, is suddenly becoming a part of you. It is a huge love affair, actually. Those moments have always been moments of enormous depth for me.

So I sat there eating my dosa, chewing slowly. At that time, this woman was still hanging around me. I got deeply involved with her. I was actually going through the whole process of her life—her pain, her fears, sufferings, and everything. It is very difficult to describe this. For almost three and a half days, I sat at the farm doing nothing. I sat there under a tree most of the time, unmindful of the need to eat and sleep. When the people who worked for me felt I needed to eat, they would bring something and keep it in front of me. Otherwise, day and night, I just sat under this tree. And this woman was all over me.

When young people commit suicide, particularly in very great distress, they linger around for a long time. People are generally scared to go to or even pass through such places where this kind of death has taken place. But it is not the place; it is the person. If we handle the person, then the place is cleared. This is when a ritual like *Kalabhairava Karma*, which we will look at later, becomes very important.

CHAPTER 4

Can Death Be Hacked?

When the body is still strong, what is meant to be can always be transcended.

CHEATING DEATH

The idea that death is a catastrophe that should be avoided at all costs has somehow set forth this quest to do all kinds of ridiculous things in the hope that we can cheat death or save someone from the jaws of death. People's imaginations have been fired on this, in part because of many colorful tales from lore. These stories have created a lot of hope in people that death can probably be cheated. To some extent, this is also fueled by the science fiction of stellar travel, where they put the body into some sort of a deep freeze or sleep mode and then wake up in another era altogether. But, fundamentally, by doing certain things you can postpone it, but you cannot cheat death; you cannot avoid death.

In India, there is a belief that if someone is on their deathbed, then you should chant the *Mahamrutyunjaya Mantra* or perform the *Mrutyunjaya Homa*, which will avert death. *Mrutyu* means death, *jaya* means victory. So the mantra and *homa* are supposed to grant you victory over death. However, people have been doing the Mrutyunjaya Homa for thousands of years, but no one has survived through all those years! No one won mrutyu. It is a silly understanding that winning over mrutyu is to live forever physically. No one has succeeded in that till now. But one who is beyond the body has won over death.

I am not trying to dismiss the ritual completely. But how it is done, by whom it is done, and how many have actually benefited from it is questionable. Definitely, to some extent, some wonderful things could have happened, certain situations where death was certain may have been averted. There is no question about that. But we should not interpret jaya as victory. *Mrutyunjaya* can mean that you have transcended the fear of death. If you transcend the fear of death, in a way, death does not matter. I have not looked at the ritual in detail, but in my understanding, probably in ancient times, they performed this to give one freedom from the fear of death. Somewhere along the way, advertisements and the commercial aspects of it took over, and they started saying you will never die if you do this.

About fifteen years ago, something like this came our way. A person in Coimbatore took his own horoscope to an astrologer for some purpose. Looking at the horoscope, the astrologer was taken aback and said, "This person is already dead; why did you bring this to me?" The person was very disturbed by this, so he consulted a few more astrologers. They all said the same thing—the person whose horoscope this was supposed to be was dead. Finally, someone brought him to us.

Looking at this person's energies, I pointed out the places in the Dhyanalinga where he should sit to strengthen those aspects of his energy system. He did that and went home. This is one of those rare horoscopes where someone clearly foresaw that he would die at this time. But due to his karma in this life or his sadhana or the way he lived his life or whatever, he had gone beyond that foreseen time of death. In some ways, he was a dead man alive. So I said, "Anyway, you crossed one line, let us cross one more," and asked him to sit in different places in the Dhyanalinga which we had marked for him. Without asking questions, he went and sat there. If he is alive and well today, it is his doing.

Recently, I came to know he is still alive and fine, and he has no clue how he survived. Now, this became a big thing, and people started asking, "Is it possible to avoid death by sitting in the Dhyanalinga?" See, people die due to different reasons. And I am not talking about medical reasons. Let us say, two people are dying of the same illness—perhaps renal failure. But, energy-wise, they need not be dying of the same cause. They may be dying of two different energy causes—the energy may be exiting in two different ways.

Accomplished yogis sometimes do certain things to avert what would otherwise have been a moment of death for them. They do this by slowing down everything in the system and entering into samadhi* states. They say this happened in the life of the Indian saint Shirdi Sai Baba. He was suffering from severe asthma, and one day he suffered a severe attack when it felt like he was going to die. So he decided to rid himself of the ailment entirely by going into samadhi. He told his disciples that there would be no sign of life in his body for some time and they should protect it for three days. If after three days there was no sign of him returning, then they should bury the body in a particular spot. That night he went into samadhi. Both his breathing and his pulse stopped. The next day, the villagers came and, being concerned that he was dead, wanted to at least properly bury him in the spot he had indicated. Fortunately, one of Sai Baba's disciples did not budge and prevented them from doing so, placing his Master's body on his lap all the while. Finally, after three days, Baba showed signs of life and be-

---

* More on this in the section "Samadhi and Death" in chapter 5.

came normal again. He lived for thirty-two years after that, because he managed to avert death at the appointed time by going into samadhi and recharging his pranic system.

In samadhi states, your sense of time is lost because it is only measured by the progress and the cycles of the physical. Let us say, you are sitting in an air-conditioned hall which is uniformly lit from morning to evening. The only reason you will know time is because of the weariness of the body. As the day progresses, your body keeps time. Every three or four hours, it will tell you that you have to go to the bathroom. It will tell you that you are thirsty. It will tell you that you are hungry. This is the only way you will know time. Without the cycles of the body, you don't know time. So if you slow down the cycles of the body by going into samadhi you may lose the sense of time, and, then, in your experience, there is no time. So what is ten years to other people may get reduced to one year because you made your cycles ten times slower.

So for the clock outside, you cheated it. But you did not cheat time because time is not in the clock. The clock is like your bladder. It keeps a count of things inside of you. It is not that the clock is generating time. Time is a completely different dimension altogether. Only because of the physical cycles, because the Earth spins, because the planet revolves around the sun, are you keeping time with those physical manifestations or physical expressions. But, actually, if there were no planets, there would still be time. Time is the platform for Creation to exist. Without it, Creation would not exist.

Now, if you slow down your metabolism, if you as much as breathe a fewer number of times in a minute, you will live longer. You will not be deceiving time. It is just that you slow down the body and stretch that time. If you distance yourself from the body, you deceive time. Samadhi works like that. But if you deep-freeze the body, you will go through life without experiencing it. Let us say, you deep-froze the body for a hundred years and then woke up. You will not gain any life because you did not live for those hundred years. If you were living for these hundred years, it means something. You did not exist, but you just popped up after a hundred years—it is like a prisoner who served twenty years in jail and then came out. There is no real gain in that. When it is so easy to reproduce and have a new body, why do you want to preserve the old body? What is the point? This is all an Egyptian dream. You should see how those mummies are now—all dried rubbish, valuable only to archeologists, not for any life process. Of course, it has become good tourism.

Now, there are some other specific situations or programs where we tell people, "Don't worry, for the next few days or weeks, we will ensure that you will not die." Once it so happened that I was in the middle of a program, and they brought in a brahmachari who had been bitten by a snake. I said, "He will not die just because a reptile bit him. That much life we have taken into our hands." And he survived. There have been some other situations like this; so, over time, some people started asking, "Sadhguru, can you cheat death?"

We are not cheating death. We are only making sure life happens, that is all! Right now, to stabilize my own system, I am using certain help from outside to do that in a certain way.* Similarly, in the advanced spiritual programs at Isha, I act like a peg for everything else because everything else is connected to me at that moment. This is why we are so horribly finicky about every small thing during the programs. We are finicky about where people sit, where they stand, when they come in, when they go out, and all that. If they get up for as much as going to the bathroom, we don't let them, because if we don't maintain the tightness of the atmosphere we will not be able

---

* Certain energy supports that Sadhguru draws from outside to keep his physical body intact.

to be a peg that holds and supports. We want everything to happen in a certain way, because once the situation becomes loose, then managing it becomes almost impossible. When everyone is focused in one direction, it is easy to do what we have to do with them. When we did not have the necessary infrastructure and conducted these programs in external premises, many big lumps the size of lemons used to form on my spine. They used to stay for two or three days because that was the kind of strain the body was under. Now that we have our own constructed places, at least one aspect of it is handled. It is so much easier to do these programs in a place which is dedicated to it rather than doing it in a place where every day something new is happening.

Almost every day, at least a dozen photographs of people who are on their deathbed come to me. People want to know whether they will die or not, or if something can be done for their recovery, whether it is the right time for them, or if something can be done for them. It is dealt with without making too much drama about it. You could create a lot of drama about it and become like a superman. But I want to be able to go out and play golf anonymously. So it is better to be like this.

In an earlier section,* I narrated how one of our teachers went to the Himalayas and died. So if it is possible to avert or postpone death in some cases, could his death have been avoided? If you attempt such interventions, there are many things you will have to do. In today's world, due to various cultural and attitudinal situations, people are not available to you in that dimension. Maybe people who are at the Yoga Center are available to some extent, and you could do something with them. But even they are not fully available. The worst part of this modern life is that everything has to be ex-

---

* "Predictions of Death" in chapter 3.

plained. Life does not work like that. Tell me, how are you alive? With all your science, explain to me, what is keeping you alive right now? I will show you how many holes there are in your explanation.

Because you have to explain everything, there are so many things you cannot do with people. They will put everything under their limited logical lens and come to their own conclusions. You can intervene in some way with only a few people. The rest you cannot touch, because without a logical explanation you cannot do anything. This is the nature of life today. Just telling him, "Don't go" would not have worked.

So was it meant to be? Not necessarily. When the body is still strong, what is meant to be can always be transcended. Maybe I would have asked him to go on a long sadhana, but he would not have complied just because I asked him to. If I had told him to go into silence for forty-five days, he would have thought that he was being punished and maybe he would have slipped out of the back door and death could have happened in many other ways.

In today's world, you cannot tell someone, "Just do this." You have to explain it to them, but it is not possible to explain these things, because, for one, it may not be logical; second, it is not so black and white. Even in your own perception, it is not like it is 100 percent certain that this person is going to die. It looks like they will die. There are certain indications that say death is close, so I think they may die. But they may not die. You see a gray area, you see danger, and you step back. That is about it. You cannot say, "This is it; it is definitely going to happen." There are some cases where you can say that, but those cases are rare. Life is not like that. There is a twilight zone always.

Now, why would a Guru, or someone who is capable of intervening, intervene at all? If there are spiritual reasons, we will intervene. Or in some moments of compassion, we may intervene. But it is not good to intervene all the time because, after all, you are not avoiding death—you are only postponing it. When you do that, what comes next may not be as good as what has come now. So you need not always intervene. But, today, twenty-first-century morality is such that they will say, "You could have intervened, but you did not. That amounts to murder." Twenty-first-century people think they are all eternal people; they are not going to die. Till you print their obituary, they are not dead! People are in that state of denial about their mortality.

The Dance of Death

Being able to raise the dead is a deep fascination for most people. For them, that is the ultimate test of someone's spiritual powers. Most people are living like the dead anyway because they are unconscious of many things within themselves. If people are living unconsciously, it is as good as death. So, in a way, the whole spiritual process is about raising the dead. In that sense, raising the dead is my work, but that is not what people are asking about. They are very interested in knowing if I can make a corpse come alive again. This is a very immature desire that stems from some historically famous incidents.

On my first trip to the United States, I happened to address a gathering where a staunchly religious man stood up and asked, "Can you raise the dead?" I said, "Why would I do such a stupid thing?" It is a stupid thing because the dead should remain dead, should they not? If all the dead came back, could we live here? Are we not glad that they are all dead? You are probably thinking of one person—your husband or your wife or your father or your mother or someone like that. But I am talking about all the billions who have died on this planet till now, including the dinosaurs. Only because they are dead is it possible for us to live here. And what kind of a fool would bring back the dead? Only someone who has no sense of life at all and absolutely no perception of life would interfere with the life process and bring back the dead. Transforming yourself is one thing, meddling and fixing life around you is another thing. Life has a certain process much deeper than you can understand. So don't cut it and meddle with it by doing silly things.

It once happened: It was the dream of an elderly couple in Texas to visit Jerusalem, the Holy Land. So they made the trip and relished every step that they took there. They took the road that Jesus walked with the cross and visited the place where he walked upon water and all that. Unfortunately, in all this excitement, the wife had a heart attack and died. Now, the local funeral director came and made an offer to the husband, "See, we can do all the rituals for your wife for just $6,000. But if you want to transport her back to Texas it will cost you $24,000, and we don't know what the funeral charges in Texas are." The man thought about it and said, "No, I will take her back to Texas." They asked, "Why? This is the Holy Land, this is the best place to bury her, and it is cheaper too." He thought about it again and said, "No, I am taking her to Texas." They asked, "Why? It does not make sense. Why do you want to do this?" The man replied, "In Texas, the dead stay dead."

Historically, there have been many people who were declared dead, but they came back to life after some time. Sometimes, they popped out by themselves from their coffins even during their funeral. So this is also one of the reasons why people are looking for some miracle to bring their dead back to life. But these were not cases of miracles or someone meddling with life but that of misdiagnosis. Today, defining death is a big challenge because science has learned that death is not an event but a process that can stop progressing or even reverse itself due to various reasons. In fact, medically, they even have a term for it—they call it the Lazarus phenomenon, when someone who was declared dead comes back to life after some time, with no explanation.

In India, there have been many instances where someone died and they took the body to a yogi or someone like that and then the dead person was revived. But these too are not "revivals" in the true sense. It is more like going to a doctor of a different kind. Mostly, these were deaths that were caused by snakebites. When one is bitten by a snake, the prana takes a much longer time to leave the body. In the meantime, if the effect of the venom wears off or if there is an external infusion of prana, then it is possible for the person to be revived. Doctors who work with snakebite deaths may have seen this: With certain kinds of snakebites, especially that of the cobra, or *naga*, family, when everything has been done and the victim has still not been revived, sometimes if you put them on a ventilator, after a while they make a recovery, just like that.

I experienced something like this in my own life. I have been bitten by cobras at least five or six times in my life. Once, it almost killed me. I had picked up this cobra, but I did not notice that there were two of them entwined together. It was not the mating season, but for some reason they were together, and when I picked one up, the other one fell on my foot and bit me four times. Its venom started to get me. It must have hit the bone the first few times, so it kept going until it hit the flesh and let the venom out. Once the venom enters your body, you experience a different kind of pain. It is not just the biting or the poking kind of pain. It is like an injection—when they pierce you with a needle, there is one kind of pain; when they inject the medicine, there is another kind of pain. So I put the cobra away and started to attend to the bite.

I knew, whatever happened, I should not fall asleep. This happened in a remote area where there were no people nearby. I had my bicycle with me, so I just took my cycle and went to the nearest house I could find. There was a lady there. I told her that a cobra had bitten me, so I needed lots of tea. She became hyper but was sensible enough to make me a pot of black tea. I drank it and managed to stay alert without falling asleep or losing consciousness. Later, I made it back home.

Initially, I thought I would tell my father because he was a doctor and he would take me to the hospital and do something. But then something in me said, "What the hell, let me see what will happen." I was feeling okay, but my eyelids were feeling a bit heavy. Moreover, I did not want to freak my parents out or bring undue attention to my activities. So I just sat down and practiced a little bit of Yoga. I was not doing the Yoga to counteract the poison, but I was feeling drowsy, so I did some Yoga. After that, I had an early dinner and went to bed. In the morning, I was a bit groggy, my eyelids swollen and heavy, but I had survived.

This may have happened because the cobra probably did not deliver a full dose of its venom, or maybe just staying awake and hanging on helped ride out its effects. There was no manipulation of life involved here. But, generally, when a cobra bites, there is a greater possibility for revival because the prana withdraws more slowly from the body than usual. However, until the point where Udana Vayu has withdrawn completely from the body, revival is a possibility, at least in principle. There are some Tantric processes to do this. But after Udana Vayu has left the body, there is absolutely no chance to revive someone.

Reviving the dead is not so big in the East, but the Tantric system in India was always big on making a corpse sit up. A dead man cannot sit up, right? But that is not true. They can be made to sit up. This is because, as we already saw, death happens slowly—the withdrawal of the life process happens step-by-step. When the lung, heart, and brain activity stops, they declare you dead, but the life process still continues, and you can rekindle that. It is by using this that tantriks make dead bodies sit up. Sometimes, this is also done on corpses that are burning on the pyre.

I have not seen this personally, but I know people, people who will not lie about such things, who have seen corpses that were burning on the pyre be made to sit up. This happens because, at that moment, when the burning begins from the outside, the life process retreats, and it creates a concentrated space where life is happening more intensely at that moment. Some people are able to make use of that and rekindle the system in such a way that suddenly the corpse sits up. For some time, it behaves as if it is alive and then falls dead when the life exhausts itself. This is possible because when the corpse is brought for cremation, there is still some life energy in it. It is not good enough to beat the heart, make the circulation happen, make the brain work, and all that, but in the cellular level there is energy, lots of energy. When the fire touches it, it inflames that in a certain way. Now, by investing a certain amount of energy into the corpse, you will be able to get it to perform some action for some occult purposes—like, how your phone battery is dead but still you can make an SOS call.

All the Tantric and Aghori practices, some of which involve sitting upon a dead body, have relevance only because of this phenomenon. Otherwise, what is the point of sitting on a dead body and doing all those things? If dead means completely dead, what is there to do with bones and flesh? They are not sitting on the body to revive it. They have no interest in reviving the body. They want to use this little spurt of energy to transport themselves into something. They are trying to extract that little life and use it. That is the basis of animal sacrifices. When sacrifices are not possible, they try to use a freshly dead body. This is not as if the dead person is being brought back to life, nor is it of much spiritual significance.

Now, in the West, some people have started a project whereby, if you pay a huge sum of money, your body is cryogenically frozen and kept intact after your death. The hope is that in the future, when there is a technological breakthrough to restore your body, you can come back to life. This is pointless.

Normally, after an injury or something like that, when a person goes into a deep state of unconsciousness, the body tries to escape the pain and suffering because it may not be strong enough to bear both the shock and the pain of it. It is a kind of defense mechanism that switches off everything. Such a person may recover, once the body is strong enough to sustain life. But in cases where life has completely left the body or the bodies are being artificially kept alive for many years in a coma, there is no person in the body. You are just keeping a heart and two kidneys and a few more organs alive. That is not really life as such. This is like when someone gives their kidney, that kidney is kept alive for a few hours somewhere else—not in anyone's body, but outside. It is kept alive artificially. A coma state is very similar. Whether you keep a kidney or two kidneys plus heart, plus this and that, it is about the same. There is no person anymore.

Technology is there to keep the body alive, and in the future, you may be able to revive it too. But your particular life coming and choosing the same body is far away. In other words, this someone taking up the same body after twenty-five years is just rubbish. If such a thing ever happens, it cannot be the same person. By accident, it could have happened that some other consciousness or disembodied being got into it. That is all. But it is such a great business idea. The pharaohs of Egypt spent the money needed for mummification then. But, even now, it is good business because you pay in advance, not on revival! Unfortunately, there is no benefit for the mummified one.

I doubt such a thing will ever happen, but something like this can happen in a different way. You may have heard of yogis leaving their bodies, going somewhere, and returning to take them on. Sometimes, it so happens that before he comes back, another yogi takes on the body and goes away. It is like you park your motorcycle and go somewhere; meanwhile, someone else picks it up and leaves! Such things may happen, but the chances are very remote.

TRANSMIGRATION

The Eastern and Native American cultures were big on transmigration—the process of someone taking on the body of another person, usually a freshly dead person. In India, it is called *Parakaya Pravesha*—entering another body. It is considered one of the *Ashtasiddhi*s, or the eight great capabilities for a yogi. There are many instances of transmigration in Indian lore. One famous instance is that of Adi Shankara.

In ancient India, there were neither heretics nor the persecution of people for their personal beliefs. Whenever people had something new to propagate, they would debate with those holding opposing views. During his time, Adi Shankara was a formidable debater. His sense of logic was astute. You don't argue with a man like that. But once a famous religious scholar challenged Adi Shankara to a debate and lost. Then that man's wife maneuvered herself into the argument. Sometimes women can be fiercely protective of those dear to them. She said, "You defeated my husband, but he is not whole. We are two halves of the same thing. So you must debate with me also." How can you beat this logic?

So the debate started with the woman. Then she saw she was losing. So she started asking him questions about human sexuality. Nevertheless, Shankara continued to debate with her. Then she went into more details and then she challenged, "What do you know by experience?" This was a trap because Shankara was a brahmachari. He realized that this was a trick to defeat him. He said, "I need a month's break. We will pause the debate here and resume after a month." He then went into a secluded cave. He told his disciples, "No matter what happens, don't allow anyone into this cave because I am going to leave my body and look for another possibility for some time."

It so happened that a king was bitten by a cobra and had just died. Normally, when someone dies, from the moment the breath stops it takes about an hour and a half for the Prana Vayu to exit completely. The other pranas will be still present and exiting slowly, but the Prana Vayu will have exited completely by then. But when the cause of the death is a cobra bite, this takes up to four and a half hours. So, in many ways, this is an ideal condition for one who wants to enter that body.

Shankara left his own body to take the king's body. He left behind his vyana in the system because his body needed to be maintained for him to be able to come back. He took the king's body to answer the woman's questions experientially. So he went through that process. When some wise people around the king saw that a man whom they had declared dead had suddenly sat up and was full of energy, they became suspicious. They could recognize by his behavior that it was not the same person. It was clear to them that there was someone else in the same body. They sent soldiers all over the kingdom to look for dead bodies and burn them immediately. Their intention was that now, because the king had come back alive, he should not leave and go back. So what if he was a different guy? He looked the same. And it was very important for the kingdom to have its king. So the soldiers were sent everywhere to find and burn all the dead bodies.

The soldiers managed to locate Shankara's body in the cave and wanted to burn it. His disciples tried to mislead them, saying that their Guru was not dead, but in shavasana and would wake up soon. Suspecting fraud, the soldiers built a pyre in the cave itself and placed Shankara's body on it. Just as they were about to light the pyre, sensing this situation, Shankara relinquished the king's body and returned to his own. The king dropped dead once again and Shankara returned and went on to win the debate he had left midway.

A person who does this kind of circus with his energies usually does not live long after that, because all this expends a tremendous amount of energy. It is said that Shankara left his body shortly after this incident, at the age of thirty-two. Actually, no one knows how or where he left his body. He was last seen in Kedarnath. This incident may have accelerated his departure.

There is another famous incident involving a yogi who was later known as Thirumoolar in Tamil Nadu. His original name was Sundaranathar. He was from southern Tamil Nadu and traveled to Mount Kailash. It is said that he was initiated there by Shiva himself. After spending many years at Mount Kailash, he returned south to meet his contemporary sage friend Agastya Muni, who had settled in Tamil Nadu. While passing through a forest on his way back, he saw a herd of cows crying. Their cowherd had just died of a snakebite. Moved by the sorrow of the cows, he decided to take the dead cowherd's body for some time and console the cows. He left his body inside the hollow of a tree and entered the body of the cowherd.

The cows became happy and he herded them back to the village. He then came back to the tree to retrieve and re-enter his own body. But to his surprise, his body was not to be found anywhere. So he continued to live in the body of the cowherd. People in the village were very surprised to see that their simple cowherd now espoused spiritual teachings and composed many spiritual hymns. His name was Moolar, so, out of respect, they began calling him Thirumoolar (Thiru is a Tamil honorific), and he became known by that name. More than three thousand spiritual compositions are attributed to Thirumoolar and they are sung even today.

Are such things possible? Very much possible. There are many more examples of transmigration in India. Is it a feat? Not really. All it takes is a little bit of an understanding of the mechanics of how life happens within you. Now, if one wants to enter the body of someone who is alive, it would take a lot more. Either the person whose body you enter into must also be accomplished enough that they can make space for the other person, or they must be extremely weakened because of disease or something and it is like they are halfway gone. If it is a full-blooded body and there is no awareness of anything, then it is not possible.

All this is occult. It is not of spiritual significance, really. It is also one way of sometimes proving to yourself or to others that such things can be done. Or sometimes these things are done to do something that you do not want to do in your own body. The reasons can vary. Sadhguru Sri Brahma also did something like this toward the end of his life, in a desperate attempt to fulfill his Guru's dream.[*]

Seeking Immortality

Immortality has always been a fancy pursuit of the affluent. When people became affluent, they felt they had everything, but still, life had not happened to them. So they wanted to hang on. Immortality has also been the quest of miserable people in the world. It is a misunderstanding that people who are joyful, people who live their lives really well, are unwilling to die and they seek immortality. If joy becomes your companion, other things may have no place in your life. If you notice, when you are joyous, you are not greedy anymore. You are very generous. You will give away anything at that moment. It is only when you are miserable that you are very greedy. Happy people are loosely attached to life. They are willing to drop

---

[*] More about this in the section "My Past Lifetimes" in chapter 11.

off at any time. People always think that miserable people want to die. It is not so. Miserable people cling to life more than anyone else. The more miserable they are, the more they cling to everything around them. Even if they live for a hundred years, they will cling a little more and a little more because they have never really lived. All the time, they were so immersed in their own misery that they never had any time to live.

A happy person does not cling to anyone. When a person is blissful in their life, they are not bothered about whether they are going to be reborn or not. They are not even bothered about whether they are going to be alive or dead tomorrow. They are so blissful. When you are really happy, you don't need anyone. You don't need your wife, you don't need your husband, and you don't need your God. When you are very happy, all gods are forgotten. God is the creation of miserable people. Because there are lots of miserable people in the world, God has thrived. If the world was full of blissful beings, God would disappear. If all of us are truly happy, God has no business in this world. We can handle ourselves. We need God only because we have created so much of misery within ourselves and above all, such a fear of suffering.

When you become really happy, happy beyond words, when your joyousness transcends all limitations, you are ready to die. You feel, "This is it; I am willing to dissolve myself and go now." Joy prepares you for death. A man who is ready to simply die when everything is well is a man who has seen life in its fullness. Lovers who have tasted the joy of togetherness, even for a short while, are willing to die. Have you not seen this? In profound experiences of joy, love, and ecstasy, you have touched the core nature of life, where the realization that there is no distinction between life and death arises within you, if not consciously, at least unconsciously. What you call life is also death; you can say I am living or I am dying right now, because both are happening at the same time. Creating a distinction between life and death is happening out of one's lack of profoundness of experience of life. However, a miserable man is not ready to die because he has been a miser about living. He never lived, so he thinks that if he gets one more year he will live better.

In the past, every king, every powerful person on the planet, always sought to somehow become immortal. But, in reality, if you really want to curse someone, don't wish them death; wish them an endless life. That would be the worst curse for anyone. If someone lives by sadhana, and through sadhana he or she extends their life, then it is different. This is not stretching life forcefully; on the contrary, you are providing life with the necessary support to flesh itself out further. In Yoga, we have always been saying that humans can live up to 160 years. But rarely in recent times have we seen anyone living up to that age.

On average, global life expectancy has gone up significantly. This is largely because of the medical care and all the supplements that people routinely take. It is causing other problems, but it is giving an extension of life. Many organs are rejuvenated because of the battery of minerals and nutrients one takes. Now, they say, if we somehow survive for another fifty years, we can live for five hundred years because, by then, technology will have advanced so much that we can culture a new heart and a new liver and a new kidney in a laboratory and refit ourselves with everything new.

Some people were telling me how they are going to live for four hundred years. They have made plans. They are making contracts with laboratories, with doctors, as to when they will replace which organ, whether it is still working or not working. They have already decided this by looking at one's genetic predisposition and other biological markers. They have already decided that at the age of eighty they will replace their heart, at the age of eighty-five they will replace their kidneys and all the bones and joints, and so on. These are the kind of plans they have made to live for four hundred years. Such people will suffer immensely for this.

Extending the life of the body may become possible, but unless you have sadhana in your life and a certain level of mastery over your system, you will not have a mind if you live that long. You will live like a zombie. Without the needed sadhana, if you stretch the body the mind will cop out. You will find many people with still-sturdy bodies but their minds are gone because they have run out of their Prarabdha Karma. It is like you have the hardware but you have run out of the software required to run it. They are unable to open up the next dimension of memory because they have no sadhana. That just leaves an empty screen.

Wanting to live long is not a problem. But this thinking of forcefully increasing the lifespan arises from a certain arrogance against life which I don't like. This happened in the year 2050: A few scientists made an appointment with God. They met him and said, "Hey, old man, you have done pretty well with the Creation; but everything that you have done, we can also do now. So we think it is time you retire." Then God said, "Oh, is that so? What is it that you can do?" They said, "Just watch this." They pulled out their test tubes and conical flasks and all that. They took some soil and mixed various things with it and produced a live baby and it started crying. "See, here it is. We can make life. So where is the need for you? You can retire." To this, God said, "That is great, but first get your own soil."

If you want to work on the extension of the life of your body, you need to do it with the right kind of sadhana, not with outside fixing. If you do the right kind of sadhana, when the body is stretched, along with it, the Prarabdha Karma will also open up. It will open up other dimensions of karmic substance, and there will be substance to keep this going. If there is no substance for the being, but there is substance for the body, you will become like a ghost. At least, a ghost does not occupy space and does not eat food. You will eat food and occupy space, but you will live like a ghost. So living longer does not mean you go on prolonging the life of the physical body by any means. For that you need the necessary karmic substance to carry on. This can only be achieved by sadhana. Now, if you do sadhana and live for four hundred years, then you would be of tremendous value to the world. You will be of value not just because you will live long, but because of the flowering of wisdom and grace that you have become. Because of the sheer maturity of life, it will organize itself in that way in your body. Your "being," or what you are, will float around effortlessly like a bubble.

In terms of sadhana, Hatha Yoga is very important because you need a good physical base. Moreover, if you are in such a state within yourself that when you close your eyes, you have no sense of time, then time is deceived by you. If the cellular aliveness is kept up in a youthful manner, the body can last because it can rejuvenate itself. Most important, if you are burning your karma strong enough, new levels will naturally open up. Without sadhana, you have no way of digging deeper into the larger karmic substance, or what you call Sanchita Karma. Such a person will not be able to sustain life-extension.

Also, your experience of life will not be enhanced in any way just because you live for a greater number of years. A reasonable number of years, yes, but simply extending years is not going to make your life any greater, in your experience. If you just say, "I am one hundred fifty years old," others may be impressed, but in your experience what is the difference? You must decide if, for you, life is an account book or a phenomenon. If it is an account book, numbers matter. If it is a phenomenon of experience, then numbers don't matter.

Seeking the Next Dimensions

People ask this question: If my life is going well, why not continue this endlessly? What is wrong with this? Why seek something else? Now, it is not because we are suffering this that we want to move on. The very nature of the being is such that it wants to go to the next dimension or to the ultimate dimension.

It is like this: After you were born, you learned to walk. It was the most exciting thing. And then you grew up, then you got married, you made money, you produced children, and you died. And again you were born, again you were excited about standing up and you were also excited about riding a bicycle and again you met your boyfriend and you were very happy and then you were disappointed and again you got married. This is happening again and again. Suppose you actually realize this, not because someone told you, but because you actually saw that you have done this a thousand times over and still are going through the same process again and again. Would you want to go through it again?

About people's lives going well: People think that if they are married, if they have a house and children, and if they have tons of money in the bank, they are living well. That is not so. Living well means that you have grasped all aspects of life. If you have grasped everything that is there to know about life, then you have broken through the bubbles of memory in which you are storing these different things. If it all bursts out in you, you would definitely like to move on to the next dimension. Once one realizes one is repeating the same thing, they will suffer. They will want to move on to the next dimension.

Or look at it this way—suppose we make you watch your favorite movie over and over again. Seven times a day, every day, for the next month. After all, it is a wonderful movie and you like it the most. You will be coming out with tears in your eyes when you watch it the first five times or ten times. Eventually you will see that it is just a play of light and sound. Once there is no involvement from you, you will simply sit back and look at it. Suppose, in addition to this, I also took you to the projector room and it really sinks into you that the whole goddamn thing is just two wheels and a lightbulb tricking you, churning up all these emotions and making you believe all this. You may still enjoy a movie, but you will not be involved anymore.

The longing to move on to the next dimension becomes urgent, especially if you look back and realize you have been in the same movie for a long time. This dimension is about "this" and "that." In your present state of mind, "this and that" or "that and that" is interesting right now. But the next dimension is just "this and this and only this." What is seemingly many will turn out to be One. This may not seem to be interesting to you right now because you can think, feel, understand, and project only from the dimension in which you exist. But that is how it is. The sooner you realize that you have been in the same dimension, the more you will long for what is beyond that. Until then, it will seem uninteresting to you.

CHAPTER 5

Mahasamadhi

Mahasamadhi is the end of the game. The cycle is over. There is no question of rebirth; it is complete dissolution. You can say this person is truly no more.

SAMADHI AND DEATH

People often make an association between samadhi and death. They think samadhi means some deathlike situation. It is far from that. The word "samadhi" has been largely misunderstood. It is made up of the words *sama* and *dhi*. Sama means "equanimity" and dhi means *buddhi,* or the intellect. If you reach an equanimous state of intellect, it is known as samadhi.

The fundamental nature of the intellect is to discriminate. This discriminatory quality is very important for survival. You are able to discriminate between a person and a tree only because your intellect is functioning. If you want to break a stone, you have to discriminate between the stone and your finger. Otherwise, you will break your finger. Discrimination is an instrument that supports and executes the instinct of survival present in every cell of the body. If you transcend the intellect, you become equanimous. But this does not mean you lose the ability to discriminate. If you lose the discriminatory intellect, you will become insane.

In the samadhi state, your discriminatory intellect is perfectly in place but, at the same time, you have transcended it. You do not make a distinction—you are simply here, seeing life in its true working. The moment you drop or transcend the intellect, discrimination cannot exist. Everything becomes one whole, which is the reality. A state like this gives you an experience of the oneness of the Existence, the unification of everything that is. In this state, there is no time or space. Time and space are a creation of your mind. Once you transcend the mind as a limitation, time and space don't exist for you. What is here is there, what is now is then. There is no past or future for you. Everything is here, in this moment.

Samadhi is a state of equanimity where the intellect goes beyond its normal function of discrimination. This in turn loosens one from this physical body. A space between what is you and what is your body is created. Death means the physical body is completely lost. There is no contact with the physical body. Samadhi means that the physical body is intact, but the contact with the physical body has become very minimal.

For the sake of understanding, people have categorized samadhis into eight different types or levels. Of these eight, they have been broadly categorized as *savikalpa* and *nirvikalpa* samadhis. Savikalpa samadhis are samadhis with attributes or qualities. They are very pleasant, blissful, and ecstatic. Nirvikalpa samadhis are without attributes or qualities. They are beyond pleasant and unpleasant. Those who go into nirvikalpa samadhi states are always kept in protected states because their contact with the body becomes very minimal. The smallest disturbance, like a sound or a pinprick, can dislodge them from their body. These states are maintained for certain periods to establish a firm distinction between oneself and the body. It is a significant step in one's spiritual evolution, but still not the ultimate.

As we mentioned earlier, sometimes yogis go into deep states of samadhis for certain periods because they want to evade certain situations within themselves, or they want more time to work out their karma. Let us say, a yogi knows that his life situation is such that the next day he will have to leave his body, but still his karmic score is not settled, his karmic account is not complete. So he does not want to go. Instead, he goes into a samadhi state for, say, a week or ten days. Now he gets a short extension to finish what he wants to finish. This is a way of turning the clock back, this is a way of deceiving the process of time. When someone makes himself neither the mind nor the body, he avoids the *Kala Chakra*, or the wheel of time. So one deceives time and stays there and gets extra time for himself.

Samadhis by themselves have no great significance in terms of Self-Realization, or knowing the true nature of the Self. Many of Gautama the Buddha's disciples went into very long samadhis. They did not come out for years. But Gautama himself never did so because he saw it as unnecessary. He practiced and experienced all the eight kinds of samadhis before his Enlightenment and discarded them. He said, "This is not it. This is not going to take you any closer to Self-Realization. It is just moving into a higher level of experience and you might get more caught up because it is more beautiful than the current reality."

If your goal is set, if you have made Self-Realization the top priority in your life, then everything else which does not take you one step closer is meaningless.

Enlightenment and Death

How are death and Enlightenment related? Death and Enlightenment are entwined in the sense that if the life energies become overly intense, you cannot keep the body. Also, if the life energies become too feeble, you cannot keep the body. Only if it is in a certain band of intensity can you hold on to the body. If you raise the intensity beyond a certain pitch, you will get Enlightened and leave. If you drop it below a certain level, you will die. This is the natural process. Most of the Enlightened people cannot hang on to the body unless they do some tricks with it. Either they should know the mechanics of the body very well or they must constantly create some conscious karma—like some desire or some longing which will look absurd in their life because it does not fit into the rest of the person at all. People may think they are crazy, but they have to carry on with it just to keep their body going.

This is the reason sadhana is inevitable if you want to work your karma out in stages. At Isha, we don't believe in sudden Enlightenment. If sudden Enlightenment happens, most people may not be capable of withstanding it. It may cause either death or absolute introverting. If you do not know this, even now, thousands of people realize in the world, but 90 percent of them will leave at the moment of Self-Realization. "Self" does not mean the body, mind, or persona that you have built, it is that which has gathered all of these. We can call it "Self," or the fundamental life that we are. The moment one realizes that the body, mind, images of oneself that one carries, are all accumulations, naturally one wants to be unencumbered, so that leads to leaving the body because one is just dropping its encumbrances. One cannot stay in the body anymore because they do not have the understanding of the construct of the energetic system to stay and continue the work. So the moment someone realizes, they will slip out of the body; that is the end. This is why most realized beings go unnoticed. It is a rare few who attain a certain level of understanding, who manage to retain this body with their Self-Realization.

There is a lot of sadhana going on here at Isha. In terms of real activity, for me, programs are a very small part of my life, though they take a lot of time. The activity is very different. There are many people here who, if I let them go, will become fully realized beings. But they do not have the mastery over their systems to retain their bodies. They will drop their bodies if I let them go. So, usually, we peg them down at the last step so that their body can run its natural course. To peg them down is not a good thing to do, but you know we have taken social responsibilities. So I always peg them down at the last step and let the body run its natural course. When it finishes a certain phase, then we will leave it to them.

So, to have reached the final step and still retain the body, one must either understand the technology of the body or one must play some kind of drama to hang on. People ask me, "What is your trick to keep the body?" I have no compulsions. I have an anklet on my foot which is actually more of a shackle. It is not just an anklet; it is like a fix. It is done in a certain way. When I say "done" it is not just the manufacturing of the anklet; many sophisticated mystical processes are performed upon it for it to become what it is. It is a live thing. If you don't see this anklet on me one day, just know that there is very little time left.

Mukti and Mahasamadhi

In the Hindu way of life, reaching God or heaven is not the highest goal. They always spoke about *mukti* or Ultimate Liberation or freedom from the cycle of birth and death as the highest goal of life. But in English, when you say the word "freedom" or "Liberation," people visualize becoming a bird and flying in the sky. If you are a birdwatcher or if you have seen birds flying, you will know that even the most magnificent birds like the hawk or eagle are constantly looking down at the ground while in flight. They are looking for something to feed on, down below. They may not even be enjoying the flight. For them, it is a survival process, just like you going to the office. So mukti, when translated, could create wrong images in one's mind.

The words *Moksha* and Nirvana are also referring to mukti. Nirvana is a more appropriate word because Nirvana means non-existence. What it means is that you are free from the very burden of existence. When I say you are free from existence, I am not talking about existence as a quantity and you are free from that. You are free from your own existence. Your existence is finished. When there is no existence, you are even free from freedom, because freedom is also a certain bondage. As long as you exist, one way or the other you are bound. If you are existing physically, it is one kind of bondage. If you leave the physical body and you exist in some other way, there is still another kind of bondage. Everything that exists is ruled by some law. Now, mukti means you have broken all laws and they can be broken only when you cease to exist. That is the ultimate freedom.

Ultimately, every seeker wants to go beyond existence. They do not want to be in the process of existence, which may mean birth and death or hanging around or whatever. Whether you are actually physically born or not, as long as you exist you are going through some process or the other. Existence is always a process. Existence is not a thing. The sun is a process, the whole solar system is a process, the galaxy is a process, all the galaxies put together is a process. If you want to be free from all processes, it means that you must cease to exist; there is no other way. Existence, as you know it, must cease; only then is there no process.

What is the use of this? When one really looks at one's life and sees, "What is the use?"—that is exactly the thought which makes one seek mukti. Right now, such a depth of "What is the point?" is still not occurring to people, because people are still children. They might have grown-up bodies, but in terms of understanding they are still children. They want to see this, they want to see that. Let us say, the memory of a hundred lifetimes opens up to you, you will see that you are going through the same nonsense over and over again. Then you will definitely ask the question, "What is the point? Once again getting into the womb of another woman, another childbirth, another nonsense—what is the use?" If you ask this question in the deepest possible way, your longing for mukti will become absolute.

Mukti means you want to become free from the process of life and death but not because you are suffering. People who are suffering cannot attain mukti. You are fine, you are joyful, but you have had enough of kindergarten, you want to move on. However beautiful your school life was, don't you want to go to college? That is all. Death means the end of the physical body; everything else continues and finds another body soon; whereas with mukti, everything comes to an end. In a way, mukti is the end of death—and birth as well.

Mukti is also called Mahasamadhi. Mahasamadhi means one is able to walk out of one's body, consciously, without damaging it. Generally, if you want to leave the body, do what you want, you cannot come out of it unless you damage the body in some way. Unless you make the body unsuitable for cradling the life that is within, life will not leave. When things go bad, people say, "I want to die," but they don't, because they cannot. Mahasamadhi means that, without using any other external means, you leave the body at will. For someone to be able to do this, it needs tremendous energy. Such a person knows where the body is connected to life, and they untie it and leave.

Mahasamadhi is when you are also transcending discrimination so that there is no such thing as you and the other. It is completely finished. Now, as you sit here, there is you and the other. It is a certain level of reality. But Mahasamadhi means that individual existence is finished and who you are does not exist anymore.

Mahasamadhi is essentially that dimension of equanimity which gathers such a level of intensity that one can effortlessly dismantle the very nature of physical existence. One can dismantle not just the physical body, or the Annamaya Kosha, but also the Manomaya Kosha, Pranamaya Kosha, and the Vignanamaya Kosha. When the life within and life without become one, naturally this dismantling happens. Once these four koshas are dismantled, that life is truly, truly no more because the fifth body, the Anandamaya Kosha, or the bliss body, is essentially consciousness or the fundamental life element. There is nothing to dissolve there. It will just mingle with life as it always did. This is the end of the game. The cycle is over. There is no question of rebirth; it is complete dissolution. You can say this person is truly no more. It is the fortune of seekers at Isha that they have been in the presence of Mahasamadhi. Its fragrance and essence permeates Isha Yoga Center.

In reality, death is not the end because there is no such thing as death. Death exists only to one who has no awareness of life. There is only life, life and life alone. But Mahasamadhi means the real end. This is the goal of every spiritual seeker. Even an accomplished yogi will struggle with it because it is not simple. Or, rather, it is so simple that one who has a mind can rarely figure it out.

What is referred to as *jeevasamadhi* is a samadhi where a person decides to close oneself in an enclosure and end one's life. One reason for doing this is that he or she does not want to trouble people after their death. They want to handle the body themselves before they go. That is how this thing started. Another reason is that there are realized beings who are free in a certain way within themselves but lack the know-how to leave at will. Even if you are liberated within yourself, even if you have attained a certain state within yourself, to leave the physical body you need the skill, you need to know the science of how this body got connected and what you need to do to disentangle from it. This understanding has to be there, otherwise it will not come. Such a person, who is liberated but cannot disentangle from the body by themselves—will seal themselves in an enclosure, so that slowly, as the breath goes away, they will leave. But there should be no struggle in the body. If there is even a little bit of struggle, it just amounts to suicide.

People who are on the Yogic path will not do such a thing. They will sit in the open and leave because they know the science of how to eject from the body, how to leave the body. Just as you drop your clothes and walk away, you can drop your body and walk away. It is possible. This is Mahasamadhi. There is also something called *Diksha Mrutyu*, where the Guru initiates one into death. It is not a deathlike experience but death itself. It is very good to do this if you have everybody's permission and are in a mature society. This is usually done when the Guru sees someone who is capable of attaining Mahasamadhi, who has the potential but does not know how exactly to do it. So you initiate them in such a way that they can leave. It is perfectly fine. For that life, it is fantastic, actually. However, it is not accepted in today's society.

A Few Mahasamadhis

We have seen Mahasamadhis of two people whom we knew and who were dear to us. One was Swami Nirmalananda, whom I knew for a long time, and the other was Vijji, my beloved wife.

Swami Nirmalananda lived in Biligiri Rangana Betta, or BR Hills, in the southern Indian state of Karnataka. In his younger days, Nirmalananda traveled outside India for many years, visiting holy men from all religions. During World War II, he was in Europe and was deeply disturbed by the suffering he saw there. He then came back to India in the 1960s and, toward the end of his life, set up an ashram in BR Hills. He spent eleven years in silence there.

I first met him when I was probably twenty-one years old. I used to trek a lot in BR Hills, mostly alone. One particular time, I was in the forest for five or six days. So when I came out I was really hungry. I had not had any food for more than twenty-four hours. I went back to the place where I had parked my motorcycle, got on, and rode up the mountain. There was not a single restaurant there, but I knew Nirmalananda's ashram was there and he would have food. In the ashram there was a little temple and about twenty-five steps leading up to a small cottage. In those days, I wouldn't get off my motorcycle for anything. So I rode up the steps and leaned my motorcycle on the wall of the cottage. I was smeared with mud and slush, after days and nights in the wild in the rains. Hearing the motorcycle right outside his room, Nirmalananda came out and looked at me. He always had a permanent smile on his face. He used to go into periods of silence, so he was in silence on that day. I told him I was very hungry. Then he did something strange.

He came out and touched my feet. I was someone who had never even bowed down in a temple, my whole life. I would never ever touch anybody's feet. It was unthinkable for me. And this man came straight to me and held my boots, which were covered in slush. I was deeply embarrassed. I knew people considered him a great man, but I did not want to know how great he was—whether this man was a sannyasi or was Enlightened or whatever. It did not mean anything to me. All I wanted was his bread, but he came and touched my feet. This somehow disturbed me. But, anyway, I was hungry, so I ate the bread and honey he gave me.

After that, I went to BR Hills and met him many times. A sort of relationship developed between us—we kind of warmed up to each other. (Actually, I was the one who warmed up—he was always warm toward everyone.) He was mostly in silence. Sometimes, he spoke to me, but mostly he would write and I would speak. Subsequently, my own process* happened and I started teaching Yoga. Many years passed and I met him again after a long gap. By then, I was fully bearded and my wife, Vijji, was with me. She also liked Nirmalananda and we visited him together a few times. We used to have long conversations during those visits.

Now, sometime in April or May 1996, Vijji, my daughter, Radhe, and I visited him. While we were talking to him, he suddenly said that the following January, at the onset of Uttarayana, he wanted to leave. I asked him, "Why?" He said, "I have lived as a yogi, I don't want to live as a *rogi*."† He was then seventy-three years old. He was all in tears and he told me he really was not clear about how to leave. He had already built a small samadhi‡ for himself. He said he wanted to sit in the samadhi and leave. He was apprehensive about whether it would happen or not and had a lot of questions about it.

Suddenly, this became a different kind of a situation. It was no more a casual visit. This was Nirmalananda's ashram. He was the man everyone came to see and I had also gone there with my wife and daughter, but now he was consulting me. Though I had met him many times, he was now moving toward his final phase and was in a little bit of confusion. He did not know how to do this. He was just a simple and very joyful person. He had realized a few things, but still he did not know the mechanics of "how" because he had no exploration of his own system. He was just aware.

So I opened up to him in a completely different way. We started discussing things which I have never discussed anywhere. I talked to

---

* My experience at Chamundi Hills. See the section "Exploring Death" in chapter 1.
† One who is sick with disease.
‡ A spiritual tomb.

him about what he should do, what he should not do. Because death always happens because of the body being damaged either by disease or injury, to shed the body that one has acquired without any sort of damage to it demands a certain mastery. So I had to go into details of how he needed to prepare himself. Vijji was there. She was listening to all of this, and she burst into tears and cried relentlessly. I just ignored her and continued to speak to him because she could be crying for joy; she could be crying for anything. The sheer intensity of things always made her cry. She was like that. As I was talking, Nirmalananda was also overwhelmed by what I was saying. He was also weeping off and on and asking me more questions. It was then that we knew that Nirmalananda would leave.

Because I knew he would leave shortly, in December 1996 we took a large group of meditators and went there to see him one last time. He had already announced the date to many people. He had written one last letter to everyone he was in correspondence with. The news had appeared in the press too. By then these so-called rationalists in Karnataka had started a big press campaign against him. They said this man was going to commit suicide and was trying to glorify himself with all kinds of nonsense. They wanted the government to prevent the suicide and all that. They even got two police constables posted in the ashram to prevent this.

When I visited him the last time, he broke down and wept. He was really pained by this. He was a very gentle being. For his temple, he would not even pluck flowers from his plants. He worshipped his God only with the fallen flowers because he did not want to hurt the plants. He would never pluck a fruit from a tree either. He would take it only if it fell down. That is how he was. He said, "I don't even pluck a flower from a plant, but they put police on me," and he wept. I said, "What is your problem? The police are sitting there. You don't worry about this." Eventually, the policemen were withdrawn, but some people were still creating a ruckus in Bangalore and Mysore.

He was supposed to leave on the fifteenth of January, but he left on the tenth itself. He left five days early because he feared that the rationalists would come and simply make a racket. On that day, he sat outside his cottage on a bench. Just a few minutes before noon, in the presence of a small crowd, he simply left. Nirmalananda was someone who needed a Diksha Mrutyu; instead, we gave him a certain understanding of Mahasamadhi.

My wife, Vijji, was deeply influenced by Nirmalananda's Mahasamadhi. She felt that, if one has to go, this is the way to go. Anyone associated with Vijji knew she was not someone who took one step at a time. She took no steps in Yoga. She did not do Yoga for her health or her well-being. She did not care about her well-being. She did Yoga only because it meant something to me. It actually meant nothing to her. Any number of times she openly spoke about it to people. People thought she was a total sacrilege. "She is Sadhguru's wife, and look what nonsense she is talking!" they felt. But she was saying what was true for her.

When all this talk about leaving-the-body business with Nirmalananda was going on in April and May, she was sitting there and silently crying. Halfway down the hill, there is a very beautiful place full of wildlife, so when we were driving back, I stopped the car there. Vijji was still crying, so I was joking about this and that. Then she said, "Whatever you were talking about to Nirmalananda, I want that." So I jokingly said, "Oh! You want to leave? That is great. When are you going to leave?" And things like that. But she was very serious. I thought, "Okay, this is no more a joke, it is getting big." Then I said, "Okay, let us see if you can do it, you just chant 'Shambho,'* let me see." The scene is very clear in my

---

* One of the names of Shiva, also a powerful mantra.

mind even now. My little car was parked by the side of the road. I was standing there and Radhe was playing around with something. This was a deserted road where only once in twenty to thirty minutes a vehicle passed by. Vijji was kneeling in the middle of the road and telling me she wanted to go. And I said, "Okay, you chant 'Shambho.'" This is all the sadhana I gave. I gave it to her casually. I did not sit down and initiate her into something fantastic or specific.

I never thought she would have the perseverance to stick to it the way she did. It takes a lot to do it because your attention should be on it for twenty-four hours of the day. Otherwise, these things will not develop in you. I knew she had certain qualities in her; when she set her mind on something, she went all out. But I never thought she would have the determination to go all the way on this sadhana. Especially being the emotional person that she was—her emotions toward me and Radhe—I thought it would be enough to deter her. But she picked it up. She started picking up so much momentum that, within a short time, she was somewhere else. She was not the same person anymore; she was going away. She was no more my wife, but a super-intense *sadhaka*.*

I tried to slow her down a little bit because nobody can sustain that kind of intensity for too long. It will burn out. I would say, "What is the hurry?" Our daughter was not even seven years old. Vijji herself had gone through a phase of problems and struggles within herself and was now blossoming into a wonderful possibility. So I said, "Things are working out well for you also, why now?" She said, "Right now, my inside is feeling absolutely beautiful and outside everyone is wonderful to me. This is the time I want to leave. Right now, I am in a space where I want to be; I want to leave

---

* One who practices sadhana or has made formal pursuit of the spiritual path an important part of one's life.

like this." I again said, "What is the hurry now? You can wait for a few years, enjoy this and then go." She replied, "Right now, you don't want me to go, but after a few years would you want me to go?" I did not know how to reason with her or stop her. I tried all means of persuasion but nothing worked.

She was already involved with the Dhyanalinga consecration. Many things that had to be done as a part of the consecration were not easy at all. "Difficult" is not the word because it would be extremely difficult for any normal person to do those things. But she gave herself to it and did fabulously well. She had set forth toward this process for her leaving. She wanted to leave after the consecration was over. For three consecutive full moon days—in December, January, and February—she wanted to cook and serve the brahmacharis. Not with a serving spoon, but with her own hands. The desire to serve with your own hands is part of Hindu culture. She wanted to do this on three full moons, and on the full moon in February she wanted to leave.

The consecration process, as it was going, was sure to be over before January 23. But I knew something was going to happen which would postpone the whole thing in a big way, putting everything at risk. So somewhere in the middle of January, I made the people involved take a vow that by the next full moon in February we would finish it. No matter what, whatever it takes, we would finish it. They said yes, but I said, "That is not enough, you have to really take a vow." I actually made them shout three times that we were going to do it. I am so absolutely committed to fulfilling my Guru's will that I am willing to get into someone's womb, be born, make that woman go through all that, grow up, all with a single-point agenda of doing one thing. I am that relentless. It was my Guru's dream to consecrate the Dhyanalinga, and somehow it was passed on to me. I had spent lifetimes trying to do this, and now that we were this close to finishing it I wanted it completed with

Vijji by my side. Without her, it would have meant starting all over again and that was almost impossible.

While the plans for consecration were in progress, concurrently, Vijji's plan of leaving was on. We had visited her parents and my relatives one last time. She tried to convey the same to the family, but no one grasped it because she was healthy and well. When she said that this was her last visit, they thought she was angry with them. We also attended a family wedding after a very long time. I had been so absent at these social occasions that many people met Vijji for the first time only then. Then, on January 21, we dropped our daughter, Radhe, off at school. Vijji had already been telling Radhe for some time that she was leaving. Radhe's birthday is in March, so she was telling her she would not be there for her birthday, and by then she would be gone. The girl and Vijji were discussing in a very matter-of-fact manner that she would not be there and how I would come and do this and do that. I said, "Why are you doing this to the girl? Leave her alone." She said, "No, no. I have to tell her. I don't want her to feel I left without telling her."

We came back from Ooty on the evening of January 21. On the evening of the twenty-third, she left. What she thought would happen on the full moon in February happened a month early. On that day, there was an exceedingly rare and archetypically appropriate planetary alignment. They say it happens once in two hundred years. It was also *Thaipoosam*[*], a day that many sages of the past had chosen for their own Mahasamadhis. So these things also factored in.

On that evening, a group of people from the Yoga Center had assembled in the shrine, as they did on full moon evenings. Vijji had already cooked for them. We were going to meditate together,

---

[*] Thaipoosam is usually the first full moon after the winter solstice.

and she was to serve them food after that. A few minutes after everyone had sat down for meditation and closed their eyes, she got up and went to the bathroom. I was a little irritated with this because once we sit down for meditation no one moves even a limb, let alone gets up and leaves. But she went to the bathroom and returned a few minutes later. She had taken off her gold bangles, earrings, and toe rings, left them in the bathroom, and returned. After some time, she just uttered "Shambho" thrice and slumped to her left. And that was it. I noticed that something was off and asked one of the brahmacharis to attend to her, and another fetched some water. But she was gone by then.

What she had accomplished is not child's play. Even accomplished yogis will struggle to attain this. Even a *gnani*[*] like Nirmalananda, who spent his lifetime in spiritual sadhana, struggled to attain this. To throw this life out of this body without injuring the body, it takes something else. One has to generate a tremendous amount of energy, which requires intense sadhana. She knew and was undergoing the methods to achieve this, and she was working toward it. But I never imagined that without my assistance she would be able to generate the necessary energy.

Moreover, there were certain things to be done, which she had no way of knowing. For example, when we initiate people into certain sadhana, we give them something like a metal ring or a bracelet to wear. They are never supposed to remove it unless the Guru says so. This is because, sometimes, during that kind of sadhana, you might accidentally slip out of your body. If there is some metal on certain parts of your body, it will prevent it. I had never mentioned this to her. Yet, somehow, intuitively, she had taken off all her jewelry at that moment. She must have seen that it was preventing her from leaving.

---

[*] An adept in the path of Gnana Yoga—one of the four paths of Yoga.

Some people ask me, "Could she have been stopped?" The consecration work was still not complete. Moreover, she was my wife and she was leaving behind a small child, so why did I not stop her? Could I have stopped her? I say, yes, it is possible. Anyone could have stopped her. You should know, not just a Guru, but anyone, can stop you. You have heard all those old stories where some sages were meditating and something would come and distract them. Why, even Shiva himself got distracted.* So a simple distraction can do it. It does not take any Guru or some spiritual capability to distract them. It is just that if they have gone beyond a certain point, then whatever you do, such things cannot distract them. Still, a Guru can hold them if he wants to, but, at the same time, if they have gone that far, who would want to hold them? You may hold them before they go to that point, but if they have gone to that point you will not hold them. There is no point holding back such a person; it is against the very grain of our existence.

Mahasamadhi should not be confused with committing suicide; as I have explained, it is different because it does not damage the physical body. It is walking away from a healthy, living body, which means you have enough mastery over your life to make it or break it. So, when someone has gained this mastery and is leaving in that way, with such intensity, you don't try to stop them. It does not matter who he or she is, whether this is your father, your mother, your wife or child; what does it matter? Such things don't exist in that plane. Somebody being a wife or a husband is only true in our psychological and physiological sphere. Yes, Vijji was my beloved wife, but when she got into a certain state I no longer saw her as my wife. She became a possibility that is transcendent and beyond personal relationships.

---

* The legend where Kamadeva disturbs Shiva's meditation by shooting an arrow of flowers at him.

Her name was Vijaya Kumari, which means "victory's daughter." The highest possible victory for any being became hers. All her life, she used to say that she was proud that she was my wife, but with this she made me proud as her husband and Guru.

VIJJI

She knew Love
and nothing more
She was Love
and nothing more
The Lord needs Love
and nothing more
She wooed him with Her Love
and She is no more

There have been many other instances of people leaving their bodies at will. One such interesting case is that of Layman Pang and his daughter. Layman Pang was a lay Buddhist famous in China in the ninth century AD. He was born in a wealthy family, but at some point he, his wife, his son, and his daughter renounced all their possessions and lived an itinerant life while being dedicated to spiritual pursuit. One day, when he was about seventy years old, he decided it was time to leave his body on a particular day. At that time, only his daughter was living with him. On the appointed day, the two of them prepared the room for his departure. He took a bath, donned his robe, and sat crossed-legged on his bed. He wanted to leave at noon. So he asked his daughter to look out the window and let him know when it was noon exactly.

Having been raised under the tutelage of her father, Layman Pang's daughter, Ling-chao, was an accomplished spiritual seeker herself. Layman Pang often commented on Ling-chao's ability to grasp things very quickly. On that day, Ling-chao sat looking out the window, waiting for noon. Suddenly, she reported to her father that there was an eclipse. "Is that so?" Layman Pang asked. "Yes, please come and see for yourself," she answered. Then Layman Pang rose from his seat and looked out the window. Immediately, Ling-chao jumped on her father's bed and, sitting cross-legged, left her body in a moment.

When Layman Pang returned and saw what had happened, he said, "My daughter's way was always quick. Now she has gone ahead of me." People say Ling-chao tricked her father to leave before him. But it may not be so. Probably, Layman Pang had prepared the ambience so well that his daughter was instinctively drawn toward the bed and the nature of the energies he had created was such that she, who was also a spiritual practitioner, was able to leave the body at that instant. Layman Pang looked at the situation and calmly went out, gathered firewood, and performed a cremation ceremony. He then observed the traditional mourning period of seven days, at the end of which the governor of the province visited Layman Pang to pay his condolences. As they were talking, Layman Pang, sitting by the side of the governor, left his body.

PART II

THE GRACEFULNESS OF DEATH

BECOME ME

I was borne in my mother's womb
but she did not create me
I eat the salt of this Earth
but I do not belong to her
It is through this body that I walk
but I am not it
It is my mind through which I work
but it could not contain me
In the limitations of time and space I live
but it has not denied me unboundedness
I was born like you, I eat like you,
sleep like you and I will die like you
but the limited has not limited me
Life's bondages have not bound me
As the dance of life progresses
this space, this unboundedness has become
unbearably sweet
Become love and reach out
Become me

CHAPTER 6

Preparing for a Good Death

> Most people in the world believe that if they die in their sleep, it is wonderful. What a horrible way to go!

DOES DEATH NEED PREPARATION?

If death is inevitable, what is the need to spend time and energy preparing for it? You must understand that what you refer to as death is a unique happening. It is the very last moment of your life. Almost everything else in your life may happen many times over, but the final moment when you transcend the limitations of your physical body will happen only once in your lifetime. It is the last thing that you will do in your life. Moving from the physical to the non-physical is the greatest moment in your life. So is it not very important that you make it happen most gracefully and wonderfully?

Moreover, let us say, you want to go to Coimbatore city from the Yoga Center. It is just nineteen miles away, so, typically, you just hop on some bus and go. You don't book a seat on the bus ten days in advance, take a huge suitcase, pack your lunch and water bottle, and all that. If there is no transport available, you may even walk the distance. But if you want to go on a long journey you book your tickets, take food, water, and whatever else you may need for this long journey. Now, if you want to go to Antarctica, you take just about everything with you, don't you? You should know, when compared to the journey after death, the journey from your birth to death is just a short one. The time a being spends in an embodied state is nothing compared to the time one spends in a disembodied state. Yet you have done too much preparation for this. You have bought enough clothes to wear for three lifetimes, footwear for eight lifetimes, and a whole lot of other things. But for the journey after death, which is a very long one, should you not make adequate preparations too?

Dying well is very important because, when a being is disembodied, whether one's experience becomes heavenly or hellish largely depends on how one dies. Not entirely, but largely so. Preparing for death is not about gathering a lot of information and satisfying one's curiosity about something to come. If you want to make use of the opportunity that death presents, you cannot approach it with fear. This is not something that you can handle all of a sudden at that moment. So it is important that on many levels we prepare for death beforehand. If you can manage this last conscious moment of your life gracefully, you will at least go through the disembodied phase well. You will not make it hellish.

Unfortunately, most people create fear at that moment. They just cling on, saying, "I don't want to die." Some people actually desperately cling on to a bedsheet or someone's hand or something. This is not a good way to go. With just a little preparation, guidance, and even a bit of help, what is now considered a catastrophe can become a huge opportunity for spiritual possibility. In a way, from a spiritual perspective, what did not perhaps happen in life can be accomplished at the moment of death if it is handled sensibly. This is because it is very easy to untie the knots of everything that you have accumulated at that final moment. But if you are unprepared or become fearful of it or are ignorant of the ways of life, you will create resistance toward it and miss that possibility completely.

Everyone should know how to die by themselves. I have been telling people that when I die, I will make sure that no one has to even carry me to my grave. I will walk to my grave. You know, they had built a samadhi for me at the Yoga Center many years ago. It is still there at the Yoga Center. We had always planned to leave at a certain time, once the Dhyanalinga was done. So we prepared this. We had many discussions about it, like, "Don't put too many steps because maybe at that time I will not be able to climb down too much," and so on. We worked out details of how the door, the bolt, and the locking mechanism should be for me to lock it from inside, one final time. We did this because I was planning to walk into my grave myself so that those four people would be spared some labor. But the samadhi structure did not get used and money got wasted—that is another matter. So everyone must make preparations for their death—not just externally, internally too. You must be able to sit quietly and die. When death is imminent, most wild animals will withdraw to a place where they just sit. They don't eat anything and they die. When even animals, creatures that crawl, have that much dignity about their death, why do human beings want drama around them? In life, they want drama, but at least death should be conducted in a dignified way.

Ideally, I would like to teach the whole population a way to live beautifully, blissfully, every moment of their life. Then, naturally, one will leave in the best possible manner. But as I am getting older, I am realizing that it is taking a lot of time and effort. So if that is not possible, I would like to at least teach them how to die well, so that they can manage at least the last moment of their lives sensibly.

It is my wish that for some reason, if people cannot live blissfully, they must at least die well. But much more is possible if one makes an effort in this direction. This possibility is available not only for accomplished yogis but also for any sensible person who is willing to take instructions that are beyond one's understanding.

People on the spiritual path often go one step further and choose the time, date, and place of their death. They are able to fix it beforehand and leave at that time because they have created the necessary awareness within themselves so that, when the time comes, they can bundle the life energies and leave the body consciously. To leave this body consciously and walk away without damaging it, just like taking off your clothes, is the ultimate possibility in your life. If your awareness has grown to such a point that you know where you as a being and this physical body which you gathered are connected, then you can disentangle yourself whenever the moment is right for you. This is the ultimate kind of preparation you can make for your death. To come to this possibility, the most important thing is to grow a constant moment-to-moment awareness that you are mortal. Being conscious of your mortality, every day, every moment will naturally blossom into this possibility of disentangling yourself from all accumulations, whether physical, psychological, or karmic. This must be brought into everybody's life on this planet, because unfortunately most people live with a moment-to-moment fear of and anxiety about both life and death, like they are going to crash in some way physically or psychologically. To create a world where people live peacefully, blissfully, and also die the same way, the most important thing is to build this awareness right from one's childhood that this is a mortal life and our existence here is on a time lease. If one is continuously aware, you will not become paranoid; rather, you will become conscious.

When we talk about making preparations for death, people ask, "What if the death is sudden? How can such a person die well?"

Death is never sudden. You may not have foreseen it, but it is never sudden. Today's movies are big culprits in spreading this fallacy of instantaneous death. They think of life as a quantity which is sitting inside that goes *pop!* when someone is shot. It is not like that. Look at it this way: Suppose I shoot you in the head right now; will all your breath go off at once? No, it will happen slowly. Once the compression of the rib cage is gone here, it will slowly dribble out. Similarly, life dribbles out, over some time. But the moment the body turns inert your experience of life is gone. Your experience of the body and your senses is gone, but the experience itself is still there. This is so even when you are sleeping. There is an experience there, but you are unable to turn inward and access this experience. Once your senses are disconnected, you have no experience of the world or the body, but the experience of presence is still there.

Now, suppose a man was shot in the head; does he also have the opportunity to die peacefully? Let us say, a man fell down from the roof and died. From your perspective, because you see the body breaking up, you may think this is a violent death. But for the man who has fallen down, he may have died a very peaceful death within himself in those last few moments. Or he may have died a violent death. The violence is not in the way the body breaks. The violence is in the way that the human being experiences it in that moment. As an outside observer, you are judging the violence by what happened to the body. But you cannot know what happened to the being. Only he knows, unless you know the ways to know it.

Someone may die surrounded by his or her family, but at the last moment they may have just looked at their fiendish relative. You may think they died peacefully in their bed, but, no, they might have become terrified and died a violent death! Someone might have died in a car crash where their body broke into bits, but at the last moment they might have just said "Shiva" or some other thing and died peacefully, we don't know. The violence of the death is not determined by what happened to the body; it depends on what happened within that person.

A man who is shot in the head is in no way at any kind of disadvantage compared to a person who is dying of some disease or old age or whatever. You need to understand this: However sudden the death is—whether it is a heart attack, car crash, air crash, or a bullet in the head—still, there are a few moments between injury and death. Even if a man's head is chopped off all of a sudden, he has still got a few moments between that injury and death. Those few moments can become moments of awareness if he has put a certain amount of awareness into his life. On the other hand, even if someone gave some people a hundred years of lifespan, it is possible that in these hundred years they do not become aware. That is the reality of life. Someone who is suddenly shot has just a few moments, but it is still the same reality. If you had lived a life of awareness, awareness of the life process itself, then it is very much possible that even at the last moment you could become aware. For this to come, you have to build a life of awareness. Only then you can be aware in your death.

That is why it is important to develop this awareness during your life so it does not matter how death comes to you—you will have the ability to die well. Some people are able to live well only if good situations come to them. Some people live well whichever kind of situation comes to them. This is so with death as well. If you develop the necessary capability, whichever way death comes you can maintain your awareness and die well. If you have not lived a life of awareness, the possibility of you suddenly becoming aware in an extreme situation like death does not arise at all. Let us say, the doctor tells someone, "You have cancer, you have got just one month to live"; how many of them become aware because they have one month's preparation time? They may just become paranoid. Only a few become aware and make use of this advance intimation.

Sleep, Ojas, and Death

There are certain preparations for death that one can do involving sleep and generation of *ojas*.* Now, is there any connection between sleep and death? Fundamentally, the dynamism of the physical has to touch the inertia of the non-physical. This is the Shiva/Shakti principle. Shiva is inertia; Shakti is dynamism. Everything in the physical Universe has to go through that. It is happening in so many ways in Existence. Whether it is an atom, an amoeba, a human being, the planet, the solar system, or the Universe—all of them are going in these cycles of dynamism and inertia because this is the most fundamental cycle. Lifespans are different depending upon who you are, what you are, but it is the same principle in operation. Inhalation/exhalation, wakefulness/sleep, day/night, life/death, creation/dissolution—all these are fundamentally the same process.

In a way, what you call sleep is also like death. You die, but you wake up with the same old goddamn body. Actually, even with sleep, if you are very tired and go to bed, after a good sleep it feels like you woke up with a new body. Death is when you went to sleep and woke up to find the body has shrunk. You have to grow it again! Now, if you are conscious during this transition between the states of dynamism and inertia, you may get off the bus. If you can move from wakefulness to sleep while remaining fully conscious, you will very effortlessly move from life to death also fully conscious, because in its fundamental essence, it is not different. It is just moving from dynamism to inertia. If you are able to move consciously from one state to another in these cycles from Shakti to Shiva, then you have transcended a whole lot of things.

You can try this with your sleep tonight. When you are falling

---

* A non-physical force generated by spiritual practices.

asleep, when you are going from the state of wakefulness to sleep, see if you can be aware at that moment. If you can be aware at that moment, then you can be aware at that moment when you go from body to bodiless state. Most people sleep without any awareness. But that final moment when you are transiting from wakefulness to sleep, if you can simply be aware, you will be awake in your sleep. If you can manage this awareness, something tremendous will happen.

Now, if you consciously bring some quality to the last few moments of your falling asleep, that will continue into your sleep as well. Let us say, you make the moment of falling asleep very loving or happy within yourself: You will see that this quality will continue through the sleep also. That is exactly what will happen with death, but far more enhanced. If, at the final moment, a certain quality is brought in, then that quality will continue.

Instead of learning to stay awake when you are sleeping, which is much more difficult, you can learn to sleep when you are awake. This is easier to get. If you do some sadhana, you can get it. This is what happens in Shoonya* meditation—you are awake but you are asleep. The body thinks you are asleep; that is why it drops the metabolism. But you are awake. When you are sitting in Shoonya, suddenly the body thinks you are gone, and in your experience your hand disappears, your leg disappears, and so on. You kind of sneaked up on the body. The body does not know you are awake, but if one thought arises, suddenly it realizes that you are sneaking up on it and the legs and hands come back. Staying awake in your sleep will take much more effort but sleeping when you are awake is a possibility. But if you learn to maintain awareness during either of these transitions, it will help you immensely to go through the

---

* A fifteen-minute meditation offered by Sadhguru.

transition from the embodied to the disembodied state. A much simpler but not so effective way forward is *Isha Kriya*.*

The process of death can also be greatly assisted if you are able to generate or gather a lot of ojas. In some Far East cultures, an Enlightened being is referred to as an *enso*. The word "enso" means a circle. Why a circle? Why do you think your automobile wheels are all circular? Triangular wheels would be jazzier, wouldn't they? Why are they circular, not triangular or rectangular or whatever? Because anything that is circular has the least amount of resistance. So an Enlightened being is referred to as an "enso" not because they are round of body but because they have generated sufficient ojas that their passage through life and death happens with the least amount of resistance.

In Yogic culture, this is sort of fondly or mischievously referred to as stealing from the Earth. This body is a loan that you have taken from Mother Earth. She is very generous with this, but when it comes to reclaiming she is very stringent. She will not let you take even one atom as a souvenir. She will collect every atom back. So the yogis learned how to steal from the Earth. That is, they convert the physical into the non-physical. Now she cannot claim it back. She cannot recognize it. This non-physical thing is known as ojas.

Sometimes there are people on certain types of sadhana who, during that time, will eat huge volumes of food. Usually, it is handled in seclusion, so people don't get to see these things. They eat the kind of volumes that no human body can consume. They eat ten people's food, but they will not gain an ounce and they will not have any kind of health problems. If you eat that much food, your stomach would burst. But they will not gain any weight because, at

---

* A simple eleven-minute daily meditative process designed by Sadhguru to help people gracefully pass through the process of disembodiment, when it is time.

that particular phase, they are transforming the physical into the non-physical. Normally, the food that you eat becomes flesh and blood. But if you do certain things with your system, it will transform the physical into the non-physical. You will develop ojas, not body. If you have sufficient ojas around you, your passage through life and death will become very effortless. You will go through the whole process smoothly.

Having ojas gives you a certain body when you lose yours. It is like you are not made for water, you are not a fish. So if you are lost in the ocean, you would like to have at least a piece of wood. A piece of wood would mean a lot in those circumstances. If you have one piece of the *kattumaram*,[*] it is good enough. If you have two pieces of the kattumaram, you can ride and go where you want. So when you lose your physical body, if you have a piece of body you will see you can direct your boat which way to go. That is the intent of developing ojas. If you have ojas, then you also lubricate your life so that your movement through this world also becomes easy.

So how does one gather ojas? The kriyas that you practice in the morning and evening are one way of generating ojas. If you are doing *kapalabhati*,[†] if you do it powerfully enough, you develop ojas. Right now, when you do kapalabhati, you may feel the general heat in the face and head. That is okay for health and well-being. If you do proper kapalabhati, it will become one-pointed; heat will get generated at one point, just at the top of your head. If you do kapalabhati like that, then ojas will develop. Right now, the brahmacharis are doing various sadhanas of Surya Kriya. If you do that, ojas will develop. The *kumbhaka sadhana*[‡] that they practice will develop an enormous amount of ojas. When you develop ojas, if you

---

[*] The original Tamil word from which the word "catamaran" was derived.
[†] A certain Yogic practice that involves forceful breathing.
[‡] An advanced Yogic practice taught to brahmacharis, which involves holding the breath for long durations.

watch carefully, you will not have a clear-cut shadow. Because of the ojas, the light will get confused or diffused. Erasing of physical boundaries not by damage but by enveloping oneself with ojas is also Yoga or union.

Why Do People Fear Death?

The fear of death has come because of a certain sense of ignorance and unawareness. Most people are terrified even by just seeing a dead body. I understand that for people who loved them, for people who cared for them, losing someone dear is a big loss. But why are people afraid of seeing a dead body? Living bodies can be dangerous, I can understand that. They can do many things to you. They can pretend to like you, but tomorrow they may kill you. But dead bodies are absolutely safe, yet people are afraid of them!

In many parts of the world, children are told not to even utter the word "death" inside the house, because they have a stupid hope that if you don't utter this word it will not enter the house. This morbid fear of death is not natural. Maybe the majority of people have subscribed to it, but the fear is not a natural process. Death is a natural process. If life happens, then death is natural. Being afraid of something natural is unnatural. The fear of death is simply because we are not in touch with reality. The fear of death has come to us because we have become deeply identified with this body. Our identification with this body has become so strong because we have not explored other dimensions. If we had explored other dimensions of experience, if we had established ourselves in other dimensions of experience, the body would not be such a big issue.

You talk of your body as if you came with it. You did not. You only gathered it. You gathered it while in your mother's womb and continued gathering it after your birth. Whatever we accumulate, we can say, "This is mine." But you cannot say, "This is me." Now, if I take the cup from which I drink water and say, "This is my cup," you will think, "Sadhguru seems to have some problem. But let me listen some more; everyone says he is wise." But after some time, if I say, "This is me," then you will definitely say, "Let me get away from this person." But you are doing the same thing with your body, which is why you make such a big fuss about shedding it.

Suppose you overate and gathered a lot of body during the next few weeks and then worked out and dropped some of it; you don't call it death. You gathered something and you put it back. No big deal. You would be happy and relieved, not distressed, about it. It should be the same with death. What you know as death is just a little bit of purging. With age, the flesh is beginning to lose its vigor, so it needs to be cleaned up. Either you put back what you gathered joyfully or you put it back crying. That is a choice you have. Death is like you picked up a spadeful of soil and threw it back. But, instead, if you look at this spadeful of soil and get very attached to it, you will cry like a child when it falls off your spade. It is like a child who picked up a little pebble from somewhere, came home, and lost it. He is heartbroken. He cries inconsolably. If all that you know is just the body, then this is what will happen to you. But if you had known something in your life that is more than the body, then shedding the body will not be a big deal for you.

What you refer to as life is essentially like a term loan from a bank. They may give you a ten-year loan, but it is not yours; you must pay it back. With some tricks, you can extend it to twelve years. If you are very tricky, you can stretch it to fifteen years. If you are super tricky, maybe you can stretch it to twenty years. That is about it. Beyond that, no one has stretched it until now. People may tell you stories that someone lived for four thousand years (probably because they want to make a movie), but no one has stretched life that much. There are ways to hibernate life so that you still maintain your intent beyond the body, and you can once again take a body and come back. That is a different matter. That is not stretching your life. That is handling the natural cycle consciously.

Now, generally, in society, people have been convincing you that, after all, the fear of death is natural. Whatever the majority of people do, they say it is natural. If the majority of the people were smoking cigarettes, people would say smoking is a natural thing, wouldn't they? This was happening in the past. Even now, certain groups of people say it is natural. A human being is not made to smoke; you are not an automobile! It is not natural for you to smoke. But people will make it natural.

When I was growing up, my lack of fear caused a lot of anxiety to my father. He would keep saying, "What will happen to this boy? There is no fear in his heart about anything." One day, I turned around and asked him, "When did fear become a virtue?" Fear is not a virtue, but people have made it so natural that they think something is missing if there is no fear. Similarly, right now, the fear of death has been made natural by society.

Somewhere along the way, the fear of pain has become mixed with the fear of death because a lot of people think death is going to be painful. This is why they ask doctors to give them something so that they can go painlessly. Death is not painful, believe me. It is very nice. It does not happen because of any particular thing. It is just happening all the time. It is just that at some point people realize that it has happened to them; other times they don't realize it. The breaking of the body can hurt. That can be painful, but not death. The disease that causes death may be painful, the injury that causes death may be painful, but death itself is not painful. It once happened: Shankaran Pillai fell off the second floor and screamed. People gathered and asked, "Why? Did the fall hurt you?" He said, "You idiots, it is not the fall, it was the stopping." In people's understanding, often one thing gets mixed up with the other.

The fear of pain is a physiological thing. The body builds this up as a survival mechanism, in anticipation of pain. It is a physiological reality and you don't want to go through that because you know how unpleasant it can be. But the fear of death has no basis because death is not painful. Yet why do people fear death? Let us say, you took a loan of a million dollars from me, and in ten years' time it grew to a billion dollars. Now, if I tell you that I am coming to your house, you will welcome me wonderfully. If I ask for my million dollars, you will happily give it back and maybe something on top of it too. You will regard me as your great friend because I gave you the money ten years ago. But if you have squandered the million dollars I gave you, if I say I am coming to your house I will feel like death to you. You will shiver in your pants. Actually, for many people, their debt collectors create more fear in them than their deaths!

The fear of death is also like this. Planet Earth is telling you it is time to pay back your loan. No interest, nothing. If you made something truly wonderful out of it, you will joyfully pay it back and go. But if you made nothing out of it except living your life psychologically, you will be terrified. Those who have not made good use of it will always try to dodge. Those who are successful in knowing and existing as a full-fledged life are willing to pay back joyfully without any problem. Those who never really lived and only thought about it are scared and bewildered.

If you really look at it, you are not afraid of physical death as such. Suppose you have grown old and God offers you a deal, "Okay, you give me this old body and I will give you a new body," who would not want to take it? So you are not really afraid of losing the body as such. The fear of death is about what you think you will lose by death. The fear of death is essentially the fear of loss. If someone is going to lose their job or all their money or someone who is very dear to them or a person whom they are very dependent upon, they will have greater fears. What they go through is just like what they go through if they are going to die. People even kill themselves rather than go through that. The real fear is not that the body is going to break one day. "What will happen to me?" is the real fear.

Fundamentally, the only thing that can get hurt, the only thing that can feel trampled, the only thing that can be abused in you is your ego or your persona. You are only constantly afraid of losing this image that you have built of who you are. That is the biggest barrier, a bubble that you are unwilling to get out of. Actually, if somehow we devise ways to disgrace you and abuse you, not physically but in every other way, you would actually wish death over that. Now death would be a gift, death would be a benevolence rather than going through all that.

Sometimes, this same fear gets translated into many different aspects. One person will make their fear of death into, "I am not worried about dying, but my children, how they will suffer!" So they will suffer with that fear. Someone else suffers from the fear of "I don't want to die" kind of thing, simply because they do not know anything beyond that. This is a fear of losing everything that I know as myself and the world and life. Have you noticed, people who have been convinced that they are going to gain by death step into it without any fear at all? If you understand there is nothing to lose, because you came with nothing anyway, the fear of death will not be relevant.

How to Deal with the Fear of Death

Mortality need not be a morbid affair, because it is the most fundamental fact of our existence. All the fairy tales, horror movies, and a whole lot of other literature are an attempt by the ignorant to make death into the most morbid fact of our lives, but it is the most natural and inevitable fact of our lives. If we don't come to terms with that, we have not come to terms with any aspect of life; we are living in make-believe. This makes one's life experience limited only to one's physical self or body.

No matter what kind of teachings other people give you, it does not matter. Someone may tell you that you are not the body or that you are the *atma* (soul) or the *paramatma* (super soul)[*] or whatever, but in your experience, this body is you. Whatever Gitas[†] they may read to you, whatever Upanishads they may read to you, your experience is still limited to the physical body. So you fear losing it. But if you explore and establish yourself in other dimensions of experience, the body will become an easy thing to handle. Life or death will not make such a big difference. Fundamentally, death means you are shedding what you have gathered in this life in terms of physical content and psychological content. You may think many things about yourself as a person, but as far as the planet is concerned, it is just recycling itself. It pops you up and pulls you back. In that pop-up, you have an opportunity to transcend this whole cycle. But whether you transcend or not is entirely up to you.

Moreover, when your experience of life is limited to the physical body, then you not only fear death but also fear life and seek security. And this fear of life in turn makes you court death, because seeking security is courting death. Have you noticed, if people feel insecure, they will just curl up and sleep? They just go back into that fetal position. The need is to go back into the womb. The womb is not really in the mother; the womb is really in death. The physical mother is just a small manifestation of that, but the real womb is in death. When people feel insecure, they want to drink

---

[*] Universal soul, according to Hindu tradition.
[†] The Bhagavad Gita and six other holy Hindu scriptures.

and sleep because sleep is just a small manifestation of death. People want to sleep absolutely like a log because it gives freedom from life. This whole "courting death" thing has come because of the need for security.

From where did the insecurity spring, first of all? Insecurity comes to you because of limited identification. You identify yourself as a body, and only because of that is there all this insecurity. Your body is a fragile bubble that you have blown. The fear of death is simply because you are existing here in this vast Existence as a tiny person. If you have tasted the unboundedness in you, if you truly experienced yourself beyond the limitations of the physical and the mental, there would be no fear. This is why there is so much emphasis on using your time and life to know that which is beyond the physical. That is why you must do sadhana. But a lot of people who have a fear of death try to become immortal. They try to beat it. This is a wrong approach. If you fear death now, you must see what the basis of this is. Instead of seeing how to transcend your limited identification, if you try to become immortal it is just distraction; it will not get you anywhere.

If your experience of life is established beyond the physical body, shedding it is a very simple affair. When you want to change your clothes, you just change them, don't you? If you don't like it, you are through with it and you walk naked. It is up to you. You need to understand, once this body has run its course it will go anyway, whether you like it or not, whether you approve of it or not. As long as it exists, taking good care of it is definitely our business. But if you are paranoid about ill health or death you will not take good care of it. In your anxiety, you will destroy the body. The very anxiety of what may happen to this body will destroy the body.

Confronting your fear of death can bring tremendous clarity and transformation in one's life. This happened some decades ago.

Once I was in Bangalore and I went to the vegetable market. I was not there to buy anything; I just like to walk through the vegetable markets. So I was walking and suddenly I saw this vegetable vendor who was all bright and lit up. I could not believe that a man like this was selling vegetables. I looked at him and instantly our eyes locked and I laughed. He also started laughing. Then I went to him and we started talking about things in general. Then I asked him, "How come a man like you is selling vegetables here?" He was evasive. He said, "I am just doing my work here." We bantered a little more and I finally found out what had happened.

It seems he was an ordinary vegetable-seller. One day, he became ill, so ill that he thought he was going to die. But each day it got postponed by one more day and one more day. For four months, this went on—every day he would think, "This is it!" But at the end of the day he would still be alive. In these four months, because of constantly being with death, something tremendous happened within him. His energies exploded into a different state altogether. He became so blissful, he cared not a hoot about whether he retained the body or not. Once he did not care, his body recovered completely.

Mortality is freedom from the mortal coil. The foundation of ignorance is mistaking the accumulated body to be oneself. Breaking that is Enlightenment. Now he came back to his vegetable shop and began selling vegetables. He saw that his ill health brought such a miracle into his life, so anyone who comes to buy vegetables from him, he blesses: "May you also become ill like me." When he says "ill," he is not wishing you ill. He is wishing that somehow, if through health it has not happened to you, at least through ill health may you wake up, because that is what happened to him.

So whatever it is—illness, death, or any calamity that happens around you—you can either use it to liberate yourself or you can use it to entangle yourself. Calamities, especially like death and illness, are a tremendous opportunity to look beyond the limitations of what you normally understand as life. It need not happen to you; if you are intelligent, you can learn from other people's experiences. You have heard about Gautama. He saw just one sick man, one old man, and one dead body, and he realized, "Any day, this can happen to me, so there is no point in running away from it."

If someone is ill, or someone is dying, I want you to sit with them and see that this could have been you and that this could be you any day. The most horrible illness that someone has gotten—we don't want it, we are not wishing for it—but you should know, any day, it could be you. It does not matter whether you are eighteen or eighty, it could be you today or tomorrow.

Now, if you are already in fear and at the end of your life, what to do? Fundamentally, the problem is that we think there is a solution for anger, there is another solution for fear, there is another solution for depression. No. There is no treatment as such for these things. This may look simplistic, but the fundamental reality is that your mind is not taking instructions from you. There are two significant faculties that human beings have—a vivid sense of memory and a vivid sense of imagination. Fear means your imagination is out of control. So it is a question of taking your faculties into your control rather than fighting fear. In reality, there is no such thing as fear. Actually, you are making it up.

Generally, people think that if the process of survival gets better, if food and shelter are taken care of, the fear will go away. But affluent societies are clearly proving that is not the case. They are making a big statement: Give us as much food as you want, as much shelter as you want; it does not matter, we will experience fear of something else. The terror that someone goes through among the civilian population in a war-torn country is much more acute, but you will see, when they get a break from the bombing, they will all play, sing, dance, and be happy, because suddenly they realize the value of life. But the fear that affluent societies suffer is endemic; it is simply ongoing, day in and day out.

Fear is not because of a situation; it is simply because your own psychological system is not in your hands. It is essentially the nature of how you keep your mind. Unfortunately, people try to handle a consequence without understanding the cause. Fear is a consequence of a certain situation within you. When you try to handle fear, you are trying to handle the consequence. What is needed is taking charge of your physiological and psychological process, paying attention to the process of how we generate thoughts, how we generate emotions, how we conduct our body, and how we manage our chemistry.

People think talking about death more openly, gaining more exposure to death, will help them overcome the fear of death. It is only partially true because it is in the way you do it. It need not work for everyone. Someone may watch people dying and get terrified, or someone else may watch a lot of people die and become callous. They just don't care. There are a whole lot of people like that. If you go to burial or cremation grounds or even the morgues, in most places the person just does not care. He thinks he is immortal. It is all a question of your awareness and how you look at it. If you are ready for it, in some way you are sensitive to it, then it could do something for you. But many people may become completely insensitive. It is always dependent on the individual person.

So are there certain practices that you can still do, certain kinds of ambiences that you can create around you so that you can gradually take control of your faculties even at the moment of death? One thing you can do is remind yourself about death—your death. Every day, spend just five minutes reminding yourself that you are mortal and today you may die. Just remind yourself this much and wonderful things will happen to you. Gurdjieff was a nineteenth-century mystic and spiritual teacher who lived in Europe. During his time, he was called a rascal saint. A rascal, because his methods were so drastic—he did crazy things with people. He gave a solution to the world: He said if you want to have the whole world Enlightened, we must plant a new organ in everyone's body. The purpose of this organ would be that several times every day this organ should remind you that you will also die. Just reminding yourself constantly that you are mortal and you may die today will take away your fear of death.

The Shoonya meditation that we initiate people into is not an implant, but it also reminds you of death. Every day, when you sit down for Shoonya meditation, you see that your personality has dissolved and there is just a certain presence. During the meditation, everything that you consider as "myself" will become nothing. It is as if you die. When you open your eyes, it is all there again. So twice a day, every day, you consciously die. If you just practice this consciously, when the time to actually die comes it will no more be a big issue. This will release you from the fear of death.

There are other practices and processes that can distinctly establish the two dimensions of energy, *Ida* and *Pingala*.* Once these dualities are distinct in your experience, the flame of *Sushumna*—that energy that is beyond dualities—is experienced. In experiencing the non-dual, the duality of life and death will become one. It is the illusion of duality and the attachment to one of them that makes death a fearful expectation—of being wrenched away from that which you know. Gaining mastery over the Pancha Pranas, the five manifestations of life energy, or gaining mastery over the five elements also takes away the distinction between life and death. Once the borders of life and death—the two dimensions of the same—

---

* Ida and Pingala *nadi*s are the two main pranic channels of the body and also represent the feminine and masculine dimensions of pranic energy. Sushumna nadi is the third and central pranic channel, whose opening has always denoted spiritual awakening.

are breached and you can consciously transact with both, there will be no room for fear.

So do people who fear death always die a terrible death? It could work out both ways, actually. Some people who were always afraid of death may just go through it just like that, without any issue when the actual moment comes. On the other hand, people who think they are very brave may not know how to deal with it at that time. There are many factors to it. The karmic content of one's life always plays a big role and what kind of life you have led until then definitely factors in. But it is also about what form the death came to you in, what kind of context. In certain contexts, people may be terrorized even if they are otherwise not disposed toward it. In other contexts, they may come to terms with death just because the context was such. This is why, in the Hindu culture, they always say that a dying person must be treated with the utmost care and respect, and there has been a great amount of emphasis on setting the right context. We will be looking at this later in the book.

How to Live One's Old Age

Every creature in the world except man seems to know how to die gracefully. If you walk in a forest—even in one that is rich with wildlife—unless it is an animal that has been killed by a predator, you will not find a carcass just lying around like that. In the forest, even in the cities, where the birds are mostly crows these days, you will not find a dead crow just like that. They all know when it is time to die, so they withdraw to a quiet place and die gracefully. It is only the human being who is oblivious to this and dies in a manner that is becoming increasingly graceless. When death comes, people who did not know how to live will definitely have problems with how to die.

In many ways, old age can be a great blessing because the whole experience of life is behind you. When you are approaching death, it is an opportunity, because when energies have become feeble and they are progressing toward dropping the body it is much easier to become aware of the nature of your existence. When you were a child, everything was beautiful, but you were eager to grow up because you wanted to experience life. When you became youthful, your intelligence got hijacked by your hormones. Whatever you did, knowingly or unknowingly, it just pushed you in that direction. Very few people are capable of raising their intelligence beyond the hormonal hijack and looking at life with clarity. All others are trapped in it. During youth, when the body is vibrant, it is very difficult to make yourself aware because you are so identified with your body that you don't see anything beyond that.

However, as you age, this recedes. As the body loses its vibrancy, you become more and more aware because you cannot identify with that body which is receding. When you come to old age, all the longings are over and the experience of a whole life is behind you. So once again you are childlike, but you have the wisdom and experience of life. It can be a very fruitful and wonderful part of your life. If you take care of your rejuvenation process well, old age can be a miraculous part of your life. Unfortunately, most human beings suffer their old age simply because they don't take care of their rejuvenation process properly. In their old age, very few people can even smile. This is because the only thing that they knew in their life was the physical body. Once the body begins to recede, they become despondent. It might not have become diseased, no terrible cancer needs to have come, but in every step that you take, age is telling you, "This is not forever." If you establish yourself in other dimensions of experience, the body becomes an easy thing to handle. Old age and even death can be joyful experiences. For this, you need to know when to leave and exit gracefully.

When death is definitely going to happen in the next week or two, it is so much easier to become aware. There are certain things that can be done to become more aware at that time. One should just lie down. Now, if you do not know anything else, if there is no help from outside, the best thing is to just simply see what you are not because even if you are unable to see what you are, you can easily see what you are not. Now the vibrancy of the body has dropped so much but the life is still on. So you can see within yourself the disparity between what is you and what is the body. It is better that you spend time just seeing the distinction between what is you and what is your body. You will pass quite effortlessly.

Even on a daily basis, one can make this awareness a part of one's life. When you are hungry and want to eat, just postpone it by ten minutes. Be conscious of your hunger; do not get busy with some other activity. Consciously postpone your meal and wait. Even when you normally sit for a meal, just be conscious of your hunger while looking at the food. Do this for just two minutes. Such simple methods can slowly establish the distinction between the experience of oneself and that of the physical body. There are, of course, more sophisticated ways of conducting this. Being hungry is a time when it is much more obvious that your body is an accumulation. Hence, there has been such significance attached to fasting in all traditions.

In Hindu tradition, they always said you should not die among your family. People used to go to the forest to die, a practice called *Vanaprastha Ashrama*. It meant that after a certain stage in life people withdrew from the family and society and retired into forests or ashrams that were set up for this purpose, and lived there joyfully. But today, unfortunately, old age means "hospital ashrama." When the time comes, the best place to die is always under the open sky, not the hospital. If you want to go into the mountains and sit there by yourself and die, that is fine. That was the widely prevalent practice at one time. Even Dhritarashtra, who was the emperor during

Mahabharata, took up Vanaprastha. He along with his queen, Gandhari, and his brother's wife, Kunti, went into the forest after the Kurukshetra War, with just Sanjaya as an assistant. They had all become old, so they chose to go to the forest to die rather than die in the palace.

Though Dhritarashtra was blind, heavily biased, and stupid in many ways, there was enough awareness in him that he should handle his death sensibly. This is the significance of cultural intelligence, or what is called *samskara*. This is missing in the world today. Kunti had suffered all kinds of hardship all her life; now her children had won the war and become emperors, so at least she could have enjoyed the palace and died in comfort. But she too decided to go and die in the forest. This is the great wisdom that was prevalent in those times, thanks to the culture of truth-seeking. It so happened that one day the four of them climbed up a very steep hill and there was a forest fire. Because three of them were old, those three could not run or fight the forest fire, so they just decided to offer themselves to the fire. Dhritarashtra told Sanjaya, "You have served me very well till now, but you are still a young man—go away. The three of us will give ourselves to the fire." Sanjaya refused to leave them, and all four got willingly burned in the forest fire.

What Dhritarashtra and the others did was something rather extreme, but the general population walked the well-charted path of Vanaprastha Ashrama, which was more calibrated and worked very well for everyone. Vanaprastha can be done in a more organized way.

The Wisdom of Vanaprastha Ashrama

In ancient India, when couples took up Vanaprastha Ashrama, they often withdrew together and lived a very simple back-to-basics kind of life until their death. This was to ensure that they died well or had a good death. Now, to the modern mind, this may sound very harsh and illogical. After all, it appears that when you are young and healthy, when you can rough it out, you are allowed to live in well-built homes with all the comforts and in the midst of society, but when you are approaching old age, when you are ailing and infirm, you are required to give up everything and live in the forest, fending for yourself? But if you look at it deeply, there is a lot of wisdom in this practice. It was one simple way to ensure that even people who did not have the mastery to drop their body at will could attain a good death.

This practice has its origins in the Varnashrama system, where they looked deeply at human nature. They took into consideration all the aspects of human life—one's needs, capabilities, and possibilities—and evolved a set of guidelines that ensured the well-being of the individual and the society. Accordingly, they designated the nature of the activity to be performed and the ideals to be pursued during each of these stages of life.

This division of stages was not hard and fast, but more broad guidelines about what to emphasize at each phase of one's life. Nor were all the stages compulsory. One could skip one or two stages and go on to the next, depending upon one's inclination.

ASHRAMA OR STAGE	AGE (YEARS)	DESCRIPTION	GOAL
Balavastha (Childhood)	0–12	The aim is to grow the body and brain to full potential. Emphasis is upon eating, playing, and sleeping during this stage.	Full development of the body and brain.

Brahmacharya (Celibate Student)	12–24	During this period, the student typically left home to stay with a Guru to acquire both spiritual and practical knowledge. The student has two duties: to learn the skills of one's life and to practice unwavering devotion to one's teachers.	Knowledge.
Grihastha (Householder)	24–48	This stage of life is dedicated to earning a living and raising a family.	Wealth and progeny.
Vanaprastha (Hermit in Retreat)	48–60	In this stage, a person hands over the household responsibilities to the next generation and withdraws from the affairs of the world. Most of their time is dedicated to gaining spiritual knowledge and wisdom.	Wisdom.

| Sanyasa (Renunciation) | 60+ | The stage was marked by the renunciation of material desires and prejudices and dedication to the full-fledged pursuit of spirituality. | Mukti/Liberation. |

Vanaprastha Ashrama does not mean challenging yourself with many harsh hardships in your old age. There is no point doing that because anyone will break under sufficiently tough conditions. Essentially, the idea of Vanaprastha Ashrama was to withdraw from a place that has four walls. You don't want to live within four walls, because it creates a certain illusion, a sense of immortality. Maybe because you are already in a box, you are already in a coffin, it feels like you will be forever! The four walls of your home create a false sense of immortality. But you will see, if you just sleep outdoors you will feel so vulnerable. Even if you don't understand this, your very body will understand this very clearly when you sleep outdoors. Maybe most of you don't experience anything because you are sitting in your room with your music turned on or glued to your phones, but if you are out in the jungle, just one storm—with all the lightning, thunder, rain, and the wind—and you will see how vulnerable the human body is. Even in just one night, if you stay out, suddenly a certain wisdom will arise within you.

So Vanaprastha Ashrama meant being in communion with the *vana*, or forest. The fundamental idea is that after living in a home all your life, now, as the end nears, you move closer to Nature and become aware of this vulnerability. People build homes in the first place not to make themselves immortal, but because a human child is not designed to grow up outdoors completely. Unlike other animals, it takes some time for a human body and mind to get to a certain level of maturity. We have seen this happen here—a mother elephant delivered a calf near the Yoga Center gate. She just stood there around the baby for three days, and after that both of them simply walked away into the jungle. This is a natural thing for them. This is not the case with a human child. A human child needs a few years of nurture and protection. So we did some things, like building a home, for this protection. And we put in more and more protection. We did overprotection and super-overprotection; that is a different matter. But, essentially, the idea of wanting to build a home came because the children cannot endure the outdoors.

So at that time, along with the children, the adults also enjoyed the comfort of four walls, which is fine. But then they had enough sense to understand, "If I live like this, I live with a lie, thinking I am immortal." So to make it very clear, not just intellectually, but in every way, the first thing is to step outside of four walls. This is why sadhus and sannyasis never sleep in any built areas. When they sleep, they will sleep only under a tree. If the weather is very harsh, they will sleep in a cave or some naturally protected place. But they will not go into buildings and sleep. Even if they build buildings, they build just the roof. The sides are open. Even if they build walls, they are always mud walls. The idea is that you must be in touch with the earth, you must be in touch with the elements. It constantly reminds the body. The understanding may not be there in your head, but the arrangement will constantly remind your body that you are just a pop-up and you will go back. This is the idea, and there is great benefit in this.

I have seen this with mountaineers—there is a certain quality about them that is hard to come by otherwise. Recently, I met a bunch of European and American mountaineers who have scaled many mountains in South America and the Alps. When I met them, I just sensed the way they are. There is a certain stillness and ease about them, which comes after an enormous amount of sadhana. It takes a lot of work to get there. But every day risking their lives, every day not knowing whether they will live today or not, has brought about a certain stillness and ease in them. You understand you are mortal; you know that, if you make one mistake, you are dead.

Just because people go to Vanaprastha Ashrama, it does not mean they are going there to die. It means they have become conscious that they have to die. Vanaprastha Ashrama is to bring a deep sense of mortality home to this body. Once this body is completely conscious it is mortal, it will arrange itself properly. Suddenly, you will view everything—property, money, relationships, and all that—from a distance. You understand that this is a web that you created for your survival. This is very important, because without that a human being will live a very idiotic life. If it knows it is mortal, it calibrates itself well. It will live much longer. It will not foolishly waste its energy.

We have seen this happening—not so much in India, but in the United States—people who moved into the Isha Institute of Innersciences, in Tennessee, became much healthier. In the Yoga Center in India, when we opened the Vanaprastha Ashrama, most people who moved in were young so it may not be so visible. But there, many of the people who moved in were already over sixty-five, some of them even seventy. You can see that in the last eight to ten years they have become so much fitter, younger, and healthier. They look much better and stronger than ever before, simply because of living outdoors. Of course, they practice Yoga, but they are also in good shape because they are constantly walking up and down, working in the forest, and being exposed to the elements.

Another reason Vanaprastha Ashrama came into practice was because it is not good for people to die at home in the midst of their family and relatives. Right now, in the world, people consider an unattended death to be bad. People think that when they die, the entire family should be around them. That is the worst way to die because you are looking at all these familiar faces and still connecting to the same reality you are now departing from.

When you are at home among family members, two things happen: First, your body gets connected with every other body there. I am not talking about physical or psychological connections—those will be there—beyond that also, your body will develop certain connections. Second, a family or a home means a whole lot of over-organization of life for today, tomorrow, and the day after tomorrow. When you live at home or with your family, you will get sucked into it. This connection with the other bodies and the over-organization of life will create an enhanced sense of the self in a person. This will make it very difficult to let go of things. Moreover, if you die among the family, you will die with a huge sense of attachment, which is not good for what happens after. You must understand, family does not mean attachment alone. If at the last moment of your life you look at your son, daughter, wife, or husband, it is not just love but many other things that will come within you because the relationship has not been only about love. Now all those memories and emotions will also come, which again is not a good thing to happen.

This is why, in this culture, people wanted to die in a space of non-attachment. They wanted to die in a way that had nothing to do with their body, their attachments, their struggles, and their things. They wanted to die in a space which was more spiritual in nature. Even in the olden times, not everyone took to the forests like Dhritarashtra and his family did. Most people moved into one of the ashrams, of which there were many in various parts of the country. In today's conditions, for the Vanaprastha Ashrama, you don't want to go into the forest and take a chance with forest fires or elephants or tigers. Before you die, they may kill you. Or even more likely is that the forest department may arrest you for trespassing! Yes, "vana" means forest. But "vana" also can mean garden. So it is best to withdraw into a protected outdoor space.

If dying in Nature is not possible, the next best option is to withdraw from everyone that you know, particularly relatives and close friends. It is best not to have anything around you that reminds you of the life that you have lived. Set aside your relationships and whatever *runanubandha*s you have. Even gods and goddesses are not necessary because that also is runanubandha—a relationship that you have created. If you have built sufficient awareness, the best way to go is that no one attends to you. If you have not built the necessary awareness, then you may feel terrified when the moment comes. You may want someone to hold your hand. It is all right. If not in awareness, you will leave at least with a little bit of love or comfort. It is okay, but you should keep this to the minimum.

So when is the right time to move into Vanaprastha Ashrama? In the tradition, they said after you are forty-eight years of age or when you have completed four solar cycles, it is time for you to enter Vanaprastha Ashrama. In today's world, that age may not reflect that stage of life. Moreover, these stages of life can occur differently for different people. So the chronological age is not the criterion. After a point in life, one should make an assessment of one's situation at every stage in life. It happened once: There were two women entrepreneurs in Bangalore. One day, the two of them met over coffee. In the course of the conversation, one of them said, "I insist that all the people who work for me must take a one-week vacation every six months." The other one said, "Wow! Why is that so, isn't it expensive to do that?" She said, "No, no, that is the only way I know who are the people I can do without."

So every once in a while, after every stage of your life, it is good to re-examine one's situation. It is good to check how relevant you are to the situation around you, what your priorities in life are, and whether it is time for you to withdraw. And as we saw earlier, moving into Vanaprastha Ashrama is not about going to die; it is to live your life with a certain kind of awareness and preparation, so that death can happen in the best possible manner. This is not an invitation to death but a profound acceptance of the human condition.

The Practice of Sallekhana

In the Hindu way of life, we say, you have three choices for living. You can live as a *bhogi* or a rogi or a yogi, but you can die only as a yogi or a rogi. A bhogi is one who is lost in material or sensual pleasure. A rogi is one whose life is contained by the disease he is suffering from. A yogi is someone who has achieved union or harmony with the Existence. You can live in any of the three states, but for dying, there are only two choices: You can either die as a rogi or as a yogi. There is no choice of dying as a bhogi.

At one time, in this culture, a large number of people chose to die as yogis. But today they are all choosing to die as rogis. There is a whole industry that has come up for this—maybe they feel that they have to support it. Currently, in the United States, a disproportionately large number of healthcare interventions are being done in the last thirty days of human life. Why do you need so much intervention at that stage? This effort is not for well-being, because this results mostly in torturing people to the extreme, knowing full well that they anyway have to die soon. So before those last thirty days—let us say, six months prior to that—you decide to taper down your life and leave. This is the most sensible way to conduct your mortal nature.

Why some people—even those who are not on the spiritual path—want to leave their body consciously is because they do not want to die with tubes hanging out of their body. They want to slowly run it down and leave gracefully, rather than go through all kinds of torture. What happens in the hospital is worse than hell. That is a fact. If you do not know this, please make a trip and spend a few days in all the general wards in government hospitals in India. You will see that this is one place you do not want to end up in. This is the reason why a lot of healthcare professionals in the United States sign the advance do-not-resuscitate order. They see the endless struggle that people go through with tubes and needles sticking in them, just keeping the body alive and prolonging suffering. They may do this for their patients, but they do not want it to happen to them when their own time comes.

In the past, people handled it differently in this culture. Let us say, you did not know any Yoga, and you were over eighty years of age and were still okay. You would probably last another ten to fifteen years at the most. But knowing that the body is becoming infirm, let us say, you took a call, "This is the time for me to run it down consciously." Anyway, you were going to run it down; you just decided to run it down consciously. So from two meals a day, you brought it down to one meal for a few years. Then from one meal you make it half a meal, and so on. This can greatly enhance one's lifespan, or bring it down, depending upon one's karmic and energy situations. But it will definitely ensure freedom from prolonged suffering. In the past, when people went to Vanaprastha Ashrama, they usually went from fruit to fresh leaf, fresh leaf to dry leaf, and dry leaf to just water, and then they stopped the water too. After that, in three to five days, they exited because they did not want to die as a rogi.

Is this suicide? Definitely not. Suicide happens out of frustration, out of anger, out of fear, or out of an inability to bear suffering. This is neither suicide nor euthanasia. This is about being so aware that you know when life has completed its cycle and you walk out of it. This is about developing sufficient awareness to separate yourself from the physicality that you have gathered. In that level of awareness, one can leave. If you do not attain such a level of awareness, then the least you should do is make the last moment very graceful, pleasant, joyful, and blissful for yourself. This will be possible if you have managed to do some preparations beforehand. If none of this is possible, then at least one can make the decision not to choose excessive medical intervention. This will be good for you, and good for the planet.

Modern societies are getting more and more obsessed with extending the human lifespan at any cost. You must understand that not everyone is geared to live for a hundred years. If you want to do that, you must calibrate your life in so many ways. Unfortunately, for most of these millionaire immortality-seekers, all they have known in their life is the pleasures of body, the joys and pains of psychological drama, and the intoxication of power in the world they live in. All of this being physical, they have not looked beyond that dimension at all. Today, with advanced medical interventions—hormones or supplements or stem cells or whatever—they are only managing to somehow keep the body alive.

When people have run out of their software, but their hardware is still on, they will become like empty shells. There are too many such empty shells like that in Western societies now. Some people who work with such people were telling me that there are these eighty-five-to-ninety-year-old men and women who have lost all their memory, but they remember one thing from their adolescent times: that they must attract the opposite sex. They have forgotten everything else, but this one thing has remained due to the chemical nature of that aspect of life that etches itself in one's system. They can barely walk; they are in wheelchairs. But whoever comes—

visitor, worker, anyone—if they are of the opposite sex, they want to grab them. Every day, in an attempt to appear attractive, they wear all kinds of lipsticks and smudge themselves with all kinds of makeup or cut themselves by trying a clean shave. Whosoever they see, they try to grab them. You see how pathetic it is? But this kind of thing is celebrated in today's societies. If you are ninety and still romancing someone, that is considered a great thing. It is not considered a stupid, idiotic thing, because that is all they have been habituated to.

This kind of situation would not have arisen if, like all other creatures, human beings knew when and how to die gracefully. So for people who do not have the capacity to shed the body at will, what can they do to exit it gracefully? How and when do you make that call? It is not the same for everyone. One person may be very strong at eighty-five, another may have to leave at seventy—it depends on many factors. Chronological age is not the criterion. To know this with some certainty, one needs a certain amount of sadhana, or insight into life. Then you will know when infirmity is coming, you will know when your body is becoming unstable, and you will feel you have completed your karma. Otherwise, you feel lost in this world, which, unfortunately, is the state of most modern people.

In ancient times, there was a lot of community support for people to consciously take this step of running the body down and leaving gracefully when the time came. In the Jain community, for example, they had a practice called *Sallekhana*, or *Santara*. The Hindus have something similar called *prayopavesa*. In this tradition, when someone felt they had approached the stage of leaving, if they were so conscious, they could decide for themselves—it was perfectly acceptable. If someone was not aware, then they consulted all the people around, including the family, the elders of the community, and their spiritual head. People then discussed and debated this.

Let us say, someone gives an application saying, "I think it is time for me to do Sallekhana or prayopavesa." So they would debate, discuss, and say, "No, this is not the time for you. Why do you want to do this?" They would list all the things that were yet to happen in the person's life and all the responsibilities that he or she had to fulfill. But the person says, "No, no. I think I have done enough of that. My body is not letting me stay; I need to go." Then they would say, "We have to consult so-and-so," who is considered a spiritual head of the community.

They would consult him together and decide, "Okay, I think it is time for this person to go. Maybe not now, but next year." So he or she would decide to go the following year, based on the society's advice. They would then be formally initiated into a process by the spiritual head. The process itself could be long-drawn and in many stages. At each stage, the spiritual head would review the progress and make sure that this was really the right thing for this person. Even if there was the slightest doubt about it, it would be called off, and the person would be diverted from this path.

Let us say, this was about me. Maybe I will say, "Okay, in another six months, I want to leave." So I may consult people at the Yoga Center: "I think I have done enough; you are taking care of the Yoga Center wonderfully. I don't think Devi* needs me or the Dhyanalinga needs me or anyone needs me. I think it is right for me to go in a year's time." They say, "No, no, Sadhguru, you must be here." I say, "Okay, how long?" They say, "Sadhguru, another twenty years." I say, "No, no, max three years..." If everyone is mature or conscious enough, we can talk about this and arrive at something. Otherwise, you just utter the word "death," and all hell will break loose.

When the entire society is conscious that death is an inevitable

---

* Linga Bhairavi, consecrated by Sadhguru, near the Isha Yoga Center.

part of our life, we can sit down, negotiate, guide one another, arrive at something, and decide that this is the best way to do it. This is just like fixing an arranged marriage in India. Let us say, your daughter has come of age—so when to get her married? The family sits down and discusses and debates about it. They ask the girl her views. They listen to what she has to say, look at the overall situation and see what is best, and finally arrive at a date. Similarly, death is also another part of your life; you should handle it so.

In the past, this was very widely practiced, though in many different forms. Even kings chose to take to Vanaprastha Ashrama and Sallekhana or prayopavesa toward the end of their lives. One of the most famous people who took Sallekhana was Chandragupta Maurya. Chandragupta Maurya was the founder of the Mauryan dynasty and the first emperor to unify India into one nation. No other emperor since has managed to create a bigger empire on the subcontinent. He ruled from 321 to 297 BCE. Ashoka[*] was his grandson. When he was forty-two years old, Chandragupta abdicated his throne in favor of his son Bindusara. He then became an ascetic under the Jain saint Bhadrabahu and migrated to southern India along with the Jain monks. At the age of fifty-five, he ended his life through Sallekhana at Shravanabelagola in Karnataka. Even today, the small stone enclosure where he lived after taking Sallekhana can be seen at Shravanabelagola.

In modern times, many eminent public figures like Acharya Vinoba Bhave chose this form of death. So just as you make efforts to live, you should also make efforts to prepare to die. You should decide, "In case I die, I want to die like this." Right now, let us say, I am going to die tomorrow. I am not planning to die tomorrow, but if it comes, am I ready? One hundred percent! Because, all my life, I prepared for it. Does that mean I am seeking to die tomor-

---

[*] Famous Indian emperor who ruled India from 265 to 238 BCE.

row? No. I will do everything to see that I live well. I always say, in life, one should have passion toward the highest, compassion for all, and dispassion toward oneself. Similarly, I would say, if you want to die well, you have to cultivate a certain amount of dispassion toward your own death. Otherwise, one will go struggling—kicking and screaming—which will not be good for what is going to come next.

All our life situations starting from infancy changed with time. Whether we played with rocks or teddy bears, whether we went to school or romped in the forest, whether we learned how to throw a spear or how to operate a computer, everything we did in our lives essentially depended on the times. But death is one constant—whether we live here today or we lived ten thousand years ago, people always addressed death the same way. Whether people looked at it with fear and terror, or with calm, or with absolute blissfulness depended not on time, but on how aware they were. Life situations can go on varying according to the times, but death is that aspect of our lives which has always been a constant, no matter which time of history we exist in.

The Significance of Dying in Kashi

Irrespective of the times in which we exist, in every society it is very important that we create spaces where people can die without incentives, where they can address their mortality as is. Unfortunately, our lives have been framed on the basis of incentives—we were told to strive in school to get good grades, or at work to get a promotion. People even created incentives for going to heaven: to float in a river of wine, or for virgins, or great food, but all incentives are just a part of human psychological expectation; they have nothing to do with reality. With this reward or punishment, carrot or stick, your life is not allowed to become a full-fledged process. It just goes from incentive to incentive, or punishment to punishment. We need to create spaces where at least when a person has to die, there is neither incentive nor punishment, but a way of dying gracefully. If you did not live gracefully and blissfully, at least you must die gracefully and peacefully.

It becomes the responsibility of every generation to create such spaces in our society where people can die gracefully. The city of Kashi is one such example. No other city in the world is as deeply associated with death as Kashi is. It is also one of the oldest continuously inhabited cities in the world. There is evidence of it being at least twelve thousand years old. But surely it is much older than that. Not only was Kashi continuously inhabited for thousands of years, it was also the most powerful spiritual magnet that drew people from far and wide. It would not be an overstatement to say that it would have been impossible to find someone on the subcontinent who did not want to go to Kashi for whatever reason.

Being able to die in Kashi is only one aspect that drew people to it. Kashi is not just about death. In Kashi, both life and death are celebrated with equal reverence and gusto. People also flocked to the place for its splendor and grandeur. Over thousands of years, people from all over India have settled in Kashi and they live in neighborhoods, each of which retains some of its original identity and linguistic flavor. Kashi, in many ways, is a microcosm of Hindu civilization and a civilizational center of India.

The word "kashi" means light. The city is a tower of light, in the spiritual sense. The idea and the purpose of creating such a tower of light was to assist you in gaining access to that dimension within you which you could not access by yourself. A cosmic possibility is manifested as a reality here—that is what Kashi means. Kashi is not the only such place that was created like this—many more have been created like that. But Kashi is significant because of its enormity, the aesthetics, and the beauty of it. In those times, they say, there was not another city on the planet which was as beautiful. It had three-story buildings, which was unheard of at that time. People were amazed by them. It was too incredible in their experience that houses were built on the riverbank with three floors. That was an engineering feat in itself.

Kashi was also the highest seat of spiritual learning. It is said that hundreds of sages, seers, gurus, Enlightened beings, and scholars lived there, imparting their knowledge to thousands of students who came from all over the country and other parts of the world as well. Every spiritual tradition, every sect and sub-sect of Hindu spirituality, was represented there. There are close to three thousand temples within the city itself. Kashi was also the original hub of art, culture, and music. Aesthetically, spiritually, knowledge-wise, and in every way, it was the most beautiful place of those times. With all these things put together, it created a powerful draw and the necessary atmosphere to attract people's focus. Many prominent saints, philosophers, poets, writers, and musicians of all times have lived in Kashi at some point or the other in their lives. Even Shiva went and lived in Kashi. When Agastya Muni had to leave Kashi, even he cried paeans about Kashi's beauty and greatness. He did not want to leave this city. But his work took him down south.

Traditionally, people did not go to Kashi only when they were on their deathbeds. That would have been dumb. People went and spent the last fifteen to twenty years of their lives there because they wanted to live in the most beautiful place. Living there and leaving their bodies there became an important part. So the original idea of creating the city was to live there. Slowly, because their business was elsewhere, people did not live there. Even then, they sought to live there at least for the last part of their lives. That is how it got the reputation of being the city for dying.

The city of Kashi is demarcated by a large perimeter that is known as the *Pancha Kroshi* route, creating a vast schematic circle. It is approximately fifty-two miles long. Traditionally, people believed

"*Kashyam Maranam Muktih,*" which means that anyone who dies within this perimeter is believed to attain mukti. It did not matter what kind of a lousy creature you had been all your life; if you died in Kashi, you would attain mukti, they said. To ensure this, Shiva takes the form of Kalabhairava in Kashi. Kalabhairava means "the dark one," one who represents limitless time and space. *Kala* means both time and space. It is a deadly form of Shiva. As Kalabhairava, he is supposed to be in a destructive mode. He is not destroying this or that but destroying time. All physical realities exist within the ambit of time. If your time is destroyed, everything is over for you. Kalabhairava does just that.

In Kashi, Shiva, in the form of Kalabhairava, is supposed to personally bestow Liberation by imparting the *Taraka Mantra* to all who die there. They say Yama, the God of death, has no jurisdiction within the perimeter of Kashi. Neither he nor his agents, the *yama-dootas*, can enter the city. Once a person loses their physical body, Kalabhairava gives them a *yatana sharira*, a special subtle energy body, for them to work out their karma. They say the suffering in this yatana sharira is forty-two times more intense than normal suffering. Because it is so intense, it is over almost instantaneously. All this is a very beautiful way of saying that the normal processes that take place after death are not applicable and something else that is super intense happens.

Traditionally, this is called *Bhairavi Yatana*. *Yatana* means "ultimate suffering." It is something that can happen to you beyond the body, but Kalabhairava will make it happen to you here. So at the moment of death, your many, many lifetimes play out in a few moments with great intensity. Whatever pleasures, sufferings, and pains that need to happen to you—spread over many lifetimes—will now happen to you in a microsecond. This happens with the kind of intensity that you cannot hold. If suffering has to end quickly, we must make it super intense; only then it will end quickly. This is about putting your karmic warehouse on fast-forward. If it is mild, it will go on and on forever. So Kalabhairava creates such phenomenal pain, which you have not imagined possible, so that after that nothing of the past remains in you. He makes it as brief as possible.

I have been saying this in many ways: Essentially, spirituality means putting your life on fast-forward. You may suffer much more because everything happens at a fast pace. What you would have stretched for ten years happens, let us say, in one month. So the intensity of the suffering that you go through is extremely acute. There may be moments of ecstasy and joy, but there is so much suffering also happening rapidly within you.

This happens not only in Kashi but in any consecrated space. In a way, once we initiate someone, we have put them on Bhairavi Yatana. We can further tweak it if they want. But they must be ready for it! A consecrated space means just this—it is concentrated life. By saying the suffering is forty-two times more intense means that life there is forty-two times more intense than the way you know it. So that means you burn fuel forty-two times faster. That means everything is faster. After some time, once you get used to it, there is no more yatana, it just burns. You are at a higher rev. That is the purpose of every consecrated space. This whole longing to die in Kashi is to empty out your karma bucket entirely at least toward the end of your life and not make Kashi another item on your bucket list. Emptying one's karma leads to all experiences happening at a tremendous pace.

Consecrated spaces like Kashi are good at doing this. Kashi is definitely not what it was, but it is still significant today. Substantially significant. However, Kashi is not the only place that is made like this. There are many other places, but maybe not of the same magnitude. The Dhyanalinga is one such place, though we cannot accommodate the same number of people as Kashi. In such places, life will happen better, and death also will happen better. Will it always lead to Moksha? Not necessarily; maybe it gets you a little closer. It is certainly better than what you would have done by yourself.

Another reason why people wanted to live the last part of their life in Kashi is because there were a lot of Enlightened and spiritually evolved people there at any given time. In every street, there was an Enlightened being to meet. And in those days they did not have indoor bathrooms. So the entire town would come to the ghat for a dip in the mornings and evenings. Given the sheer number of such spiritually accomplished people who visited the riverbanks, invariably such a person would notice someone whose death was near and he would do what was spiritually necessary for them. Moreover, these people would also know a specific person or ask around for someone who could do what needs to be done for the dying person. Because of this possibility, even if they lived a life of ignorance, even if they had no sadhana in their lives, people who died in Kashi were assured of a very good quality of death.

Kashi is also known as *Mahasmashana*, or "the great cremation ground." Usually, cremation grounds are situated away from the village or city. They are at a distance from human habitation because, unless you are on the spiritual path and it is a part of your sadhana, it is not conducive for the living and the dead to be in close proximity to each other. In Kashi, the city itself is built around this great cremation ground.

Even today, around the clock, the ghats are full of burning bodies because they cater not just to the people of the city but even to those from distant places. Whenever there is a death within a radius of about a hundred miles, the body is taken to Kashi to be cremated. The idea is that the person may have been unable to live in Kashi, or even die in Kashi, for some reason, but they want at least the body to be cremated in Kashi and the remains immersed in the Ganga River. They say the cremation fire has been passed on from the beginning of time and has never been extinguished since. There is a family that has been living on the ghats there for many generations, whose responsibility is to keep the fire going and provide it to each and every cremation that happens there.

So, over time, from people wanting to live in Kashi to wanting to die in Kashi, they wanted to be at least cremated in Kashi. But today people just want to visit Kashi at least once in their lifetime, and that too as tourists, not as pilgrims. Of course, the city of Kashi itself has undergone a sea change. It is no longer in its ancient, glorious form. Modernity has taken a serious toll on its structure and form. Even then, the entire atmosphere has some impact on people. More than a karmic influence, it may bring some psychological realization—an intellectual realization from seeing life being conducted in a completely nonchalant way. What is usually done behind the scenes, in seclusion, is conducted openly there. You don't have to go to a hospice to die. You can just sit on the riverbank and die. You can be cremated on the riverbank too. People see it as normal, very normal. So even just visiting such a place has a certain impact. Though terribly mutilated, Kashi remains a powerful possibility even today. The time to build new towers of light has definitely come.

CHAPTER 7

Assistance for the Dying

A bodiless being is a completely defenseless life. That is why that aspect of life must be conducted with utmost responsibility. When someone gives this being a little bit of help at the last moment, it will go a long way. Most of their sadhana for the next time will be taken care of at that moment itself.

THE IMPORTANCE OF THE LAST MOMENTS OF LIFE

Why is the moment of transition from an embodied state to a disembodied state so important? Let me give you an analogy. Right now, when you are in the body, you are like a river, going in one direction. When you become disembodied, it is like you evaporated and became a cloud. Whichever way the wind blows, you will go that way. You have no direction anymore. At least the river is clearly going toward the ocean, but we don't know where the hell the cloud is going. Whichever way the wind blows, it will go that way. Leaving the body and losing the discretionary mind is like that. If you had a discretionary mind, you could go either this way or that. But once you die, you are just fluff, floating around according to your karmic tendencies. You know, didn't they always tell you that angels float around in the clouds? Well, they used the correct analogy!

The significance of being a human is that you have the ability to discriminate and choose the course of your life. If you don't employ that, then you are not much of a human being. For example, let us say, I am hungry. But if food comes in front of me, I can discriminate and say, "No, I don't want to eat it." Because of the discriminatory capability within me, it does not matter how much compulsion arises in my body; if I don't want to, I will not eat. That is all. I can discriminate. Without this, you become like air; you will move by tendencies alone.

When you lose the body, your ability to discriminate is gone. All the memory and other mind-stuff are still there; only the discriminatory process is lost. At that moment, if you create even a little bit of unpleasantness, then the unpleasantness will multiply a millionfold. If you create a little pleasantness, the pleasantness will multiply a millionfold. Why is this so? Let us say, today, you get a little angry; you can use your discriminatory mind and control it. But if you did not have this discriminatory mind, the little anger would flare up into madness. The moment of death is a significant factor because whatever is the content of one's mind at that moment—pleasantness or unpleasantness—it could multiply manifold because of the lack of discriminatory mind. This is why it does not matter which part of the world you come from, which culture you come from; every culture holds that when a person is dying you must allow them to die peacefully.

During this phase of disembodiment, if your pleasantness multiplies, we say you are in heaven. If your unpleasantness multiplies, we say you are in hell. Hell and heaven do not exist as geographical places but as human experience. You don't have to be disembodied to be in hell or heaven; even when you are alive, they can exist for you. The advantage of being here with the body is that sometimes, when you get into hell in your experience, you can employ your discrimination and get out of that pit. Similarly, sometimes you get into heaven in your experience, but through your discrimination, however pleasant the experience is, you can drop it and move on to the next thing. Even when in the body, someone who loses their discrimination will stay depressed for long periods of time if they get into depression, while pleasant experiences will turn into addictions.

In Hindu culture, great importance was given to how a person who is dying should be treated. They said a person must die in the right space, in the right atmosphere, with the right kind of emotion and with the right kind of thought. When someone is dying, they said you are never supposed to say, "Aiyyo, Amma!"* You are supposed to say "Rama" or "Krishna" or "Shiva"† or something like that. The idea is to generate some impulse to think beyond oneself. It is a phenomenally scientific process. It is not an emotional process, because this last dimension of thought and emotion that you create becomes the major tendency in that being. They said, "Even if it is your enemy who is dying right now, you must create an appropriate atmosphere and see how he can die peacefully. Don't do ugly things." Maybe you shot him in battle, but you take off your hat when he is leaving, or you say, "Ram, Ram," or whatever you know. This is because these tendencies will go on for lifetimes. Whatever life they might have lived, at that final moment, if they generate the right thing, they could go into a good trip, rather than going into a bad trip. So this is a tremendous opportunity to enhance someone's life.

When someone is dying, at that moment the whistle has already been blown and the game is over. There is no point kicking now. Moreover, your enmity lasts only as long as they carried this body. Once they shed the body, the drama is over. They are no more your enemy, nor are they your friend. He or she is just a piece of life, and a life has to be treated as a life. When the play is on, each one of us watches, relates, and reacts in many different ways. When the cur-

---

* Cries of distress.
† Names of major Hindu deities.

tains fall, all stand up. Only one in slumber remains as he was. Everyone else, even those who did not enjoy the play, stands up and acknowledges that it is over. It would be fantastic if every act of the play was appreciated or at least looked upon with respect. If you did not succeed in that, at least the last scene—that is what death is—should be appreciated.

That is the reason why, when you see somewhere that even the dead are not treated with respect, something within you is shaken. It is not the body that needs to be treated with respect but the being who is exiting slowly who needs it. It does not matter how they lived; at least the leaving must happen well. Every human being must have that much intention. This is the least you can do for that person or the life that we are. Everywhere in the world, people are reasonably aware of it, but for the Hindus it has been a very conscious process.

In the Kurukshetra War,[*] the Pandava prince Arjuna was the most skilled warrior, but it was his brother Bheema who was considered more valiant and feisty. But that glory got tainted because he desecrated the body of an opponent. In one of the battles, he was pitched against Dushasana, who was instrumental in disrobing Draupadi. So Bheema had taken a vow at that time to avenge Draupadi's humiliation. On the day of the fateful battle, Bheema not only killed Dushasana in a brutal manner but he also tore open his chest and drank his blood to fulfill the vow. Warriors from both sides were aghast at this act of Bheema. Though he was only avenging an earlier injustice, Bheema's reputation was tainted forever by his "dishonorable conduct" because he violated the war code by not treating the dead body of the enemy with respect.

Another reason why the way we conduct this moment is very important is because a bodiless being is a completely defenseless

---

[*] The last war in the Mahabharata.

life. That is why that aspect of life must be conducted with utmost responsibility. When someone gives this little being a little bit of help at this last moment, it will go a long way. Most of their sadhana for the next time will be taken care of at that moment itself. If you look around, you will see how much struggle people go through just to be loving, or to drop hatred and anger. Sometimes, when I see people struggling with these things, it beats me as to why they struggle like this. Even to drop their old feelings and habits, they struggle. But when you help a person die well, all these things are washed off, just like that. You are born with the right quality. This is the simplest way to ensure a being is reborn pleasant.

This is not all. Even after one leaves the body, we can guide that being. If that person has sufficient trust in you, during the last few moments you can make them accomplish a certain sweetness of one's existence, embodied or disembodied, if you can create the right situation for them and help them to die well. This is a huge contribution to that being's life. Moreover, if a person truly dies well, then there is no next time for them. That life moves into the nature of limitless freedom. But all this cannot be done with one's emotions or good intentions. Just because you wish someone should go to heaven, they will not go to heaven. If you want to do such things, then you need to have a different level of understanding, awareness, and mastery over life. Otherwise, those things are out of the question.

Helping Suffering People Die

When someone is suffering deeply, should we not help that person die? See, when you were born, your mother suffered immensely. So if we believe it is okay to relieve someone of their suffering by killing, we should have killed her or killed you at that time. Do you think people on their deathbeds are suffering as much or more than those in the labor ward? Not necessarily. This question is coming up these days because we are seeing more and more people surviving as vegetables here for a long time. This prolonged suffering would not be there if you did not unnecessarily interfere with the process of life and go on medically pushing death. Without this, no one will stay beyond their natural time.

Does it mean that when you get a disease, we should withdraw all medical support? No, many people have bounced back from all kinds of hopeless situations. Many times, people thought someone would die, but they just bounced back and lived on. So should we not give these people also a chance? Who is to decide who should be helped to die and when? If there is a 100 percent medical prognosis that there is no way to recover, they can withdraw the medication. But where is the need to push someone into death by injecting a poison or something else? If you withdraw medication, if the body is not fit for life, life will move on. It is not for you to decide whether the body is fit or not unless you are conscious of the extent that you can drop it and go.

If you are afraid of old age and suffering, why don't you start doing some sadhana now to prepare yourself so that you can leave when you want to? Why do you want to wait for that moment and ask your son or daughter to give you poison? Please see, asking them to poison you is not fair to them. Even if out of their compassion or love they give you poison, can they ever forget it? You will go anyway, but why are you burdening those who have to live for a long time with all these things? You can live in such a way that you don't need anyone's mercy. You can live your life to a plan. You live as long as it is effective and you leave gracefully when you have to leave, not through mercy killing. Why don't you pursue these options?

Right now, it may seem that this mercy killing is fine. In society today, people may think it is a revolutionary idea. There are always people who want to be progressive, who are advocating mercy killing. If you are really progressive, why don't you empower individuals to shed their body at will? This is what I am doing—helping people grow into such a capability that they can terminate their life by will when the time comes, but not by poison or by a pillow.

These days, there is another kind of situation: Because of modern medical intervention, there are more and more cases of people who remain in vegetative states for a long time. And some of them bounce back to life even after many years in that state. So the people around them go through an enormous struggle trying to decide whether or not to pull the plug on their loved ones. This happened in Morocco: Shankaran Pillai had aged a little bit and was watching some program on the television about old-age homes and hospices. Watching the program, he told his wife, "Darling, if it ever happens that I become vegetative, I want you to pull the plug. I don't want to go through all this. You must just pull the plug." She looked at him and got up and pulled the television plug. So this decision to pull the plug can be very tricky.

Now, about the people who bounce back to life from vegetative or near-death states, don't think that they died and were put back. That is not true. It might have so happened that the life force was so shocked, it became more projected outward than inward. Even in the conscious state, you are partially outward-projected, mostly inward-projected. Inward projection of life energies gives you organic unity and stability of life. Outward projection gives you a strong presence and expression of life. This seesaw is naturally happening with all life, including human beings. But human beings with a certain mastery can make this into a conscious choice regarding this dimensional shift. Therefore, at that moment it might have been so that you were mostly outward-projected, partially inward-projected. So life was making a decision, "To be or not to be." This is not a philosophical question but a practical question about whether the body is fit enough to be or not be. So after doing this to-be-or-not-to-be seesaw for some time, if it chose *to be*, it is not because of medical workers or a miracle. Maybe the medical workers made the body a little more hospitable than what it would have been, but it is always life which makes the decision to stay because the body is still hospitable.

If one has an enhanced perception, it is possible to make an assessment of a patient's life chances based on the vibrancy of the Pranamaya Kosha, or energy body. It is possible to say whether a person's life energies are intense enough for recovery to happen. On the other hand, even if the body is not obviously unwell but the patient's pranic energies are at a low ebb, recovery is impossible, no matter what the intervention. It is a question of software. If the software has run out, no matter what you do it will not renew itself. But not everyone has the perception to make such a decision. It is therefore best to let life take its course, rather than allow people to issue a death certificate for the living.

Now, there are two kinds of vegetative states. In one condition, the body becomes so inert that you are not able to get it going, but the mind is active, the emotion is active, and all perceptions are intact. This is torture for the person because the body refuses to move. This can lead to a lot of suffering because they can see, they can hear, they can smell, they can understand, but they lack the ability to do anything. They want to get up and walk but the body has become inert. Now, it is a very difficult decision for anyone to make. Moreover, many a time, the person understands all the things that are spoken around them—whether to pull the plug or not and all that—it is a very bad situation. It should not happen to anyone, but when it happens, how to deal with it? This is a hard decision to make—there is no particular way to do it because it depends on individual sensitivities.

The other kind is where the body seems to be reasonably vibrant and active, digests food, and everything is happening, but the mind has become inert. So the body cannot act. The body is still kept alive because you are keeping it going with all the medical processes. This is like an empty shell that is kept alive—incapable of any response. If this is the case, you can wait for five cycles of twenty-one days and then take a call. After that, if things are still the same, you can pull the plug. You can be 100 percent sure that the life cannot be revived. Well, this may sound very drastic to you, but these days many honest doctors are asking the relatives to take the patient home when they know there is no point continuing to meddle with them. But those who just want to serve bills to you would be interested in kicking the can.

Today, advances in palliative care and pain relief have reached a point where most of the pain that a person experiences on the deathbed can be removed with appropriate medication. But people ask: Will the use of painkillers somehow affect the quality of death that is imminent? Is there some merit in going through the full suffering on the deathbed? These questions arise because of all those moralistic teachings in the world that enduring pain and enduring suffering are virtues and a way to atone for one's sins. This happened: A new batch of people landed in heaven. All of them were golfers. They asked, "Is there a golf course in heaven?" Saint Peter said, "Of course." They asked, "Can we see it? Is it okay?" He asked the Holy Ghost to drive them in a golf cart. So he drove them through a fabulous golf course, full of flowers, greenery, and everything. When they crossed the third hole, they saw that there was a pit full of fire and people were burning, screaming, and yelling. They looked at this and asked, "What is this? We thought there was no suffering in heaven." The Holy Ghost said, "They are religious people; they insist!"

So when someone is on the deathbed, is it okay to use painkillers? If it is a non-sedative painkiller and if you are able to maintain a reasonable amount of consciousness, it is perfectly fine to take them. Why do you want to go through pain if there is no medical need to suffer it? But if the painkillers are overly sedating and you are not even barely conscious, then it is not the best way to leave.

About Dying at Home

I would like to see a day where people come to *Kayantha Sthanam** and say, "I think it is my time. Is there a place here where I can stay and die and go? No one needs to carry me up here." That would be a good day. Go there, sit happily, don't eat or drink anything, just die. No funeral, just cremation. That would be an Enlightened world. Well, that is a faraway thing, that will not happen right now, but at least you must create spaces where people can die peacefully with a certain focus.

What is happening today in homes is that, though everyone is going to die, unfortunately no one is qualified to handle death. How is that? In the United States, you will see in every dining hall there are first-aid instructions as to what to do if someone is choking on food. But why is anyone choking on food? I have never heard of anything like that in India. No one chokes on food in India, though, generally, people in India are hungrier than Americans. People are choking on food probably because they are talking and eating at the same time. When you try to input and output simultaneously through the same channel, something gets confused. If people just shut up and eat, I don't think anyone will choke on their food.

Anyway, for something like choking while eating, there is so much care and effort to inform people about how to handle it, but there is nothing done on how to handle death. Everyone knows

---

* Crematoriums run by Isha.

people are going to die. You know your grandparents are going to die, you know your parents are going to die, but when it happens, no one knows how to handle it because somewhere they are trying to avoid it. They think by not talking about it, by not preparing for it, it is not going to happen. Very few families have the sense to prepare and say, "Okay, this person is going to die, let us prepare for that." It is time we prepared ourselves to do at least a few things to ensure that this person who is dying does not have to go through unnecessary suffering.

Now, even when someone is medically dead, they are not existentially dead because death happens slowly. So there are certain preparations that can be made to reduce the choppiness of the moment and assist the withdrawal of life during that time. If you are dying at home, it is best you withdraw into a clean, white room with mild-blue light. No photographs, nothing. If there is a tinge of blue around you, this will help you to die well. Another simple thing you can do to help is to have a lamp burning twenty-four hours of the day, next to that person. A ghee lamp is preferable, but you can also use butter. This creates a certain aura so that the choppy nature of withdrawal can be regulated to some extent.

Next, you can have a chant or something with the right kind of sounds going on. These should be the kind of sounds that will touch the fundamentals of who you are. It would be even better if they are consecrated sounds or chants or mantras. And better still if you have internalized it beforehand. Internalizing a chant can be a very powerful tool in life and in death. This happened in the life of the southern Indian saint called Swami Ramdas. Ramdas was initiated into the worship of Lord Rama by his father, through the chanting of the mantra "Rama, Rama, Rama." Over time, his mantra practice became deep. Once when he was still an unrecognized sadhaka, he was wandering through the countryside. It was evening and some benevolent person in a village offered to host him for the night.

Ramdas ate the dinner that was offered to him and went to sleep. But in the middle of the night, the host realized that someone was chanting "Rama, Rama, Rama" quite loudly. He was annoyed as he wanted to sleep. So he went to check on Ramdas. He was fast asleep. But the owner could still hear the sound of "Rama, Rama." So he slowly went toward Ramdas and sensed that the sound was emanating from Ramdas's body! His practice of mantra was so intensified that even while he slept, the body was just reverberating "Rama, Rama, Rama."

Such incidents where people have internalized sounds or mantras have happened in the lives of many other saints. This also happened with my Divine Guru. I call him Divine because the element of divinity happened to me only because of His Presence. Palani Swami never told anybody his name—maybe even he didn't remember. Because people saw him in many fantastic states around the Palani Hills, they called him Palani Swami. Just by sitting in one place, he drew such large crowds that the local temple priests became a little resentful. They were irked that this man who did nothing, who begged for his food from others, was drawing so many people. Meanwhile, they were sitting in the temple from morning till evening, doing their rituals and duties, but people were not going there; they were going to this man. So they wanted to find something against him. One day, they accused Palani Swami of uttering "Shambho" when doing his morning ablutions, which is something that is considered a sacrilege. So they brought him before the village panchayat and charged him with desecrating God by taking his name when going out to relieve himself in the morning. Palani Swami simply sat there before this ignorant bunch of judges, with eyes closed and mouth closed. Then loud reverberations of the sound "Shambho" could be heard among the gathering. And that was the end of their prosecution.

So you can internalize a chant like this, where your very energies reverberate with that sound. In order to reach the point where it is internalized, you need a certain amount of loud chanting initially. If you do that in your day-to-day life, it can be a great support when death is approaching. We have created a collection of sacred chants called *Vairagya*. It has five mantras. Listen to the album over and over a few times, paying attention to each one of the mantras. Each one runs for ten minutes. Figure out which mantra really draws you. Just listen repeatedly. When you feel that one of them is really grabbing you, just go by that. Keep this mantra going all the time—in your car, in your home, on your iPad, iPod, phone, everywhere.

Simply keep it going on and on for some time. Initially, you chant it loudly like a song. Slowly, see if you can close your mouth and still keep the same reverberation up. Initially, unless you chant it sufficiently in the louder form with some volume, you cannot take it inward. You must create that memory of the reverberation substantially in your system, where, even if you close your mouth, the mantra continues. After some time, if you just remind yourself, it flows because you have created a memory of that reverberation.

Now, the dying person may not be able to do the chanting themselves. At the moment of death, it takes something for a person to be aware enough to say what they want to say. Most people die in unawareness. So in this culture, if someone is dying, people around always start a chant like "Ram, Ram" or "Aum Namah Shivaya," or whatever they know because they want the dying one also to utter a consecrated sound that creates awareness. So when someone is dying at home or elsewhere, you can set up a chant of one of these mantras at a very mild volume. If they have already chosen their chant themselves or internalized it, that can be used. If they had not chosen one, *Brahmananda Swarupa* could be played for everyone. This will make sure that a choppy withdrawal of life can be avoided.

We could make more powerful body-exiting mantras available because reverberations can do wonders for a life that is already organizing itself to exit. If you cause powerful reverberations of support, life will organize itself very well, and you will become loose inside the body. So you can at least have a few days or a few hours of experience where you are not the body 100 percent. This will be a wonderful thing for any human being. But it will also affect people who are around, so no one should be there when this is being used. Moreover, we don't know how people will use it. There is no way to ensure that it will be used responsibly. They may use it in their car when they are driving, and they may exit by crashing! So it is best to not attempt these things with the masses and instead use something general like the *Vairagya* chants.

Of the Pancha Pranas, Udana Vayu can be influenced by the right kind of reverberations. As we mentioned earlier, Udana Vayu withdraws between six and twelve hours after the breath stops. By chanting and lighting *sambrani*,[*] one can create the conducive reverberations for Udana to exit swiftly. Otherwise, cremating the person's body before their Udana exits can cause a certain level of turmoil.

Now, what to do if someone is dying in an ICU or something like that, where the doctors will not allow lamps and chants and things like that? First of all, people should not go to an ICU to die. Hospitals are for people who want to bounce back to life, not for people who are dying. But if such a situation is inevitable you could do a few things at home, but they are not as effective. For example, you can keep some clothing of theirs—something they have used—wrap it in a white cloth and keep it in front of their picture and

---

[*] A type of incense.

light a lamp. You could play the chant there. It will have some impact, but not the same as being in their physical presence.

This lamp and the chant should continue for up to fourteen days after one has been certified dead because one may be medically dead but not existentially dead. Death happens slowly. The withdrawal of the life process from this lump of earth—the body—happens step-by-step. For all practical purposes, the activity of the lungs, heart, and brain stops, so they are declared dead, but it is not yet so. Even if the person's body is burned, they are still not gone because their movement into the other realm has not yet happened.

Now, when the moment of death is approaching, it is best to move the dying person out of the house into an open courtyard or open space. There you must keep them, preferably on cloth, with minimal clothing, covered by a sheet, upon wet soil, in a north–south alignment with the head to the north. This is to be done when death is certain and you want it to happen with ease. If the body is still in the house, inside constructed atmospheres, the being does not leave the body with ease.

The body that we carry is a loan from the planet. We have not borrowed anything from anywhere else, apart from this planet. It is Mother Earth's breast upon which we have fed for so long. When the body comes in touch with the soil, there is an intelligence in the physical body which knows it has to merge with this. It naturally starts organizing to leave. That organization within the system also relieves one of fear that something unknown is happening, and there is a systemic flow of our physical nature that brings one to a certain level of calm, and maybe even blissfulness. As one who wants to live well needs to organize oneself, one who wants to die well also needs to organize.

Why put the head toward the north? Traditionally, in India, they tell you not to sleep with your head to the north. This is valid only when you are in the northern hemisphere. If you go to the southern hemisphere—say, Australia—you should not put your head toward the south. Mostly, this body is designed in such a way that if you remain vertical, it is ideal. Now your heart is located three-fourths of the way up because pumping the blood up is difficult, pumping it down is easy, and all the arteries and veins that go above the heart are very thin. Blood vessels going down are much thicker. As they go toward the brain, they become almost hairlike. So when you lie down, the blood can be pumped into the upper portion of the body much more easily. The heart also makes some adjustments once you lie down. But despite that there is a certain effect.

Now, iron is an important constituent of your blood. If you are anemic, your doctor prescribes you iron supplements. As you know, the North Pole has a very strong magnetic pull on the rest of the Earth. Now, if you lie down with your head toward the north, it will pull your blood in that direction, so there will be increased blood flow to your brain. This is not too much, but enough to impact the system. This is why, when you sleep with your head toward the north, you will have disturbed sleep. You can also have nightmares because of disturbed sleep. Old people may even die in their sleep if they put their head to the north. Or they can have a hemorrhage or stroke and things like that. So when you live in the northern hemisphere, you should not put your head toward the north.

However, when a person is dying, you should place the head toward the north because it eases and aids the disentanglement process of the being from the body. During the last moments, even though the physical body has lost its vibrancy, life still tries to stay there and do things, not knowing what to do. But the moment you place it outside in north–south alignment, it just knows it is over. So it will leave the body effortlessly. It also aids in maintaining a conscious state during the transition. These are some simple but effective things you can do to assist someone who is dying.

Rituals from Death to the Disposal of the Body

We already saw that when it comes to death, the usage of language is significant: You do not diagnose someone as dead, you *declare* that they are dead. It is significant because there is a difference between the two. When you declare them dead, it is only for you that they are dead. As far as that person is concerned, in a way, all that has happened is that he or she is disembodied—they have lost their body. All their life they lived thinking they are the body, never realizing the physical mass that we carry is an accumulation from this planet. When suddenly one slips out of the body, one tends to hover around it, as there is no discriminatory intelligence. It is in stages that life came into the body and it is in stages that it will go away.

It is believed in Hindu culture that the moment we are sure that someone is dead, we must do certain things because the situation is rife with possibilities for us to help the departed being. A person who is knowledgeable about the intricacies of the process of death can do a whole lot of good for the departed, but even ordinary people who happen to be around the dying also can make a huge difference in easing the journey of the departed by doing certain things, whether they understand it or not. This will be good for the dead person and also good for the living.

THE LAYING OUT OF THE BODY

Even after death has happened, it is good to place the body in a north–south alignment, with the head to the north. As we said earlier, as far as the dead person is concerned, all their life they lived thinking they are the body, experiencing that they are the body. Suddenly, they popped out and they are confused. Confused existentially, not psychologically. They do not have a discriminatory mind to think. They do not realize that it is over. They linger around because the body is still there. They tend to make attempts to get back into the body, which is unfit to sustain life. This can lead to a certain energy in that place which is neither good for the person nor for the people living around that space.

When you place the body in a north–south alignment, with the head toward the north, the being will be pulled away from the body. Once you do this, certain changes happen more quickly in the physiology of the body that has been discarded. The being realizes that it is futile to hang around that particular body because it cannot access it anymore. A certain distance arises between the being and the body, which is very conducive for what has to happen next for the being.

TYING THE BIG TOES TOGETHER

The next thing to do after death is to tie the big toes together. This is because when you are alive, life energies are deeply infused into every cell of your body. When death happens, these energies recede slowly. Functionally, it may be dead, but it does not die totally; it dies slowly because all the cells in the body are not dead yet, and they are still making an effort to live. They will try to draw energy from outside. When they try to draw energy, certain forces may enter the body. In order to prevent these things, people tie the two big toes together in such a way that the outer surfaces of the big toes are touching each other.

Even now, you will notice that if you put your big toes together, your anal outlet and the Muladhara Chakra will always be tightly closed. If the Muladhara Chakra is not closed, the remaining aspect of the prana tends to leave from that chakra, which is not desirable. Moreover, if the Muladhara Chakra and the anal outlet are open, it tends to become a lower passageway for the being to enter the body again. This can cause a very negative situation, which is not at all good for that being, nor for the living.

Once the Muladhara Chakra is closed, the being cannot get in and repossession of the body cannot happen. This wanting to possess the body through the Muladhara Chakra need not necessarily be by the being who has left the body. There are other beings who seek such a passage. If someone wants to do certain occult practices where freshly dead bodies are used, it is always the Muladhara which is made use of because that is the easiest passage. Other passages will not be as easily available. So tying the toes together will also protect the body from being used by people who are into occult practices, which would bind that being in so many ways.

There is also a practical aspect to this. If you don't tie the toes together, when death happens, the legs will naturally tend to move apart and spread wide. Once rigor mortis sets in, you will not be able to bring them back together, and handling the dead body will become difficult and awkward. So tying the toes together will prevent the distortion of the body.

WASHING AND CLOTHING THE BODY

In certain communities in India, where they are still aware of these things, the first thing they do when someone dies is strip the body naked. The next thing to do is wash the body with water. One reason is that the person may have been injured and ill during the last moments, so you want to clean that up. But it is not just for hygiene purposes that you give them a wash. See, even when you are alive, if someone tries to give you a bath and they pour water on your face, you will feel like you are being waterboarded. It feels like you are drowning. If there is even any little activity happening in the body, it will all cease. The idea is not to just clean the body, but to facilitate the complete withdrawal of life from the body as running water has the ability to clear many aspects off the body.

Now, once again, you lay the body in north–south alignment in an open space. The body is kept naked, with just a white cloth covering it. This cloth is also for the people's sake, not for the dead body's sake. There is nothing to cover, there is nothing to expose for a dead body, but the living people have issues. So one white cloth, just a sheet, is used to cover the body. Why a white cloth? The color white reflects all light and most of the heat—two factors that can hasten the decomposition of the cells. This hastening of decomposition is not advisable at this stage, as certain aspects of prana are still partially functional in the body. Black or colored cloth will absorb both light and heat, and should be avoided.

Unfortunately, these days, people have begun clothing and dressing up the body elaborately. Undertakers in the West actually do more makeup for dead bodies than what people would do for Hollywood stars. It has become very lucrative. But in this culture, when you go back to death, you go back naked, as you were born. Even if you did not realize it when you were alive, it is at least a realization for the other people who are watching. It is a knock on their head to tell them that these things do not matter anymore.

THINGS NOT TO DO AROUND A DEAD BODY

There are many customs and rituals for the dead in various cultures, but there are some things that you should definitely not do around a dead body. One thing is that you should not sleep near a dead body. This is so because, in sleep, everyone is far more susceptible to everything than in wakefulness. We already saw that death is a process and it continues for quite some time. If you have kept the body for six, twelve, or twenty-four hours or whatever, the process is still on, and life is still exiting. So people who are sleeping near the body become available to such things, which is not good for them.

Another thing is that one should not cook or eat near a dead body. The very nature of food will draw that energy in that direction. So if you are cooking or eating near a dead body where the life energies are still exiting, you will be eating your own relative in some way. This may sound very extreme, but it is so because food will draw these energies. This is why, traditionally, people don't cook in the house where death has occurred for a period of fourteen days. People bring food from outside, for the people there. But it is not good to eat there either.

The very process of eating itself makes a person vulnerable to influences. The moments of eating and sexuality are the times when a human being becomes far more vulnerable than other times because, essentially, human structure has to open up in some way to take it in. This is the reason why you must bring down the number of times you eat so that you retain the integrity of the system. You can clearly observe this: Those who eat all the time, even if they eat less, will not have integrity of system. It is not about how much you eat, but how many times a day you eat. Even the medical experts unfortunately used to advise eating many times during the day, though they have now transitioned to recommend intermittent fasting with large time spaces in between of not eating, which has always been the Yogic way—to bring down the number of times you eat.

Sexuality, food, and even constantly sipping water opens up the body to various influences that will not always work positively for people. It is in this context that a yogi opens his or her body only when absolutely needed and that too in a structured and disciplined manner. Constant ingestion loosens the general integrity of the subtler dimensions of the body. It is not that they become obese; that is not the point. It brings about looseness, not of character, but of the physical, mental, and energetic integrity of the system. Particularly the neurological system, which is the basis of all we experience in the world, becomes more susceptible to fluctuations from one extremity to another, from joy to misery, from a sense of assurance to fear, rather than a sustained high. It leads to a depletion of strength or vibrancy or capability simply because they are opening their system too many times in a day. Also, you do not eat simply anywhere and everywhere. Always, in the Hindu way of life, you never want to be seen by strangers when you are eating. You don't eat with just anyone. You eat only with people who know you, with people who have good intentions for you. But today, even if it is your enemy, meetings happen over dinner. But at least around a dead body, you should avoid eating.

One should also avoid unnecessary touching of the dead body. Whatever touching you need to do should be to clean or bathe or move the body, but one should avoid unnecessarily holding the body, hugging, and all that. That is not good for you or that life which is exiting. One more thing is that you do not leave the dead body alone. In Hindu culture, if someone close to you dies, you are supposed to keep a ghee, butter, or sesame-oil lamp burning near the body. People are supposed to sit and watch—no one leaves a dead body alone. The lamp's flame has a purificatory effect and is like *Klesha Nashana Kriya*. If it is a regular death, the lamp is to be placed at the feet. If it is an elevated exit, then the lamp is to be placed at the head to have a purificatory impact upon the exiting energy. If there is qualified help, then they may choose to light the lamp over a specific part of the body. The lamp can be lit even up to fourteen days after the body is cremated or buried.

PAYING RESPECTS TO THE DEAD

In almost all parts of the world, if someone is dead, people who knew the person come and pay their respects for who he or she was.

But in Hindu culture, a dead person is generally treated as a Divine being and one bows down to them. It does not matter who they were when they were alive. When they were alive, maybe they did not deserve any kind of respect, but now that they are dead, people bow down to them. This is not out of joy that the person is gone. They bow down to him or her because he or she is no more that person. Now what is left and what is hovering around is of a different nature. This is life. This is the basis of life, and with that you don't argue. You don't question its wisdom. You just bow down because it is way beyond you.

THE BELONGINGS OF THE DEAD PERSON

When a person is dead, the articles of clothing that have been intimately in touch with their body, such as the underclothes, must be burned immediately. Other clothes, jewelry, and other articles are distributed not just to one person but among many people within three days. Everything is distributed as quickly as possible so that the being gets confused. It will not know where to hang around anymore. If you were to give a bundle of their belongings to one person, the being would go there because the energy of their own body still exists in the clothes and they are attracted to it. This is done not only to settle the dead but also to settle the family and relatives so that they too understand that it is over. It does not matter how involved or attached you were to someone—when it is done, the game is up.

TO BURN OR BURY

You will see that, if someone very dear to you is dead and their body is there, you will keep on hallucinating, "Maybe they are just sleeping, maybe they will sit up, maybe some miracle will happen. Maybe something else will happen." You know, this will go on unnecessarily. You will see people crying and a big emotional drama happening. But the moment the body is cremated, you will see everyone becomes silent. Always. Because now everyone knows the game is up. The cremation of bodies has also come from a certain understanding of life. The idea of burning is that no trace of you should remain. Once you are gone, you are clean gone. Nothing of you should remain. But if someone exits their body consciously, or even if not consciously, they at least left gently or seeped out of the system, then you can bury them. But if they were jolted out of the system, you must burn the body.

Traditionally, in India, you will see agricultural families bury their dead because most of them would have died of old age—they would have seeped out. *Kshatriya* families, which were the fighting class, always burned their dead because most of them were jolted out of their body either in a war or while fighting somewhere. Even otherwise, these were people who lived flamboyant lifestyles of drinking and doing this and that, so most of the time they broke the body in some way. Such bodies must be burned immediately. But now there is no one to identify all these things, and moreover, even if you put them in a coffin and bury them, they will not become part of the Earth for a long time. So, I would say if someone dies when they are still young and vibrantly alive, it is better to cremate them. Only if someone dies of old age can you bury them.

If you understand life very well, absolutely well, you can exit the body in such a way that you exit completely, you gather everything and leave. If you leave like that, then you also can be buried. You have completely exited, so there is no hurry. We can even keep you for a day or two and then bury you. Usually, people build samadhis for such people so that the energies that they have left behind can be made use of by other people.

Even if we bury someone, we should put a layer of salt and turmeric beneath and above the body. Don't think we are making a stew out of them; the idea is that we want the body to deteriorate as quickly as possible. If you put it in the ground without these things, the body remains intact for a long time and unnecessarily certain processes happen, which are not good. Also, in India, another fear was that there were people doing various kinds of occult sadhanas, who were always looking for a freshly dead body. If you bury the body and go, as soon as you go they will come and dig it up. In recent times, you don't hear much of such things, but it used to happen often in the past. If you put salt, that body becomes useless for them. If they know you put salt, they will not dig up the grave.

There are also certain cultures which practice feeding the carrion to scavenger birds. As we know, among sailors, there is a practice of burial at sea. These practices have come out of convenience. Certain religions originated where there was hardly any wood to burn, hence burial has become big. There was no question of burning because fuel was extremely precious in desert lands. Moreover, burial was easy in the sand. A pit could be dug with bare hands and covered up. Perhaps the custom to bury the dead in a box came into existence because wild animals smelled them and dug out the bodies. Slowly, the boxes became more and more elaborate. With the passage of time, today most coffins are more and more ornamental, made of hardwood, steel, and even concrete. If you bury a body in these types of coffins, they will just rot inside. They will not become a part of the earth for a very, very long time. This is not good.

Another reason for avoiding burial is the question of what you leave behind. You should experiment with this and see. Enter a burial ground and see how it feels, then enter a cremation ground and see how it feels. If, let us say, five cremations have happened today, the cremation ground will be very active, alive with energy.

This is a lot of life, but if you don't have a balanced mind, it can be a very fearful kind of energy. Fearful not because of anything else but because in some way it reminds you of your mortality. It is almost like there has been a sacrifice here—that kind of energy. Yogis and tantriks wanted to hang around such places because they had learned to use that energy in a positive way. So what cremation leaves behind is something that is quite alive, but this is not the case with burial.

If you go to a burial ground, you will see there is a rotting kind of energy. "Rotting" may not be the right word because it is not because the body is rotting. It is a slow release of that same energy. Besides, because the energy hangs around for too long, it has intermingled in so many ways with too many lives and the net result is a very stale kind of energy. Burial grounds do not cause fear in you, but very easily a certain sadness or depressive mood can set in in a person just by visiting there, even if no one dear to them was buried there. This is like the feeling you get in a general ward in a government hospital. It is neither life nor death. This is not a good thing to leave behind for future generations.

BRINGING HOME THE BODY

People have this strong sentiment that wherever the person died, his or her body should be brought home for burial or cremation. At one time, this would have had some relevance because many traditional people in this country would not eat anything grown in a place that was beyond a day's walking distance from their homes. Nothing from outside that area was consumed. Whenever they traveled, they also carried their food with them. They did not want to eat food from anywhere and everywhere. So they developed a strong resonance and a very existential relationship with the land on which they were living. If you lived like that, dying in that place and being buried in that place could be very important.

Today, we eat things which come from around the world or at least around the country, and moreover, we are loitering all over the planet. So where you are buried does not matter so much anymore. It is more an emotional thing. And if you are already in a foreign country, we don't know how much of that country you carry. So, existentially, it does not matter where you dispose of the body, but emotionally, it does matter for people. Moreover, there is this element of practicality too. All the family and friends who would have wanted to participate in the funeral are more likely to be around your own home, so it makes more sense to bring the body back because many of them may not be able to travel to the place where this person died.

CLEANSING THE HOUSE

Whenever a death occurs in a place or a dwelling, generally there are some cleansing processes that are to be done. This is not just for some hygiene reasons; you want to wipe off that energy completely from that place. If you want to cleanse the homes or dwellings, you can do *Punya Pooja** or something similar, which will work very well. You can also cleanse it by taking a vibrant fire, like a camphor fire, all over the house. Just like we do klesha nashana for the individual body, you can do klesha nashana for the entire house. Doing some chants in that space also could be very beneficial.

This need for cleansing is not just for the places where death happens. Traditionally, even if you attended a funeral, you had to bathe, cleanse yourself properly, and change your clothes before you even entered the house or touched anything there. In some cultures, the clothes you wore to the funeral were never to be used again. They were burned because they gather a certain aura of death, and you don't want to carry that and walk around.

---

* A cleansing ritual offered by Isha Yoga Center, to cleanse a space, usually a dwelling or a workspace.

TONSURING THE HEAD AFTER CREMATION

A common after-death Hindu ritual is tonsuring the head of the male relatives of the deceased. This shaving of the head came into practice when people generally kept a lot of hair on their heads. Today, they cut it every month or so, so whether you shave or not may not make much difference. But normally people used to have long hair, and hair is one thing that can easily gather a certain amount of aura. You know that hair gathers static. People who have a lot of hair have static—it will be crackling sometimes in certain weather. Hair has this capability. Similarly, if you have been in the house where death has occurred or you are related to that person, you gather an aura of death, particularly in your hair. It hangs around you.

So if you have a lot of hair, you shave it so that the aura is gone. This is the reason why they tonsure the heads of newborn babies also. When you were in your mother's womb, you gathered that aura. After birth, the aura of that is still there. If it stays with you, you will not grow well. So, we wait for four to five months, so that the baby is reasonably grown and stable in health, and then we shave the head. Shaving the child's head also aids in the development of the brain by moving energies toward the head region.

SPREADING THE ASHES

After the death has happened, it can take up to forty days for the being to completely leave the body. Even if you have burned the physical body, the being will look for certain elements of the body like the ash or maybe their used clothes or something that belonged to them. It could be the sweat or smell of the body because still the realization has not come that it is over. This is not desirable, so we want to eliminate it. One of the things that is done for this is to scatter the ashes as widely as possible.

After cremation, if you keep the ash in one place, there is a tendency for the being to look for that. So they are put in a river where they get really spread out. That way they cannot be found. The effort is to do everything possible to make the being understand that it is over. This is also for the living to understand that it is all over. Otherwise, you will keep the ash in a pot in your house and you will become unnecessarily emotional about it.

Another reason why you disperse the ash is that you want to prevent its misuse. Usually, occult practitioners gather ash from the cremation ground when they want to do those types of rituals, where they want to attract a disembodied being toward them.

It is because of all these reasons that when someone dear to you dies, you want to make sure this ash is scattered as wide as possible. You don't want your dead relatives to come searching for it or become victims of sorcery. So you take the ash and put it in the rivers. Or you go to a mountain and, where the wind is strong, you throw it into the air so that it spreads all over.

DONATING ORGANS

I would say, even if you have not lived your life in a useful manner, in death at least you could be useful! So if someone can use the dead body, it is fine. We already saw that all people don't die the same way, just as all people don't live the same way. If you look at it technically, people can die out of any one of the chakras. One can die in any one of these dimensions. If one has died in a certain way, by consciously exiting the body, then it is not good to dismember one's body. But if people have died in normal ways, it is all right to do it. The problem again is, who is there capable enough to decide this? Moreover, when someone is dead, can one go and tell someone, "Okay, your father has died in a bad way, so you can cut open the body and donate the organs"? It is not socially advisable or even possible. So it is better that organ donation is open for everyone rather than making exceptions to it. Moreover, if it is going to be useful for someone, maybe it is better to do it. Strictly speaking, there are some disadvantages for certain people if the organs are taken out, but it is okay if someone is going to see through your eyes or live better through your organs.

Now people ask: If one is on the spiritual path, can one donate organs? I think, except for the kidney and a few other things, you are donating the organs only after you are dead. So donate it; what is the problem? The question is: Is the little bit of gouging the body that they do after death okay for a spiritual person? After one is dead, anyway you burn the body or bury it. If you bury it, the organs will get donated to the worms or plants. They also make use of it. If you take away an eyeball, the worms will not miss it. If you die in an accident or something, where the body is broken but still all these organs are fine, we can take them. It is all right. It has nothing to do with spirituality. It is only an emotional problem. If something is useful for someone, if they can see or live making use of it, it is okay. Moreover, for a person to die with the intention "Let my body be useful to ten people," that is a good thing.

Some people donate their entire body for research purposes. These bodies will be preserved for a long time and cut open to the maximum. If they start cutting the body within the first eleven to fourteen days, there is definitely a little bit of harm to that person. If that is the case, then we can do something so that they completely exit. After that, how their body is used, it does not matter. But I think it will be well beyond fourteen days before they start cutting it for education or research purposes. At that time, it is just like a piece of vegetable. Whether you give it to the doctors or bury it or burn it, it makes no difference to that individual.

Now, some people worry that if karma is encoded into even the minutest aspect of our lives, then do the organs that are received through transplantation also bring the karma of the donor along with them? People have been doing blood transfusions for ages now. Blood is far more vital than any other organ and in fact goes all over the body, to every organ. It has access to everything, including your brain. But people are doing fine with blood transfusion, so this should also be fine. Definitely, there is something that you acquire, but the benefit outweighs the risks. Is it the best thing to do? No. But is it something that you do if it is needed? Yes. If the organ is not suitable, or in some way not going well with the body, it will anyway reject it.

The problem is that we have too much emotion about these things. Your kidneys are just filters. If you own a diesel car, every ten thousand miles or so you replace the fuel filter. So, similarly, you are replacing your kidney filter. Since your filter has already been used, it is a secondhand filter. So is there a problem? Maybe. So, now, they are trying to grow new filters in the lab. When you need it, you can have it ready-made. It is a good new filter. You can put it in because the body is a mechanical thing. Maybe you will turn spiritual more easily if you have all organs replaced because you will have no sense of your own body. It is a good thing because you don't have to tell such people, "You are not the body!" They know they are not their heart, they are not their liver, they are not their kidney!

DEMATERIALIZING THE BODY

All the after-death rituals are mainly for the right disposal of the physical body and for assisting the being in its future journey. However, there are people who help themselves and do not require any assistance from anybody for this. These are highly accomplished yogis—they not only leave their bodies at will, they also dematerialize them. It is as if they do not want to trouble anyone with the cremation process! Such a body does not get destroyed, it gets dematerialized. It has moved from Creation to non-Creation.

The whole process that you see in the Existence is from non-Creation to Creation, from unmanifest to manifest. But here the reverse is happening. A yogi with enough mastery of the five elements can do that to his body.

There have been many yogis like this. When they leave, some people leave ash behind, but many times all that is left is a small puddle of water. How is this done? Essentially, this body is a play of five elements: 72 percent of it is water, 12 percent is earth, 6 percent is air, 4 percent is fire, and the rest is aakash. With aakash, you don't have to do anything. If you know how to dematerialize these other things, especially the earth, you will evaporate right here. These people dematerialize water also, but because it is a larger part of your body, some amount of it usually gets left out. A little lack of perfection, that is all. This has happened with many of our meditators who have powerful Yantras in their homes—on some days, in the morning, they find a puddle of water near the Yantra. The previous night they would have cleaned everything and lit a lamp and all that, but in the morning, there is a puddle of water there. There is nothing to worry about. This is because some disembodied being has used the Yantra to dissolve its karmic body completely, and in the process, there is some water left behind. It is perfectly all right.

There are also some instances in recent history where such dematerializations have been reported. In the year 1873, a Tamil saint named Ramalinga Adigal, popularly known as Vallalar, delivered his last discourse and announced that he would be "leaving." In January 1874, he went to his one-room residence. Before retiring, he placed outside the lamp he had used to light his room, and asked people to meditate with lamps lit from that lamp. He requested that nobody should open his room, and that if they did, they would not find him there. The then British government forced open the room in May, and, as expected, the room was empty. There are many such instances where saints and yogis have chosen not to bother people with their bodies.

Another such incident is supposed to have happened as recently as 1952 in Tibet. There was a famous Master named Sonam Namgyal. He was a simple stone carver of mantras and sacred texts. He did not belong to any established spiritual schools or tradition. He composed his own songs and chants and sang them instead of the traditional ones. No one had any idea what he was doing. They say he had been a hunter in his youth and once when he was wandering in the mountains he had received teachings from a great Master. Once, he fell ill, and instead of becoming saddened or burdened by it, he became increasingly happy. He called his family and everyone nearby and said, "I am going to die soon, and all I ask is that when I die, don't move my body for a week. You can attend to it after that."

As predicted, he died within a few weeks, and after that his family wrapped his body and placed the body in a small room in the house. At that time, they felt he seemed lighter and smaller for his size. Over the week, when they looked into the room, it seemed that the body was getting smaller and smaller. On the eighth day after his death, the funeral had been arranged, and when they uncovered the body, there was nothing but his nails and hair inside. He must have wandered into India and learned this from the Himalayan yogis at some point because this is clearly the hallmark of Indian yogis.

Dematerializing of the body can be done through occult processes also. It has very much been in practice for centuries, particularly in North American tribes. Once, in Mysore, I saw this happen. I was riding my motorcycle and had stopped at some place for no real reason. It was evening time and suddenly this bearded man appeared in front of me, with just a towel wrapped around his waist.

I looked at him and he became a flame, just a burning flame. He burned for ten minutes, and then, *poof*, he was gone. Then this guy started appearing in so many ways to me during a certain period. I would try to offer some money and, *poof*, he would disappear just like that.

It happened another time also when we were preparing for the consecration of the Dhyanalinga. This was again in Mysore. A friend of mine had opened a new showroom for watches and had asked me to visit it. Vijji and I decided to go there one day. I parked the car and we were walking across the road. When we were about to enter the store, a man approached us. He was also wearing just a small piece of cloth around his waist. He came and asked for alms. I looked at him and immediately knew he was not a beggar. So I pulled out my wallet, took out all the money that was there, and put it in his hand.* I did not even see how much money was there. I just took it all and placed it in his hand. The next moment he was gone, he vanished just like that.

Vijji, who saw the whole thing, was aghast. She got so terrified, she could not sleep for a few days. She could not digest that this man was standing there and then he vanished—just like that. I did not pursue this. I regretted I kept the wallet—I should have just given everything to him. I had a few things other than money in it, so I kept it.

These are people who have mastered a certain element. They exist as that. Their manifestation as a physical body is probably not totally in their control and they cannot stay that way for long. This is why it is a momentary manifestation and then it is gone. So either through mastery over the elements, or through *Vamachara*, people are able to pull off such things.

Regardless of what one may believe or not believe, there is no

---

* In the Indian culture it is considered good fortune to be able to give alms to holy men.

question that the building material that makes up our bodies is from this planet. The question is, when its job is done, how do we dispose of the body and allow it to return to its source? Some part of it merges back with the soil, some with water, some with air, some with fire, and, if there is no karmic substance, then some with aakash. If there is karmic substance, the aakash part of it will stay. The best way to return the body to its source, if one is conscious enough, is to dematerialize the body. The next best is by cremation, next by burial in the earth without a box. Putting it in a wooden box will delay the process, but it will still become part of the earth. Enclosing it in concrete is bad and enclosing it in a metal box is worse. Trying to preserve it with mummification is the worst thing to do, as you are not willing to allow the body to become a part of the earth. The wisdom of one's existence is that once we are done with the body, it must become quickly integrated with its source.

CHAPTER 8

Assistance for the Disembodied

As we have responsibilities for the living, we have responsibilities for the dead.

WHY AFTER-DEATH RITUALS ARE NEEDED

Earlier,* we already saw that when a person dies, the life energy does not leave the body all at once. For all practical purposes, one may be dead, but if you are a doctor who has seen enough deaths around you or if you are an undertaker—you would know that death is a process that happens over a period of time and is not an event that occurs instantaneously. This is because, during the process of disembodiment, the Pancha Pranas do not exit all at once but recede in stages. It is like this: You were not just born one day. It took a little more than nine months before you could become a full life. Similarly, even one's exit does not happen just like that. Life exits the body in stages. Usually, a person who is dying can do with some help at this stage. Everyone dies, and at some point in our lives we all will lose someone who is dear to us. So we would definitely like to see that something nice happens to them.

---

* See the section "The Sequence of Death" in chapter 2.

Suppose you are living in a rented house and your landlord asks you to vacate. You vacate, but in parts. You may take your furniture, but leave your kitchen things; you may take your kitchen things but leave your bedding, because you are still not done with the place— you want to keep coming back and stay connected to the house. When the landlord sees this, he will throw everything out. In a way, that is exactly what needs to be done with you.

If it is a yogi who has done enough work on his or her five vayus, when they leave, they will gather everything and go. They do not want to linger with a dead creature, so when they vacate, they do it completely. This is a good way to leave, but to leave like this, one needs certain mastery over one's energies. If a person leaves like this, there is no need to do any rituals because he has already exited completely. But if you don't know how to vacate, if you are too attached to the dwelling in which you have been and you try to vacate in installments, someone else can push you out a little bit.

This process can be very effectively done within the first three to five days after the death. Up to eleven days, the possibility is still pretty good. Up to fourteen days, it is possible, but after that it becomes difficult. If the one who has died is very young or very vibrantly still alive after one left the body, then it is possible to do something up to forty-eight days. After that, our ability to access that disembodied being diminishes.

When they are still confused and in a transitory state, they are more accessible. It is like when you have some really big problem confounding you in your life, then you come to me and plead, "Sadhguru, please do something." Now, you are easy to deal with at that time. But when you are doing a little better and in comfort, no one can talk to you! These beings are also like that. In fourteen days, they will settle in their new accommodations, and it will be a little hard to convince them after that.

Moreover, if you do certain things and dismantle the Vyana

Vayu, which is exiting the physical system, the subtle body will not get the Vyana Vayu that it needs to preserve itself. So it will start crumbling. Even now, if we remove the Vyana Vayu from your body, it will crumble. The body will start dismantling itself. When you take away the Vyana Vayu or limit the amount of Vyana Vayu which is getting into that system after death, the preservation quality goes away. Now it becomes desperate to seek a new body. So these rituals interfere with the process of Vyana Vayu exiting the body and don't allow it to proceed further. Now, it is almost like they have gone to a new place or a new country but they don't have an ID yet. So they cannot find accommodation, nor can they go anywhere. They will start crumbling.

Death rituals are not just to assist the dead person in his or her journey, they are also for the benefit of those who are left behind, because if this person who dies leaves a lot of unsettled life around us, our lives will not be good. It is not that ghosts will come and catch you. But it will influence the atmosphere. It will psychologically influence those around. It will also influence the quality of life around. This is the reason every culture in the world has its own type of rituals for the dead. Generally, a lot of it is to settle certain psychological factors of the near and dear ones left behind. In some way, they did have a certain relevance and science behind them too. But, probably, no other culture has such elaborate methods as the Hindus do. No one has looked at death with the kind of understanding and depth that this culture has. Right from the moment that death occurs, or even before it occurs, there are whole systems to help a person die in the most beneficial way. Having looked at life from every possible angle, they want to extract the most out of everything toward Liberation, or mukti. If death is going to occur, they want to make use of even that to attain mukti, in some way. So they created powerful rituals for the dying and for the dead.

Today, these rituals have become even more important because almost everyone on the planet is beginning to die in unawareness, without the necessary understanding of the life mechanism within themselves. In the olden days, most people died of infections and diseases. So people created a whole science to help them beyond their body. When they were in the body, maybe the people around them could not figure out what the ailment was or the person did not get the necessary treatment or something else happened and they died. So at least after his or her death, they wanted to help them in such a way that they did not hang around for too long and dissolved quickly. This is how the whole science behind these rituals evolved. Unfortunately, today, it has mostly become a meaningless ritual being done without the needed understanding or expertise.

When we do not take care of the dead properly, the adolescent children in that society will suffer immensely because of this. The first thing these disembodied beings go toward is adolescent life because that is the easiest and the most vulnerable human life around. Adolescence is like a human version of molting, where growth is very rapid, not only physiologically but in every other way. Because of this, during this period, life is very susceptible to influence. If there is any positive or negative energy around, adolescents are the first people to absorb it.

Among adolescents, girls are even more susceptible to these things than boys are. But preadolescent children—up to eight to ten years of age—are generally immune to these things. Nature has given them that protection, so you don't have to protect them much. It is mostly children between ten and twenty years of age who can get affected. When I say "affected," I am not referring to their hormonal stuff or them losing their way with drink and drugs. That can also happen, but there are other kinds of influences that they can come under. Today, you can see how much upheaval children are going through just to face adolescence. In the previous generations, adolescence was never such a struggle. One reason for this is that we are not taking care of those who have departed in an appropriate manner. It is like loose software hanging around and adolescent life naturally tangles with that. So either because of conscious knowing or by instinct, people in every culture in some way tried to create protective atmospheres for the adolescents.

Many traditions always kept the places of their dead as sacred, and women and children were never allowed to enter those spaces. Whether it is the Mayans or the Native Americans or people of Latin America—women and children were not allowed in these places. In India, of course, there were elaborate guidelines for these places as to who could go and when and all that. This is not just for psychological reasons. This has an existential impact on the system and those who are more vulnerable will be more affected by these things. So in this culture, after the body was disposed of, there were elaborate processes to clean the person too.

Unfortunately, over a period of time, people distorted and exaggerated things in such a way that these rituals have become largely commercial, with some kind of ritualistic circus being conducted. There are still a few who can do it well, but they have become very scarce. For some people, this is a potential for perpetual business, because whatever the state of the economy, people will continue to die. So when there is such an opportunity, they just cannot let it go. Entrepreneurship comes alive, not even sparing the dead.

Runanubandha—The Web of Debt

If you want to understand how dead people can affect our lives, you should first understand what runanubandha is. It is like this: It takes many things to make an individual human being who he or she is. Of these, the aspect of bonding is one of great significance. However, modern societies have grossly neglected it. With everything that our five sense organs come in touch with, in some way, knowingly or unknowingly, consciously or unconsciously, we establish a certain bond with it. This is not just with the people around us but also with the very land that we walk upon, the air that we breathe, and just about everything that we see, hear, smell, taste, and touch. This is because none of these things happen without investing a certain amount of energy in it. You cannot see something unless you invest some energy in it. You cannot really listen to something unless you invest some energy in it. You cannot taste or touch anything unless something of you is invested. With this investment comes a bonding. In traditional terms, this is called runanubandha.

Runanubandha exists because the body has its own memory. It is a certain kind of physical memory that you carry within you. It is different from the genetic factors that are transmitted from parent to child. You pick up runanubandha through the course of life in many ways. One common way is through physical contact. The body remembers any kind of intimacy you have with any physical substance. This is the reason why, traditionally, in the Hindu culture, people learned to greet one another with folded hands with great warmth, without physical contact, because they do not want to acquire that extra runanubandha that can create bondage and impede their Liberation process. Contact with certain types of substances also has more of an impact than others.

Traditional Hindus never take certain substances like salt, sesame seeds, or oil from someone else's hands because they want to avoid developing runanubandha. If you so much as use someone's clothes, you could develop runanubandha. At the Yoga Center, all the brahmacharis wash their clothes separately. This is because all of them are doing sadhana and everyone has their own specific characteristics. We do not want it all mixed up. Another way to prevent a mix-up is to coat the clothes with soil in every wash. Sadhus and sannyasis always use finely sieved red earth to dye their clothes. The clothes are originally white, but because they are constantly washed with filtered earth they turn mud-colored. This is to ensure that the only runanubandha that they have is with the Earth—not with the people or things around them.

Another way you develop runanubandha is through relationships. Even if you so much as hold someone's hand, you develop runanubandha. Of all the relationships, sexual relationships have maximum impact in terms of the amount of memory that they leave upon you, compared to any other kind of substance you come in touch with. This is not a question of guilt or ridding yourself of guilt. Guilt is a social phenomenon. What you feel guilty about essentially depends upon the norms of the society you live in. If you feel guilty about something in one society, you may not feel guilty about the same in another society. This is not about social conditioning—this is an existential reality.

Since Hindu culture is essentially oriented toward Liberation, people took enormous pains to ensure that they kept their runanubandha only to the extent that is absolutely necessary when they were alive. When they were physically present here, because people had a variety of relationships—blood, sexual, or transactional—a certain physical sameness happened. So there was a runanubandha with the person. When the person died, efforts were made to obliterate the runanubandha with this person as much as possible. That is how conscious the culture has been.

You must break this relationship with the dead person for you to be able to live well, because the nature of life is such that at times you can become susceptible; then both the right and wrong kind of things can enter you. If this runanubandha is not properly broken, as can be seen happening in modern societies, it will definitely affect your physiological structure. It weakens your body and your psychological structure in such a way that not only will you suffer from grief, but it will also lead to certain derangement of life. This is why Hindu culture evolved many methods in the rituals that were performed after death to consciously dissolve the runanubandha. Only in distancing yourself from the dead can you truly understand and enact the profoundness of the statement, "Leave the dead to the dead."

Kalabhairava Karma—An After-Death Ritual at Isha

For a long time, we used to provide this service for the dead, personally, for people who approached us. If at the instant a person died, someone sent me their picture, there is something that I would do for them in the first three days after death. Sometimes we could do a lot, sometimes we could do only a little. Sometimes we could even do an absolute job depending upon who it was. We would not tell them what we had done, but we would do something for sure. Till now, we have done this for thousands of people. But as the number of these requests increased, we thought this service needed to be scaled up. Now, at the Yoga Center, we do a proper ritual called the Kalabhairava Karma. This will greatly aid and assist the journey this departed being has to make now. All it requires is a photograph of the dead person and a piece of cloth used by them. It would be good if the blood relatives of this person are present while the ritual is being performed at the Yoga Center.

So how is it possible that with just a photograph and a piece of cloth we can assist the person who has died in their journey? One way of understanding life is that everything that you know as life right now is in some way an imprint of a certain memory. Now, when I say "memory," I am not talking about just remembering something in the conscious mind. It goes beyond that. You are in the human form, with two hands, two legs, and all that because of the Evolutionary Memory. In this human form, there are specific manifestations like the skin color, the shape of the nose, the shape of the eyes, etc., because of Genetic Memory. Even when these things are the same or similar, each human being is different in some way because of individual Karmic Memory. There are layers and layers of memories like this. Now, these memories are present in the mind, body, and the energies of a person and play out in so many ways.

Essentially, what you call "individual lives" are these small bubbles of memory—different levels of memory that have become different kinds of creatures. Of these creatures, a human being has the most complex memory. It is only because of the complexity of memory that the abilities of humans have been enhanced, and as a consequence, their sufferings also have become enhanced. For example, other creatures do not suffer their memories like human beings. Sometimes they suffer a singular memory. Some birds and animals suffer one particular memory—maybe its partner died or maybe something else happened—they become depressed. They just remember that one thing and they suffer that. But a human being is not like that. He or she can remember a million small things and suffer a million times over, because human memory is very detailed and there is a vividness to it. There is a certain reality to it that is more real than the real. For most people, what happened yesterday is more real than what is happening right now. That is their experience of life. They live by memory. When you live by memory, you live with one foot in the land of death and another in the land of life. That is torture!

If you want to look at it in a very rudimentary manner, let us say, you walked in your garden. Now, if you bring a sniffer dog, just by smelling the ground he will know which way you went. They can do this for up to three or four days, sometimes even longer, if there has been no disturbance. This is because you leave puddles of memory when you walk—because our individual scent is a consequence of the unique nature of our complex memory structure. That is why a dog is able to track it down. So if with just a few moments of your contact with the ground you are leaving puddles of memory for a creature like a dog to pick up, imagine how much memory you are leaving behind throughout the span of your life. How much memory do you think the clothes that you wore, the places you sat on, the places you slept on, the objects that you were in touch with, and such other things carry?

Once a person is dead, in Hindu culture, we always want to wipe out the runanubandha because we know yesterday has a power of its own. If you do not liberate yourself from it, yesterday will rule your tomorrow. Yesterday ruling your tomorrow means tomorrow never comes. Someone said this very forcefully: "Leave the dead to the dead." Leaving the dead to the dead does not mean ignoring those who died. It just means whatever happened yesterday, whatever happened in the previous moment, you must always be conscious that it is dead. After a person dies, maybe they have attained mukti or they have gone somewhere else, we don't know, but either because you were born to them or you were in touch with them in some way or the other, their memory imprints are on you. These imprints are not just in your mind but also in your body and energies as well. So one important aspect of death rituals is that you must become free of this.

Becoming free of memory and losing your memory are two different things. If you lose your Conscious Memory, you may no longer remember them, but it does not mean you have become free of it. This will start to work within you in many unconscious ways. Therefore, we want to distance ourselves from our memory. We don't want to lose it; we just want to carry it a little loosely on us. That is all. So with these death rituals, you do some things to free the departed but it is also important to free the living. Some distance must happen.

If there are too many puddles of strong memory, it will also trouble the dead. Close relatives, particularly if they had very loving relationships with them, will bother the dead. That is why, in this culture, when someone wanted to die, they went away to a place where they were not among family. You don't want to be with your family when you die because, till the last moment, these attachments will go on. You want to be away, alone, clearly understanding that all the relationships we have made in this world are essentially of memory. Once these memories are wiped out, no relationship exists. It is now easy to establish that dimension within us, to become conscious of that dimension which is beyond memory, which is life itself. So for the departed one, we want to shave off as much memory as possible so that their process of Liberation becomes smoother, easier, not tangled up here and there.

The fourteenth day after a person has died is an important day while doing the rituals for the dead. This is the day when all the blood relatives of the person who has died must assemble and perform some rituals. On such an occasion, in traditional settings, you will see the relatives of the dead person taking account of who has come and who has not. They keep tabs on whether everyone has come because these are people who have strong memories, or runanubandha, with the person who has died. They have to attend, and in some way wash their memory and release the person. For fourteen days they would have collected all the little bits and pieces of memories that this person has left behind; now they want to assemble the whole thing and dissolve it. This residual memory should not live on; it must go, dissipate in every possible way. So everyone who carries a piece is required to be there.

Those days are gone when the whole clan assembled when someone died. In today's conditions, this is no longer feasible. Only one or two people come for Kalabhairava Karma. Furthermore, they grumble, "Do I have to come? Can I send it by DHL? Can I FedEx it?" We do not know where all the memories of the person who died are stuck. So we do whatever best we can. In such cases, one simple thing to do is that you take a whiff of their memory and put it in a place which is naturally about disentanglement. Normally, they tie it in front of a Shiva temple because he is an ascetic—untouched by anything, always smeared in ash. So with Kalabhairava Karma, we use a photograph of the dead person and a piece of clothing that was in close contact with their body. Both these articles will have strong imprints of the memories of the person. Now we do a process to dissolve as much of this memory as possible. What is not possible, leave it to Shiva. We don't want to put these articles on the Dhyanalinga, so we burn them and tie the ashes in a cloth to the tamarind tree outside the Dhyanalinga entrance to take care of whatever is left.

Kalabhairava Karma is not a dig-and-clean process. We just mop up the surface so that nothing holds as far as possible. For most cases, this itself is enough. It is not good to put a number to these things, but it is just my guess that maybe around 10 to 15 percent of the people would need very strong processes to release them. For another 60 to 70 percent, you can release them with a very simple process like Kalabhairava Karma. For another 10 to 15 percent that is in between, if some residue of that person is placed in a powerful space, which we are doing, it will do the job.

If we want to do a total, thorough cleaning, which may be necessary sometimes, it will need a different level of involvement from both the parties—the person who performs the ritual and the relatives of the departed one. This gets complicated. It will need a much higher level of involvement and it does not always work out well. In case it does not work out well, it could be an unnecessary disturbance of life for those who are living. We don't really want to rake it up, so we just wipe clean everything that is on the surface.

This is what Kalabhairava Karma does. (Kalabhairava Shanti,* on the other hand, is mostly for the people who are living, but sometimes it is for the dead also.)

Now, if a close relative who carries a very strong memory of that person comes and spends enough time in the Dhyanalinga, even if there is no ritual, it may still work for that dead person. This is not because of the Kalabhairava Karma; this is the nature of the place. Even when we are alive, when we say that the Dhyanalinga will make you meditative, what we mean is that it will stop the endless mental diarrhea that goes on in a person. When mental diarrhea stops, it means the memory that is of the rotting kind gets reduced. Now, if there is no food in the stomach, there will be no diarrhea, right? Similarly, if there is no memory rotting inside, there will be no thought process; it develops a distance from yourself.

Dhyanalinga does not care whether you are living or dead. All he knows is to separate the chaff from the grain. He wants to separate what is you from what is not you. He does not care whether you have a body or not. So if the relatives who carry a strong enough memory of the dead person spend enough time in the Dhyanalinga—say, two or three days around the full moon or new moon days—it could work well for the person who died.

THE SCOPE OF KALABHAIRAVA KARMA

Generally, all around the world, when these after-death rituals were performed, there were two components to it: One was to handle the emotions of those who were left behind, and the other was to direct the departed being in a suitable manner. So in some cultures, some scriptures were read aloud to give people an understanding of what

---

* Another ritual offered at the Linga Bhairavi, near the Isha Yoga Center.

was happening, to allay their fears and reassure them that everything was all right. There were also some chants and rituals performed to soothe their emotions. In some cultures, there would be someone reading aloud about what was happening to this person and egging them on to be brave and to move on to the next stage, and so on. But once you drop the physical body, you don't have the discriminatory mind, so there is no comprehension of language. And there is no sound or silence. So there is no question of this person understanding this or that. That is for the living. With rituals, you can draw the being to something, you can direct the being in a particular direction, but you cannot talk to it.

The scope of what can be done with these rituals is wider. For example, there are people who direct these beings to be reborn specifically into either a wealthy family or the same family or a royal family. Such things can be done, but it is ridiculous because there is no guarantee that just because one is born in a rich family one is going to live well. There are too many complexities of life which decide that. Moreover, those kinds of manipulations are not good to do and it does not work well for that life either. The best thing is to make that "life bubble" thinner and leave it. It will find its own way to a better place. So I am personally only concerned about peeling that life off as much as possible; if possible, all the way, but at least enough that you can make it into a thinner bubble than what it is. What will happen, how it will be reborn, is not for you to worry about.

Let us say, there is a wind blowing. Depending on how light a certain substance is, it will land somewhere. A piece of paper or a feather may go far but a twig or branch may fall just a little away from you. Sometimes if the weight and the shape are right, then the feather may travel and not land for months at a time. The important thing is to make it light. How far it will fly, what will happen to it, where it will land, and so on, is subject to life. It is something that you don't try to direct because those kinds of manipulations can lead to lots of troubles. Now, once someone is dead, people are very interested in knowing where the departed person is—in heaven or hell or whatever. Some people claim to be able to tell you that. You can determine whether a being is comfortable or in struggle. Accordingly, you can do certain rituals for that being. But determining geographically where it is, is rubbish because there is no geographical "where."

If Kalabhairava Karma is done within the stipulated time, it will find its target. If it is done later, it may not be as effective. But it will shorten the time the life just hangs. It reduces the limbo time for sure. By how much? This depends on each being. If you go back to the bubble analogy,* it depends on how big the bubble is and how thin the skin of the bubble is. But if it is done within eleven to fourteen days, we dismantle it to a large extent. If you want to take the bubble analogy further—after it has lost the body, by itself, the bubble may float around for a long time. It will keep on floating because it does not want to lose itself. But once Kalabhairava Karma is done, a quick cycle will happen. Kalabhairava Karma not only shortens the hanging-around time but it also makes it a more pleasant journey.

Can we liberate people with these rituals? Can we give somebody Mahasamadhi through Kalabhairava Karma? It is possible, but not always. There are various aspects to it. Unless that bubble is so thin already, it is not necessarily a Mahasamadhi. If there is such a being who is such a huge bubble but somehow could not burst by its own nature, Kalabhairava Karma may burst it and it could become Mahasamadhi. But otherwise, it makes the bubble very thin and fragile, so that it will want to find a physical body quickly because it cannot last long by itself. In any case, we can definitely hasten their journey.

---

* See the section "A Bubble of Life and Death" in chapter 2.

If you want to do Kalabhairava Karma for yourself when you are alive, it becomes Kalabhairava Kriya. Basically, Kalabhairava Karma is being performed so that after you are dead, we mop up bits of your life that are sticking around here and there. Kalabhairava Karma is being done to you because you are not a yogi and you are unable to do the mopping up yourself. A yogi will withdraw to the forest and die alone somewhere there because he has done everything that he needs to do for his life. No one has to do anything for him later. Everything is finished. No Kalabhairava Karma is needed. When he is gone, it is a complete evacuation of the space that he occupied. If you do not have that kind of mastery over your energies, you could do Kalabhairava Kriya. It can be taught to people, but it will need an extreme sense of discipline about who you are and how you manage your energies and system.

It once happened: A cardiac surgeon had some trouble with his car, so he took it to the mechanic. The mechanic said it would be fixed in twenty-four hours. The following day when the surgeon went to collect the car, it was not ready and there was no responsible answer for the delay. Six days passed like this, and every day the mechanic asked him to come the following day. After a week of this, the surgeon asked the mechanic, "Why are you doing this to me? I need to go to work, I have things to do and I don't have a car." So the mechanic strutted around a little and said, "Well, you are a cardiac surgeon. What do you do? You fix the engines, just like me. But why are you paid fifty times more than me?" The cardiac surgeon then realized what the problem was. He said, "I fix the engines when they are running. Can you?" Kalabhairava Kriya is like that.

Doing something for the departed is one thing. Doing the same thing with oneself, when the engine is running, is another thing. If you want to release this thing when it is still running, it takes a different level of discipline. If you show such discipline in everything that you do with your life—that you are not clumsy, you are alert to every small thing, then you can do Kalabhairava Kriya. After that, when you leave, no one has to do anything for you. It will definitely be a great thing to do in one's life, a fantastic thing to do for oneself. But it will need a sense of discipline, which is a very scarce material in today's world.

Traditionally, they said that if you do Kalabhairava Kriya for yourself then you cannot go back to your home or village and live a social life. You have to live the rest of your life away from any community, like an outcast. It is not that this person is an outcast. They just no longer belong there because they have created a genetic distance. They have got nothing to do with the family or the community because it is over for them. You can create distance to such an extent that even the fundamental physiological features of your system can change. It can be done.

Once we started conducting Kalabhairava Karma at the Yoga Center, people started asking if they could do Kalabhairava Karma for their dogs or cats also. Please! There is no need for that. Existentially, one fundamental difference between animal life and plant life is that a plant does not have a subtle body. There is a lot of reverberation in it, but there is no subtle body for a plant. A plant may gather an aura around itself. Certain trees or plants gather much more than others, so those plants and trees have been identified as sacred plants in the Hindu culture, as we want to benefit by being near them. But the plants do not generate it, because they do not have a subtle body.

All rituals done after death are about transporting the subtle body to the right place. When the subtle body is not well defined, there is no need to do anything nor is there a possibility to do something. An animal has a subtle body, but except in the case of cows and cobras, it is not very defined or very evolved. So we generally ignore the subtle body of all other animals. The subtle body of those animals can easily merge and mingle with Nature; it does not really transport itself.

Cows and cobras are different because they have a more evolved subtle body. The subtle body of the cow has evolved through emotional competence. If you observe a cow, you will see that it is capable of a range of emotions. Sometimes it is almost humanlike. So that gives them a subtle body. On the other hand, the subtle body of the cobra has evolved through the sharpness of reverb perception. Most snakes are "stone deaf," but they manage to listen through the entire length of their body. Theirs is truly "ear to the ground" hearing, which is phenomenal. Out of this ability they too have developed a subtle body. So there is some meaning in trying to do something for them after death. This is why these two animals are especially revered in this culture. Traditionally, the carcasses of cows and cobras are never left just like that; they are either cremated or buried. Even if you find one lying around, you are supposed to bury it or cremate it.

Now, for those of you who have been initiated by me, it is true that there is no need to go through any death rituals. However, what if you were a "missed case"—someone who went through the initiation process, but missed it? For those of you who have been initiated by me, I would like you to finish your process when you are alive, when life is still alive and kicking in you, so that you don't burden me when you are dead. I am willing to attend to you when you are alive. If you are incompetent, I am also willing to attend to you after you are dead. But why don't you make yourself competent in such a way that here and after, you will be fine? You should live in such a way that there should be no need for any after-death rituals for you. You should promise me that you will not trouble me even after you are dead! Hereafter, things should happen the way they need to happen for you.

Training People for Death Rituals

If some things are not there in our lives, we can manage without them most of the times. But after-death rituals are something that no society can live without. They are absolutely necessary because you cannot do it to yourself. So is it possible that we can train people to do these after-death rituals? Very much so.

Coming to the necessary awareness to attend to somebody else's passage with one's awareness and energies is not for everybody. The purpose of the ritual is that what is done with the highest level of awareness can be made systematic, so that anybody who has the necessary integrity of intent can deliver the ritual without really knowing the workings of it. Just as you can use a phone without knowing how it works, or a watch without knowing how it is made, rituals allow for systematic outreach for something which otherwise demands great awareness.

In India, people who handled the dead and those processes were called *chandalas*. In pre-Aryan times, theirs was considered one of the top professions in society. Over the next few thousand years, a stigma became associated with this and it became the lowest profession in the social hierarchy. In ancient times, untouchability was very much prevalent in India. People of certain castes were considered untouchables and others would not touch them. But even the untouchables would not touch a chandala because he was considered the lowest of the lowest. On the other hand, Adiyogi Shiva himself always kept himself in the company of chandalas because he thought they were the highest. He saw that their understanding of life and knowing was far better than that of all the other people who were conducting other things. So if you get into this service we will have to give it a new look, we will have to dress you up differently. We have to make you deliver this whole thing in a completely different way than the way it was traditionally done. Otherwise, shaking off the stigma and being able to be useful to people will be very difficult.

It would be best to do this without rituals, but to train people to conduct a ritual is so much easier than training people to do the same thing without a ritual. The main problem with rituals is that when the level of integrity drops in the social fabric, all rituals will turn corrupt. These rituals were created when the sense of integrity and commitment for one another was so strong that there was no room for any kind of misuse. But when the general fabric of integrity has gone down in the social structure, then all rituals will be under suspicion because there is room for misuse.

Right now, if I teach someone how to handle the dead, they might want to display to their friends how they can make the dead dance or do something fanciful. Or they may want to become a "medium"! Moreover, even if you are clear that you do not want to do any such thing, people will try to influence your judgment when someone is dead. They will come and fall at your feet and say, "Do something, I just want to say one thing to my father, I wanted to say this for the last ten years, but I did not. I want to say it now." Because they cried and begged you, if you start setting up a conference call, then it is all finished. That amounts to misuse. If we teach you rituals, you will not be able to do all that. You have to just do the ritual and go home. Only if we generate people who are responsible enough to not do even one thing more than what is necessary, these things can be done. But rituals may not fit into today's world.

In some cultures, women have traditionally been prohibited from entering the cremation grounds or performing these rituals because they could be susceptible to certain undesirable influences. But if what you are doing is just a ritual in name, then women can also do it. If it is a process where genuinely something is happening where you are handling a disembodied life, then involving women in it is a little bit of an issue. There are various reasons for this. One reason was in those times a woman would be pregnant at least eight to twelve times in her lifespan. So most of the time, she would be either pregnant or breastfeeding. At such times, she should not be in such situations, particularly when she is pregnant. Even today, this is followed—if death rituals are being performed, they don't allow pregnant women to be present there. Even if a woman is free from pregnancy and breastfeeding, she may still have her menstrual cycle, which again makes her vulnerable. This is the reason why women were kept away from cremation grounds. But if she is free from all of these situations, then there is no issue in her doing these rituals.

A woman will need to take much more care in doing such things than a man. A man's biological structure is stable in a certain way; a woman's biological structure goes through certain phases, so she has to take much more care about these things. There are different kinds of biological responsibilities for male and female bodies. Instead of understanding and appreciating this, we have imbued a mentality in the world where we make every small difference into a discrimination. As a result, this whole gender discrimination has come up. Otherwise, these two aspects are complementary to each other and that is how it should be. If a certain discipline has to be maintained, you should not compromise that discipline for anything. Then even women can do it and in fact it is well known that it is far easier to help women to organize and discipline themselves than men. Women have a natural capacity to absorb order due to the deeper sense of survival instinct that is needed to fulfill their reproductive responsibilities.

We had the means to do all these things in this country, but now we are all English-educated, so we are ashamed of these things. At Isha, we hope to build a group of people to whom we can impart certain things. We are also nurturing and educating some children, hoping that they will grow in the right tradition so we can teach them some simple things about life which are very vital. Maybe they will not become engineers and doctors but we hope that they will grow into these things. We are also in the process of training some meditators in doing these kind of services. If you are willing to offer this, then we can train you to do these things properly. But you should never make it your profession; it should be done only as a service. When someone has lost their body, they are completely helpless; they need help and they can be helped, but not with corrupt, contaminated hands. It needs someone who cares and someone who has the necessary sense about it.

The Death of Infants

Is the death of infants any different from the death of adults? In a certain context, yes, because the way life manifests in a child is different from the way life manifests in an adult. If the child dies when the mother is still breastfeeding it or is under forty months of age, its life is not yet a fully established life, in a sense. So it is not the same as the death of an adult. Actually, it is strange, but you will see the parents also generally recover very quickly from the child's death in such cases. If a child above four years of age dies, the parents' pain and suffering will be much more. If you say this, people will get very upset; that is different. But if you just observe them, you will see the impact is much less, because even in the parent's consciousness, it is not fully established as a life. It is still in the process of taking shape.

When your child is an infant, that is when your contact with the child is big-time. By the time he or she is four, they start running around. You cannot hold them; they want to be all over the place. They want to see the world. But before they are four years old, they are so much with you. Yet, in spite of being physically connected to them, your connection to them is not so strong because they are not physically connected to their own body very strongly. So the same has not happened within you very strongly. If you observe life very carefully, you will know this. These days there is a lot of medical intervention to help, but until recently a lot of children would die before they were four years of age, without any ailment. They used to simply die because life was still not fully established. When this happens, there is a sense of loss but not much pain involved for the parents.

In children, until about forty to forty-eight months, the quantum of Prarabdha Karma for this life is still not decided. Life is still trying to make a judgment. This is why there is so much emphasis in the Hindu tradition on what should be done during this time. There is an entire system of rituals during preconception, conception, birth, and thereafter. This is just to ensure that this becomes a life which will take on the maximum Prarabdha Karma. Taking on the maximum is significant not because you want it to take on more suffering; it is to make it a bigger bubble, with more possibilities. But more possibilities also mean possibly more challenges, which may in turn mean more suffering. When something comes with more possibilities, there is a possibility of more things going wrong—that is the risk. So if this life becomes sure-footed, it takes on more things. If it is not so sure-footed, then it takes on fewer things. You will keep it as simple and limited as possible. This is the nature of life. This is so even internally.

So if life becomes stable enough and capable enough by the time it is forty-eight months, it will choose a much bigger Prarabdha Karma. Once in a while, it happens by itself in nature, but generally you want to create such situations where you can blow a big bubble so that the new life takes on a big possibility. In today's world, people think possibility means how much money you will make. Bigger possibility need not necessarily mean one is going to do well in the eyes of the society. In some way, it becomes a life that you cannot ignore. Most lives are ignored. No one may notice whether they existed or not. But once the bubble is big, whether one is in a desert or a forest, a village or a city or wherever they are, they will be noticed because they are a bigger bubble in some way. Is it big enough for the entire world to notice? We don't know, but if one becomes a little larger bubble, it is a bigger possibility.

Generally, most people will not remember anything before four years of age because infancy is a time when life has not yet decided how it wants to shape itself. It is still exploring whether to expand or contract and what to do and how much. If there is a very threatening and difficult kind of situation, it may contract so that it feels safer with less Prarabdha Karma and more robust surface. It does not want to stretch itself. This is why, irrespective of which culture you come from, they all insist that if you come across a child, whatever your troubles are, you must smile at the child, you must interact lovingly with the child. Even in the most remote tribal cultures, this awareness is there because you must create that comfort so that it expands as much as possible. If you create a bit of un-conduciveness, it may choose to contract. We do not want that to happen. These are not decisions anyone makes consciously. This is the life's own intelligence making these decisions.

Sometimes another kind of death happens in slightly older children. In some children, sometimes the quantity of Prarabdha Karma for this lifetime is not decided properly, so they die unexpectedly. You may have come across some children who are otherwise very healthy but die suddenly for no apparent reason. Their Prarabdha Karma not being decided properly could be one of the reasons for that. You may have also come across some children of extraordinary intelligence who do things absolutely beyond people's perceptions and sometimes die before they are six because their Prarabdha Karma was not properly fixed. Too many lifetimes of information begin to burst forth in them. Generally, one needs a different level of awareness and a certain dispassion to handle that but when it happens in a child, the body cannot sustain it and it just collapses. These are some reasons why the death of an infant is slightly different from the death of an adult.

The Parent-Offspring Connection in the Afterlife

In India, when people die, they want to have their children around them. People particularly want sons to be around. This is the reason why, in India, people desperately want to have a son. This is because there is a certain "life connection" between the children and the parents, and if you make use of it in doing rituals for parents, they can be much more effective. Daughters too are effective for this purpose, but people depended more on the sons for this role mostly because, in the past, it was only possible for the son to be around when they were dying. When the daughter came of age, she got married and went to someone else's house. When the parent died, she might not have been able to come immediately because of the distance. She need not be on another continent; even if she was just a hundred miles away, by the time she came the cremation would have been over. Moreover, she would have her own children, husband, and family. She could not just drop them and come away. She would have to make arrangements for her absence. And she could not travel alone because everything would be forested, so someone would have to escort her. Making all these arrangements would take considerable time and she would not be able to return in time. But the son lived with the parents, so he would be available. So, they said, the son must be present for the rituals and it is sufficient for the daughters to come by the twelfth day.

So, what is the nature of this connection between the parent and the child that could be made use of at that time? Generally, people's interactions with one another are physical, mental, or emotional. It never goes beyond that. But when a person dies or when a person sheds his or her body, all that is gone. The mental structure is gone, the emotions are gone, the body is for sure gone. So everything that you knew as yours is gone. So for all practical purposes, the children are as much a stranger to you as anyone. But once you bear a child, a certain space of who you are is occupied by that being whom you refer to as your child because you provided a body for this being. It is because of this connection that the parent has with the child that we can do certain things, which can help parents after they die. If the child does the right things after the death of the parent, he can even liberate the parent through this connection. People who lived completely unaware and did not do anything about themselves depended on their children to liberate them. And that became a whole tradition by itself.

However, the reverse is not true. You cannot use the parents to liberate their dead offspring. We already saw in the previous section that when children die before they are four, the death is not the same as an adult's because that life is still establishing itself. After the child crosses somewhere between forty and forty-eight months, physiologically your connection with the child increases dramatically and it happens in your body. Most people don't decipher this. They experience something happening within them before four years of age. But after four years, they are involved with so many child-related issues—where he is going, where he is, his school admission, this and that. Because of these things, they miss this experience. Otherwise, at that time, they would notice that something clicks in them because something in that body has clicked in. When that clicks in, you come to a certain ease because it becomes a part of you; you don't have to consciously hold it, a natural holding happens.

You must understand that you are only a provider of the body for your child; you cannot create a being. It is not in human hands to create a being. When that being really latches on to the body that you provided, something clicks on within you and occupies a certain space within your own system. This is how, if we just check someone's energy, we know whether they have had children or not. This is how, sometimes, an astrologer in India is able to tell you how many children you have, whether they are surviving or not. They will give you a brief synopsis of your children, their characteristics, their names, and everything, because your children occupy a certain space within you. If you observe carefully, you can see these things in that person.

Now, this physiological connection is very strong until the child is twenty-one years old. After that, it starts dissipating once again. It is because of this, as a child grows up and becomes close to twenty-one, if you look at them they look like absolute strangers. You cannot believe you bore them. You will wonder: Are these my children? Is this the same little baby that I brought up? You cannot recognize what they are doing because you don't have an abode in them, but they have an abode in you. This is a beautiful natural system of caring for the offspring, bringing them up and also being capable of releasing them when you have to.

If someone comes up to me and says, "Bless my children," I ask, "How old are they?" If they are below twenty-one years, we really bless them because if they are below that age you can bless a mother or a father and have a deep impact on the children. But if the children are over twenty-one years of age, we just banter with the parents, joke with them, and send them away because it is no use blessing them for their children. The children will have to come themselves.

This is why, if your parents die, we can do something for them through you. But if your children die, we cannot use you to do something more for them because they don't have that little space within them that is occupied by you. It is always so that the future generation occupies a little space in the past but the past generation will not and cannot occupy any space in the future generation. This is the very nature of things. So, if for some unfortunate reason your children happen to die, you can perform Kalabhairava Karma for them. It will definitely do something significant for them. But don't try to do this and that to try to influence them. It will not work. However, if you turn inward and if your way of being becomes pleasant, though your thoughts, your emotions, and your actions have no influence over your child who is no more, that being will experience pleasantness. This also is only until that life finds another body.

People get confused when I say these things, but if you are a little observant, you can sense when this departed being has found another body. You may have seen this happening with many people who have lost children: Until a certain point they cannot believe that they will ever recover from the death of their children, but suddenly one day it does not seem to affect them as much. If the parent observes the way their body behaves, how the breath behaves, the nature of their hair, their fingernails, the texture of their skin, they will know when this being has found another body. It will show. A close observation of the breath will reveal that the pattern of breath has moved from being tense and short to a distinct level of ease. This will also reflect in various other ways. The natural hydration process of the skin will change from dryness to softness due to the respiratory action of the epithelial. There are many more indicators; I will not go into them because people will start looking and start imagining all kinds of things. Now, once that life finds another body, then it is gone for good. You have nothing to do with it. Now someone else claims them—"This is my child"—and a whole new drama begins again.

The Importance of Death Anniversaries

Recognizing the needs of human beings during their lifetimes, ancient sages created a set of samskaras—rituals to purify and refine a person in order to assist one's passage through life. There are about sixty-four samskaras, but the most important of these are sixteen in number and are known as *sodasa-samskaras*. These samskaras start from the time of one's conception, and are to be performed by one's parents, and end with post-death rites to be performed by one's descendants.

The post-death rites are known as *antyeshti* and are to be performed by the son of the deceased. It ensures the future welfare of the dead and frees the living from the debt or obligations they owe the parent. Some of the post-death rituals extend throughout the lifetime of the descendants, though on a progressively smaller scale. These rituals are typically performed as *shraadha*, on each anniversary of the last deceased ancestor and days of special significance, like the new moon days, eclipse days, etc. Today, these rituals are commonly misunderstood as remembrances, but they are mainly to assist in dissolving one's *runa*s, or debts, to the ancestors.

Some of these rituals are purely for sentimental reasons, to remember the dead, acknowledge their contribution to our lives, and so on. Let us say, someone died. Maybe the person's children or grandchildren were very young at that time. They have no memory of him or her. So the parents want to bring back that memory to them so that the children can relate to that because you want children to be rooted in something. Whatever that person was, this occasion is to say a few wonderful things about them so that the children connect to that. It is a kind of legacy for them. That is one aspect of it. The other is to genetically distance yourself from the ancestors or to dissolve your runanubandha with them.

One important aspect of spiritual development is that you must distance yourself from your Genetic Memory and Evolutionary Memory. If you do not distance yourself, the same things will repeat themselves. What happened in your grandfather's life may recur in your life. Maybe you are in a different time, so you look different, but the exact same things may be happening. Maybe there is a difference in the environment, or the activity that they pursued and you now pursue may be different. So, on the surface, people think everything is different. But, experientially, the same thing may be happening because it will repeat itself. You will become a cyclical process. You will not be a fresh life. When you are not a fresh life, there is no question of release. There is no question of going beyond, there is no question of exploring something else.

So the most important reason these anniversary rituals are done by Hindus is not for remembrance but to distance yourself from your ancestors. You want to distance yourself from the dead. The annual kriyas are created in such a way that you try to curtail your Genetic Memory as much as possible. The brahmachari initiation[*] is also similar. In India, if you want to take *sanyasa*,[†] the first thing is that even if your parents are living, you do all the kriyas and karmas for them. It is not about them falling dead, that is not the intent. It is just that you create a distance between you and your Genetic Memory. Now you are one step closer to being released.

Ancestor Worship

Our debt to our ancestors is huge. But for the successive layers of knowledge and effort, human civilization would still be very primitive. So it is customary in most cultures to express one's gratitude

---

[*] Referring to the initiation process of the brahmacharis at the Isha Yoga Center.
[†] Formal renunciation.

to the ancestors. In some cultures, this ancestor veneration takes on a different proportion and turns to worship. Ancestors are granted demigod status and are looked up to for guidance and protection. They are therefore worshipped. The Native Americans are big on ancestor worship, as perhaps are even Australian aborigines and African tribes. However, in India, the rites and rituals for the ancestors are for a different reason.

In India, we distance ourselves from our ancestors; we don't worship them. Here, people either think of taking care of their ancestors or they distance themselves from them. But ancestors taking care of you is not so prevalent in India. In other cultures, this worship may have come about because there has been so much occult practice in those cultures. Their rites and rituals were largely occult, not spiritual processes. There must have been situations where the dead ancestors assisted them in battles and some other critical situations. They probably knew how to access and make use of that. There definitely would have been such situations. Because of that, the general belief that all ancestors will support you might have arisen. That is true here also.

Well, I myself have said that after I am physically gone for eighty years, I will be here in a presence bigger than the way I am right now and see that everyone who is here is seen through in some way.* There have been certain other beings who guided the subsequent generations. So similar things must have happened there. Based on that, there must have been a general belief that every ancestor was capable of doing it. Some might have done this for sure, but generally speaking, every ancestor is not capable of this.

The collective knowledge of past generations definitely benefits us in a million ways. If a strict code of how we intermarry is carefully managed, as it was in ancient India, our ability to access and

---

* Refer to the section "Will I Come Back?" in chapter 11.

benefit from the cumulative knowledge of past generations will be greatly enhanced. This is not in terms of the rigid caste system but on the basis of genetic compatibility. Many business families have exhibited this in phenomenal ways. Some of them also created deities that support this accumulation of knowledge in energy forms and managed genetic intermingling with great gusto. In many ways, this was more stringent than their religion. In many places, the land, rocks, and the very space was managed with care. In certain cultures, they do not want to disturb even the soil and rocks that were witness to their ancestral glory because these were tools for retaining their knowledge.

However, in this age of machines and unbridled travel and intermingling, it may not be very practical. Today, your children trust Google more than what you or your forefathers have to say. We have moved from intuition to information.

Of Heaven and Hell

Those who have made a hell out of themselves are always aspiring to go to heaven. When life feels like hell, we hope that when we go up there, everything will be fantastic. Now, what is in heaven? According to Hindu lore, the food is very good in heaven. If you are a foodie, you must go to the Hindu heaven. Nala, the greatest chef, will himself cook for you, and no matter how much you eat, the vessels will always be full with food. If you go to another place, white-gowned ladies float around the clouds playing the harp for you all the time. If you like that kind of ambience, you must go there. And elsewhere you will encounter virgin problems. If that is what you are looking for, you must go there. But how to get to heaven?

This happened in Alabama. At a Sunday school, the teacher was going full fire, but the audience was not like you; they were tiny tots, part of their "catch them young" policy. The teacher was going all out and the children were sitting shell-shocked. Suddenly, he stopped for dramatic impact and asked: "What do you have to do to go to heaven?" Little Mary in the front bench stood up and said, "If I mop the church floor every Sunday morning, I will go to heaven." "Absolutely!" he said. Another little girl said, "If I share my pocket money with my less-privileged friend, I will go to heaven." "Correct!" he said. A boy said, "If I help people who are in need, I will go to heaven." "Correct!" he said. Little Tommy in the back bench stood up and said, "You gotta die first." Well, that is a qualification. If you want to go to heaven, you must die first.

When you die, depending on your culture, you will be buried, cremated, or offered to the birds or animals. So you left your body here and went to heaven. Without a body, what are you going to do with good food and virgins? You know they talked about that special *patra*,[*] where however much we eat, it doesn't get empty—you must understand that is because nobody who had a body went there! Whatever bodiless people eat, it will stay right there, so naturally the vessel was always full. And that is also why they remained virgins forever.

We have been dealt these kinds of stories for a very long time. For thousands of years, you can't be telling the same story. At least come up with a better story—a heaven where Wi-Fi is free! There is nothing wrong in enjoying a story, but believing a story is stupidity. How long will you tell yourself fairy tales? It is time as human beings we show some evolution. You must stop the bloody stories and start looking at the truth about your existence.

Right now, some people want you to believe that the moment you die, you go to heaven and there will be a party organized there;

---

[*] A vessel. Here it refers to the Akshaya Patra, a vessel in Hindu lore that is said to provide an endless supply of food.

all your relatives and friends are waiting for you and you will have a great time. You must understand that when you die, you lose your body, but still you are here. You do not go anywhere. It is just that the dimensional shift from being embodied to disembodied, or from physicality to a subtler physicality, has happened. It is not a geographical shift from here to heaven or here to hell or wherever it is. And the most important thing is, what happens after is not based on God's retribution or that he is angry with you and that he must hang you or burn you in fire or fry you in oil.

The large-scale marketing of heaven and hell as destinations for the afterlife was done by the religions of the world to bring control in society. When they did not know how to control individuals or groups of people, they came up with an idea: "Okay, if we cannot punish you now, we will get you there. And for all the goodness that you show, if we are not able to reward you here, we will reward you there." Or if you were miserable, they said, "Aw, don't worry, when you go there, everything will be okay." They provided solace. If someone is in a deep state of suffering, you say, "Don't worry, when you go and sit in God's lap, everything will be okay." It is a psychological tool. It is fine when people are in extreme states. But don't brand it and sell it everywhere, because it is not going to work like that. If you really make them believe everything is going to be better somewhere, you will only mess up life here.

Now, slowly, heavens are collapsing in people's minds because if you just ask three questions about it, it will collapse. The human race has come to a point in time where human intellect is firing like never before. More people can think for themselves today than ever before in the history of humanity. Once human intellect becomes active, inevitably it will ask questions. I think in the next twenty-five years, in a maximum of forty years, the scriptures and heavens will collapse completely. It is already collapsing in many ways in individual minds. Still, people don't have the courage to voice it or it is not articulated in their mind yet, but it is collapsing. Today, the grip of heaven and hell upon people has all but worn out. Compared to the number of people who believed that they would go to heaven in the previous generation, the number of people who believe they could go to heaven in this generation has fallen very drastically. Everywhere in the world, that hope is collapsing, and in the coming few decades it will collapse even more rapidly. This has many consequences for the world.

Human beings seek heaven basically because they seek pleasantness. If right from your childhood you were told that God lives in heaven but it is a horrendous place, you would not want to go there. You would say, "No, I will pray from here itself, but I don't want to go there." So, essentially, a human being seeks pleasantness in their experience—physically, mentally, and emotionally. He or she wants the very life process and surroundings to be pleasant. If these things happen, are we fulfilled? No, it is just that if you have learned to be pleasant, only then can you explore the different dimensions of life. If you are in different states of unpleasantness, your whole life will go in just seeking happiness. People are just wasting their whole lives to achieve something called happiness. Actually, it is not even happiness; they have given up that too. They just want peace of mind today. This is the highest goal in their lives.

So once heaven collapses in people's minds, people will try to maximize their lives here. The initial maximization happens with greed and desire. But when people get frustrated and realize that having more does not make life more in any sense, they want to have the alternatives right here in a big way. They are getting drunk and drugged right here. This is not about looking at it morally. It is about the kind of damage it causes to human intelligence and human consciousness. Health, of course, is a concern, but if someone does not mind dying a few years younger, I have no problems. But the damage these chemicals cause to human possibility is our problem.

When this happens to 90 percent of the human population, the next generation that we produce will be of much lesser quality than what we are. That is a crime against humanity because the whole movement of life is such that it should get better and better.

This is not just about conscious consumption of recreational chemicals, this is about our food, water, and air being chemically poisoned. Your body is the most fantastic chemical factory; all the needed chemicals for joy, bliss, and health should be produced there, from within. Once you get into a state where chemicals influence your body from outside, it becomes a crutch that you become dependent on. Not that it cannot be dropped, but it becomes very hard to drop it. Trying to turn people around once the real damage has happened is not going to be easy. Try counseling an alcoholic or a drug addict and you will understand what I am saying. You cannot turn them around just like that, because that is the nature of chemicals—it makes you feel enhanced artificially, either in terms of health or emotional states.

So, it is important that the raising of consciousness happens and we are able to teach people how to sit here, totally blissed out and stoned by themselves, without any substance. Otherwise, in the next fifty years, so much of the human population will be on some kind of chemical. Not that everybody will be hooked on recreational chemicals, but most people will not be able to live without chlorine in the water and other chemicals in their food. What works as a poison for microorganisms also works as a poison for human beings; it's just that the dosage is relatively smaller, so it won't poison you to death, but it does poison your life. With this poisoning, the possibility of you becoming aware and knowing the nature of your existence becomes less and less, because your experiences and your existence are dependent on chemical infusion.

Existentially, there is a little bit of a basis for the notions of heaven and hell. It is because your life does not end with death; it only takes on many other forms after that. It can take on pleasant forms or it can take on very unpleasant forms depending on many factors. It is these pleasant forms that we refer to as heaven, or *Swarga*, and the unpleasant forms as *Naraka*, or hell. As we already saw earlier,* these are not geographic locations—they are forms taken by the being after the body is dropped. If you go beyond all forms, then we say it is mukti, or Liberation. A spiritual seeker is not interested in going to heaven. They neither want to go to hell nor heaven. They want to go beyond this duality of both hell and heaven.

The first thing that Yoga attacks is heaven and hell. As long as there is heaven and hell, the technology for inner well-being is meaningless. The process of moving toward one's Liberation is meaningless, since now there are two places to go—either you end up in a bad place or a good place. Your whole life becomes focused upon somehow earning a ticket to the good place. You don't have to bother about how you live. Humanity has lived as grossly as it has mainly because of the assistance of religion. They preach, "It does not matter what you do, if you just believe this, this, and this, your ticket to the good place is set." So if you do not destroy the heaven and hell that is functioning within you right now, there is really no movement toward truth.

There is a beautiful story in Yogic lore: There was a yogi who was over eighty-four years old and he started going about declaring to other yogis around him, "You know, I am going to die and go to heaven shortly." This whole thing amused the other yogis. One day, they stopped him and asked, "How do you know that you are going to heaven? Do you know what is on God's mind?" So the yogi replied, "I don't care what is on God's mind; I know what is on my mind." Yoga gives you the technology to make yourself pleasant whatever the ambience may be. That is all he was trying to say. Both

---

* Refer to the section "The Importance of the Last Moments of Life" in chapter 7.

hell and heaven are still part of the duality. What we refer to as Liberation is total dissolution. You neither go here nor there. You don't go anywhere because you just dissolve. This is why, for a spiritual seeker, neither God nor heaven is the goal—mukti, or Liberation, is.

CHAPTER 9

Of Grief and Mourning

> I want you to understand that your grief is not because someone has died. One life going away does not mean anything to you. Thousands of people in the world die in a day. But it does not leave a vacuum in you. You are still partying. The problem is, this particular life going away leaves a hole in your life.

The Essential Nature of Grief

Overcoming one's grief after the death of a loved one is becoming a big thing in today's world. But you must understand that your grief is not because someone died. One life going away does not mean anything to you. Every day, thousands of people go away. In the world, even in your own city, so many people are dying, so many people are attending funerals, so many people are in grief. And yet that does not affect you. It does not leave a vacuum in you. You are still partying in the same city. The problem is, this particular life going away leaves a vacuum in your life. Essentially, you grieve because someone who in many ways was a part of your life is gone. So one part of your life has become empty and you are not able to handle that emptiness. It is like this: A group of you were playing a game, and now suddenly one person has dropped out. There is a gap in the game because of that and you are not able to handle it.

Your problem is that this particular death leaves you incomplete. You built your life around someone, you made plans in your mind—"I am going to get married to this person, I am going to have two children, I am going to make these children do this and that," and so on. But now, when this person vanishes from your life, suddenly all those dreams are shattered. You don't know what to do with yourself. You are disillusioned. If you are disillusioned, that means your illusions have been destroyed. When your illusions are destroyed, the *maya*[*] is gone—this is the time to arrive at reality. Unfortunately, most people make this into a very painful and destructive process within themselves.

Grief is just about your incompleteness. This is a very cruel thing to say, but it is true that most people will suffer more if they lose all their money or sustenance than if they lose their spouse, parent, or child. It may sound brutal but it is a fact. This is why grief can happen to you even without anyone's death. People can be in grief simply because they are not successful. People can be in grief because they are not able to get what they want. People can be in grief if their house has burned down. People can be in grief if their car is lost. A child can be in grief if his teddy bear is gone. A child may miss that teddy bear more than his parent. He may grieve for his dog much more than for his grandfather. I have seen this happen and people were shocked. But it is very human. The boy's connection with the dog is deeper than with the grandfather. What to do?

You must examine why it is that you feel incomplete if you lose someone. This life has come as a whole. If you know this life the way it is, there is no question of incompleteness. This is a complete life. If this is an incomplete life, that means the Creator has

---

[*] Literally, "illusion." Refers to the illusionary perception of the world.

done a bad job. No, it is a great job—far greater than most people realize. It is too fantastic a job. If you had experienced this life the way it is, then nothing would leave a hole in you because this is a complete life. Then you would not fill this up with your profession or your car or your house or your family or something. This life can interact, relate to, be with, and include so many things. But still, by itself, it is a complete life. This is the way it is. If this is the experience and state you are in, then whether you lose your job, your money, or someone who is dear to you, you will not grieve.

Does it mean you will have no feeling for the departed ones at all? No, you will have immense love for them. Right now, when they are here, a little bit of a problem always exists between two people. However dear and close they are to you, if you stay too close to them for more than four to six hours, you want to get away for a bit. You just make an excuse and go and sit in the bathroom at least! You need some excuse to get away from them, however close and wonderful they are. When people are embodied, two bodies cannot be close all the time. After some time, the bodies have to get apart. But when they are disembodied, immense love will come forth because this barrier of the body is gone.

You have known many things together, done many intimate things—many wonderful things have happened between two people. But as long as they were alive, you hold some small point or the other against them and resist. Now those small points of resistance have evaporated with death. Now there is no problem; they will not speak, they will not argue with you, they will not disagree with you. You must see only the wonderful side of who they were. They had problems, all right; they had a nasty side to them. But all those things are only because they had a mind and body. So if someone passes away, you should be completely overwhelmed with love. But, unfortunately, you become filled with grief. Grief is a crippling force because it leaves a big hole in you. Then you don't know what to do next because you have not experienced life the way it is.

Grief can also have an existential basis to it. But this is only in those cases where a parent has lost a child. This is more so with the mother than the father because she has a deeper biological and existential connection to the child. So if the mother loses an offspring, especially below twenty-one years of age, there is an existential basis to her grief. Beyond that, it is just purely psychological. The loss of a child is suffered most if the child is between four and twenty-one years of age. Till four years of age, this memory is not too well imprinted. Post twenty-one years of age, this memory begins to unlink. If the death of a child happens in between, then the physiological memory in the parent goes through a withdrawal syndrome and the suffering that one goes through is very physical. Of course, this varies from one individual to another based on emotional and psychological connection and dependence.

With siblings, sometimes they might have developed a certain energetic connection beyond emotional relationship—if such things have happened, if one person is drinking coffee, the other person who is far away will smell coffee, or if one person goes through some pain, the other person also goes through pain without knowing why. In such cases, the grief that is caused by loss will not be purely emotional, it will be existential.

The physical manifestation of grief is also possible between two spouses who were very deeply connected. When one of them dies, then a certain withdrawal happens in the body of the other which they may suffer. Such people may exit within six months of the death of their spouse. This is not necessarily out of psychological trauma but because of the intertwining of lives. But that is not always true. Very few people get that close. Most of the time, grief is more psychological than existential. But the psychological is not any less important. Human emotion is a powerful part of one's life. The psychological and emotional parts are not any less significant than the physiological part. They are equally powerful or more powerful, I would say.

Going Beyond Grief

We don't wish for it, but if it so happens that our children or siblings or someone whom we deeply love dies before us, how do we go beyond the grief? When we talk about going beyond something, it is not about forgetting about it. You cannot forget your child. You cannot tell yourself, "It is all right, it is all natural." You cannot. It is true that something that is very precious to you, something that means a lot to you, is gone. But the fact of life is that when something slips beyond the realm of what you call life right now, once it crosses that boundary, it is not yours anymore. I want you to understand that when your parent, child, or friend is dead, you can neither care for them nor can you be uncaring toward them. Both these things are only for the living. In other words, they have crossed a boundary line, beyond which it is not your realm or business.

You must understand that your connection with people is very physical. Some connections are not physical, but for almost 99.99 percent of the people, their connections with other people are all physical. Someone is your mother, someone is your father, someone is your husband, someone is your brother, or someone is your wife—all because of the physical. You may have emotions attached to it, but emotions don't mean anything on an existential plane. If I just wipe your memory out, your emotions will be forgotten. You give them enormous importance, but emotions are very much on the surface. Even your deepest connection is physical.

Now, your brother or friend or child or parent or whoever died, when they were alive, what are the things that you knew about them? Their body was familiar to you. They may have revealed some parts of their mind to you. Even that they would not have revealed completely to you—don't have such illusions. They would have revealed some aspects of their emotions to you. They did not reveal anything else to you. Now, when they died, they did not carry their body and go. So one major part of familiarity is finished. Whatever the content of their mind, the memory of who you are and who they are was also left behind. Once someone leaves their body, whether you like it or not, they have nothing to do with you anymore. You can sit here alive and still think someone is your brother. But for the one who has left the body there is no brother, sister, father, mother—he or she has gone beyond that. Only when you are embodied do you have a mother, a father, a brother, a sister. After that, there is no such thing.

When someone dies, people think they must forsake their enmity with that person and their friendship should be nurtured. That is stupid. Someone who is dead is neither your friend nor your enemy. It is over. The business is over. You are unwilling to come to terms with it, so grief sets in. As you slowly come to terms with it, grief recedes, doesn't it? Anyway, after ten years you will forget them. Usually, it does not take ten years, but even if it takes ten years, after ten years you will eat well, you will laugh, you will make merry, you will do everything. I am saying maintain eleven days of mourning and after that, you do all that, what is the problem? Somewhere people feel guilty that they are still alive when someone has died. But you will also die. You just have to wait. This seems like a very brutal approach, but that is the fact of life.

We must decide in our lives whether we want truth that is liberating, or we want fancy lies which give solace. If you tell me you want solace, I will tell you a different story. If you tell me that you want the truth, you want liberation from this, then it is a completely different thing. It is not with any insensitivity that I am saying this, but it is time to accept it the way it is. When death happens, it is time to look back and cherish what has been, and it is time to accept it and look at what you can do with the life that is here.

Right now, let us say, your son or daughter or grandson or someone who was very dear to you passed away. Instead of sitting and making a wreck of yourself, why don't you look around you? There are so many other sons and daughters and grandsons who have no one to care for them. There is enough opportunity for you to express this love and care in a million different ways. There is so much life around you which needs this care, and you have a need to find expression of this love and care in you, so please do that. If you don't do that, your grief will be forever. It will remain bottled and torture you for all your life. For one son that you lost, you can take up ten as your own and find full expression of your love and parenthood. You will find that it will become a foundation to make your life much more beautiful than it would be with just one son. You could make it like that. You have to take that step. Otherwise, you will simply go on with something that you cannot change.

I want you to remember that what is happening within us—it does not matter for what reason it is happening—is being created by us. If we are willing, we can change that too. As long as you are alive, it is important that you see how to contribute to the living because other than doing a few rituals within the stipulated time, there is nothing that you can do about the dead. Moreover, if you believe that the person you are grieving for has enriched your life, show that enrichment in how you live. If you are going to cry for the rest of your life, then it means this person is now the biggest problem in your life, doesn't it? Someone entered your life and left—if they have enriched your life, you must live joyfully. Acknowledge them for whatever they have done for you, don't make it look like they poisoned your life and left.

I want you to understand: However big one is in the world, tomorrow morning if I fall dead or you fall dead, the world will go on just fine—maybe better—without us! It is good that people die. Should we bring back the dead? Right now, your emotions are such that you will naturally say, "Please bring back my brother who has died." But why only your brother; shall I also bring back your grandfather and his father and his father and everyone? Can you imagine what would happen to the world if all those people wake up and start walking? It is good they are dead, isn't it? It is not right to think that someone should not die. People should die. We want them to complete their whole course and die. We don't want them to have an untimely death, that is the only concern. But that understanding is not there today as people are so terribly attached to their physical bodies. This is why even if they are ninety or a hundred you still don't want them to die.

You must understand that, whatever situations happen to you in your life, you can come out of it with greater strength, or you can be left broken by it. This is a choice that you have. This is a choice every human being has. We do not have a choice all the time about whether this situation should happen or not. We can influence it only to some extent, but many situations will happen beyond us. But each time, we have the choice whether to go through these situations gracefully or go through these situations in a broken way. This is a choice we always have.

Now, is it possible to do some rituals to overcome grief? Yes, we can. There are things you can do, but is it worth doing it? You must understand that creating rituals for everything is taking steps backward. Doing a ritual means you are not willing to do anything, you just want someone else or something else to handle your grief. When there is a way, where with a certain attitude of mind and awareness, you can come out of it, why do you need to go into rituals? It is okay to use rituals for certain aspects of life, but not for every aspect of life. If someone dear to you dies, you must learn to handle it rather than expecting a ritual or some other intervention to release you. If someone is in such a hopeless state, yes, we will do something but that should not be the mode for a society. It will become very entangling after some time.

One of the tools you could use to overcome grief is to perform Kalabhairava Karma. Kalabhairava Karma will distance you from your Genetic Memory. If it is done properly, there is a clear distance that is created. Suddenly, it is okay, because there is a distance between you and the dead relative. This is why many people who come to do Kalabhairava Karma experience that afterward suddenly they feel light, as if a huge burden has been taken off them. Kalabhairava Karma is not a ritual to handle your grief, but because of what it does, it can handle grief also.

Articles of the Dead

Once a woman whose grandmother had passed away a few months earlier narrated an incident that kept bothering her. One day, she wore her grandmother's clothes while cleaning her closet. She was also wearing her grandmother's ring that she had inherited. She felt that her grandmother was communicating her disapproval of this and she had been experiencing her grandmother's presence around her. Moreover, she had taken up some of her grandmother's habits too. For example, she had taken to smoking, even though she was not a smoker until then. Her grandmother was. There were a few other things like this, and she was bothered by it. She wanted me to help her become free from this.

Generally, a lot of such things are people's imagination going wild, but sometimes there could be a basis for it. If you want to be free of such things, the first thing you should do is to stop relating to the dead. You need to understand this: However dear they were to you, however intimate they might have been with you, the moment they shed their body their general sense of mind, intellect, and emotion, which was the basis of your business with them, is finished. All the things that you knew about them are finished. Some other sap is still on, but you never had any relationship with that sap. Your relationship is with the other aspects. All those aspects were shed when that person died. So the only thing that you do when someone dies is you cherish the beautiful moments that you had with them—that is all. If there was something beautiful, you cherish that; otherwise, forget about them. Don't try to work your guilt and your problems through the dead. It can become very complicated.

You must leave the dead to the dead. You have no business with them unless you have a certain level of mastery over your own life. You should not even look in that direction because you could completely mess up your life by trying to do something silly. And anyway, it does not matter how attached your grandmother was to her clothes and whatever else, she could only wear them as long as she had a body and you know clearly that she has lost that. So she has no use for it. Someone who does not have a body does not have any business with food or clothes or anything. Only if you have a body must you go toward food and clothes. Once you lose your body, what business do you have with food and clothes? Even when you have a body, you should not go too much toward it, but at least you have a good enough excuse to do so! You have to cover your body at least, so you want to cover it nicely, that is all right. But when you have lost the body, what are you going to wear clothes upon and walk around in?

Generally, when a lot of emotion is mixed up in the situation, there will be so many things which will happen within you and outside of you. When you go to your grandmother's place, just do whatever work needs to be done, do your sadhana, be with your grandfather who is still alive, and stop trying to be with the dead. See how to enrich your life and your grandfather's life for those few moments that you are there, rather than doing all kinds of fanciful things with your grandmother.

It is possible that there is a certain residual element of your grandmother that is left behind in her clothes. And they may cause some things to happen. But there is no need to play into it. All these things were taken care of in India by various customs that were built into the culture. People accepted these things as a normal happening. When a person died, all the clothes that were closely in touch with that person's body were burned. They were never kept. The clothes that the person occasionally wore were given only to a blood relative, no one else. And even in such an instance, the clothes were not worn for the first year.

These things were done because a certain amount of our energy gets into whatever we are in touch with. If you give it a certain kind of opportunity, these clothes will start behaving funnily. Your grandmother need not come, these clothes will start acting funny by themselves. You are familiar with static, where clothes gather electric charges by being in contact with certain substances. Similarly, whatever is in close association with your body will get a certain amount of your quality. The first preference of people who want to do some occult practices on you is to get hold of your hair or nails. These are actually parts of the body that are discarded periodically, so it is easy to get direct access to you through them. If they cannot get that, the next thing they seek is some clothing which is in close contact with your body. Of these, the first target is underwear. This is why people used to take enormous care to ensure that their underwear was never left accessible to others. These days it is all going to the washerman, otherwise, traditionally, in our homes, it was all put in a covered basket. It must be washed inside the house—never be taken out because with this clothing itself, people can do things to you. It is because of this quality that these clothes carry that even when a person dies their clothes can crackle up a little bit if a certain kind of energy is on.

There have been instances where things actually moved around. Especially the things that they intimately used—they start moving around here and there by themselves. It is not that this person has come and moved things. It is just that the energy that was associated with those objects is sort of withdrawing. In the process of withdrawal, there will be a little bit of extra movement. It is like when you switch off your car engine: When it is just dying down, it makes a little extra shake in the car. It is stopping, so actually it should recede, but that is not what happens. Similarly, when life shifts from one mode to another, there will be a little extra reverberation. That extra shake is mistaken to be ghosts walking all over the place.

If you do something like the Kalabhairava Karma for this person, it will ensure that no residue of that person remains. Now the dead can be packed and sent, and the living can continue their life. If the living get involved with the dead, they will lose their lives in so many ways. All this spooky stuff is sort of intriguing, but it can consume your life in so many different ways that will not be very pleasant. This does not mean some dead person is trying to suck your life out. No. Just your involvement with the dead can do that. Unless you are sufficiently established and possess a certain level of capability, you should not look in that direction. It is not necessary.

Empathetic Death

This happens with some birds, and it also happens with animals and human beings: If they were a couple or were very close, when one of them dies, within three to six months the other will also die. One reason why this happened is because in India, when people were married, their energies were bound together in a certain way. This was at a time in this country when tradition did not allow separation. At that time, people took the liberty of tying them up at the level of the energy because anyway the couple would not separate. These things are not to be done frivolously, just like that. Much consideration must be given to the consequences of such actions.

You may know this: Traditional Hindu women were required to wear toe rings after marriage. In Tamil Nadu, it is called *metti*. This is because marriage was supposed to be such a huge experience for the woman that there was a possibility that she would leave the body. Usually, they were married off at the age of eight or ten. The husband and wife would live separately and would not see each other till they were fourteen or fifteen. During this period, while the boy was physiologically and psychologically trained and conditioned to protect this person who is dedicated to him, the girl (being more emotionally competent) was emotionally and psychologically conditioned to believe that her husband was her God. This possibility was built up in her mind. When she was physically mature, she was brought to the marital home. So when she comes and meets her husband, it would be such a huge experience for her that her life would explode within her. At that time, it was possible that she could slip out of the body. To prevent this, they put some metal on the girl's body, in the form of metti. Wearing metal on the body always prevents such an accident. This is also done when we put people through certain types of sadhana. They are given a metal ring or bracelet or some ornament like that. They are not supposed to remove it without the permission of the Guru. This is to prevent them from accidentally slipping out of the body.

In this culture, whether it is business or marriage or having children or family—everything was used as a tool toward your Liberation and mukti. Because of this, they nurtured the newly married girl and boy in such a way that for four to six years they would not have seen each other, but were made to believe that when they met something very big was going to happen. So, in the child's mind, this grew into such a big possibility. It is not just two bodies meeting, not just two minds and emotions meeting; they did a certain process where the marriage was two lives being merged into one.

When a woman got married, she wore something called *mangalsutra* around her neck. *Mangal* means auspicious, *sutra* means thread. The mangalsutra is an energy thread which you are supposed to replace every year. Someone who knows what it is gives you a live mangalsutra, which matches the energies of the husband and wife in such a way that they are not just bound in body, mind, and emotion, they are bound as two lives as well. It is like, if you have the right kind of sutra, your kite will fly well. Similarly, the mangalsutra was to make your marriage more purposeful and successful. But today people wear thick gold chains fashioned as mangalsutras, which cannot replace the actual sutra or thread that they are meant to wear. That sutra was to make you fly in marriage, but this gold chain is a symbol of slavery. Unfortunately, this is the shift that has happened.

In those days, people understood that in a marriage, how the bodies, minds, and emotions matched was not important. What was important was that two lives were entwined so that there was a kind of bonding. For this, they employed many tools. Many couples would have never spoken to each other before the marriage, but when married in this manner, their marriage created a bonding which was inexplicable because marriage was a scientific process of binding two lives in such a way that there was no question of incompatibility. It did not matter even if you married a devil. You still bonded and felt ecstatic within you, simply because of the union within yourself and not because of what the other person was doing. When you are like this, what your husband or wife did was immaterial. Just the way you were was an explosive experience. As human experience is 100 percent from within, one could touch the peaks of life irrespective of the quality of one's partner.

Since marriage was done this way, when one person left, many times the other person also left a short time after that. Today there is statistical evidence of a disproportionate number of spouses dying within six months of each other, but this is more because of the disruption of life than any other reason. Let us say, a couple lives to their old age. When one of them dies, because we have all moved from living as large joint families to nuclear families, often there is no one left to care for the survivor. Now, because of this disruption in their life, the wish to die becomes very strong in them. While they were both alive, though both were ambling around, they were there for each other. When one person dies, the other person just wants to go because there is usually no other support, unless they are living with the children who are very loving and taking care of them. One life following another in death is not necessarily because of loss of companionship or emotional debacle. Two lives that lived in tandem, that were tied together energetically, tend to dismantle in response. This does not happen at the level of thought; it is deeper than that.

Large-scale Death and Its Consequences

We saw that if a violent or unnatural death happens, then the being hangs around and this in turn impacts the place. Now, in the case of wars, where a lot of people are killed violently, are there any negative consequences in that place? This has to be looked at in two parts: If you look at the ancient wars, they were fought with swords and spears, with men running full speed into one another. I don't think there is much fear in such a situation. Death and destruction happened rather quickly. This is often true even with modern warfare. In that sense, there is not much of a residue of this kind.

It is only if you gave them an opportunity for fear—if they were cornered or something, then they were terrorized. But this did not happen on such a large scale in ancient wars. However, if you take World War I or even World War II, most of it was fought in the trenches. Those trenches were terrible places of fear. People were cold and hungry, their fingers and toes were eaten up by frostbite, pain, and all that. Their fear was because they were sitting there, waiting to die. Instead, if you went out with your rifle, screaming, then either you died or the enemy died. This would be a different thing. This is like a car accident. If you are driving full speed and suddenly *boom!*—either they die or you die. But when they were sitting and waiting in those trenches, only a small percentage of men would not have much fear—these were people who had a larger vision that they were doing this for their country and all that. However, there were many others who did not have such a sense of sacrifice but just became pawns in the game of war. They would have wondered why the hell they were born in this country because they were now in the trenches and might get killed at any moment. Such people would have been in extreme fear.

Whether they died or not, that fear would have left behind an enormous negative force. I think Europe has seen that kind of long-term fear and suffering more than any other land on the planet. So many lives falling apart will have an impact anywhere. But when people die of fear on a large scale, very morbid manifestations may happen. It can be psychological and mixed up with what people go through in terms of life or energetic turmoil. Most of all, one thing that will happen is that they will not know joy, they will not know love. These two things will become difficult when all these things happen around you. They may know passion, they may know sexuality, they may know pleasures, but they cannot know the simple joy and simple bond of loving someone. So complicated expressions of the simple human traits of wanting to be joyful or loving will manifest.

Something like this is said in the Mahabharata after Kurukshetra.* The Kurukshetra War was a terrible war. It is said that more than a hundred thousand people died in the war. For the population of those days, a hundred thousand people is a huge number to die, that too just by swords and arrows. If you have to kill a hundred thousand people with no bombs, no gunpowder, just with swords and arrows, then the amount of fighting that happened must have been enormous. The strange thing is that we know so much about the war and there are detailed accounts of every little thing that happened there. After the war, the Pandavas ruled the kingdom for thirty-six years—but we don't hear a single word about it. In the entire story, the real story should have been after the war because that is why they fought the war—to decide who should rule and how—but not a word is heard about it because nothing significant happened in their lives.

They did not live a joyful life. They simply lived and ruled. They must have done something for the kingdom—expanded it,

---

* The place where the final battle of Mahabharata took place. Often, the war is also known by the same name.

perhaps, but nothing significant. Nothing significant happened in the human experience because there was a certain barrenness in their life. This would not be just for those five people and their family but for the entire population as well. This was not because they were affected psychologically from having lost someone. Yes, that impact would also have been there, but above all, it was just the effect of the gore of death all around.

Today, they say, because the place was so soaked in blood, it is good to die in Kurukshetra. People go there to die because they believe it is a good place to die. Maybe someone made this up or maybe it is good, I don't know. But at that time, definitely, the next few generations after that would have this gore of death in their samskara.* So they could never have really known the joy of bonding with people, nor the simple joy of living. They would have slogged, they would have built, and they would have done things. Here and there, they would have laughed, they would have lived, they would know everything, but there would have been no real sense of joy. Where enormous amounts of human blood are spilled, the impact stays alive in the soil for a longer period in temperate climates than in tropical climates. It is not just the grayness of the weather; one who is sensitive to life can feel the difference in the liveliness of the soil and water, particularly the soil.

So can this be undone? Yes, it can. Creating many consecrated spaces would be one way of doing it. If you create really powerful consecrated spaces that are strategically located, it could undo a lot. But there is nothing like *Gnanam, Dhyanam, Anandam!*† Gnanam is awareness about the truth. Dhyanam is meditativeness. Anandam is blissfulness, which is a consequence of the two. Really, these things are not simply slogans. They can change the world!

---

* The residual tendencies of a being.
† A slogan that was once used to popularize Isha Yoga in Tamil Nadu.

Mourning Period

In many cultures, there were stipulations as to what people who were closely related to the dead should and should not do for a certain period of time after the death. This was mainly to create a karmic distance between the living and the departed so that both could continue their respective journeys without much encumbrance. For example, in Hindu culture, those related to the dead person would not consume meat or drink alcohol along with their clan that is of the same blood, as consuming meat or alcohol together strengthens the bondage, or runanubandha. This is also one of the important aspects of plant-based diets, that it reduces your runanubandha and leaves you more of an individual than part of the clan, which is a very essential factor for one's individual Liberation. Liberation can only be individual; a crowd or a group cannot go through this.

In a previous section[*] we saw how we create runanubandha with everybody and everything we interact with in our lives. But runanubandha is not at the same level for all relationships. So, depending upon the strength of the runanubandha, to that extent the death of a person affects another individual. For example, sometimes, without knowing why, someone wakes up in the morning feeling a pit in the stomach. This could be due to various reasons, but it is also possible that someone who has strong runanubandha with you is in some distress or has died or whatever. You may not know this person, you may have never met him or her, but just like that, your system is reacting to what is happening to that person. It is very much possible. The problem of speaking about these aspects is people will start imagining all kinds of things. Tomorrow, if someone is not feeling well, instead of seeing a doctor or examining what

---

[*] See the section "Runanubandha—The Web of Debt" in chapter 8.

they did not do right the previous day, they will start imagining that someone they love must have died somewhere and all kinds of confusion will start.

In Hindu culture, there is a peculiar tradition of mourning that depends on being genealogically related to the dead person in a particular way. Such people are supposed to avoid going to temples or participating in social events or celebrations for forty days. This is because, in ancient India, they followed the system of *kula*, which is like a clan, but with a much more genetic basis to it. Kulas were created mainly to maintain a clear genetic pathway through generations. Through this connection, they created runanubandha on the physical and genetic level as well. Kulas were maintained and sustained primarily by creating *Kula Devata*s, or the deity for the kula. Each kula had a deity with specific rituals related to that deity. In ancient times, not everyone went to every temple. There were some temples that were for general well-being, which everyone visited. But for specific purposes, people went only to their Kula Devata. Not only that, if a certain kind of genetic pathway is maintained, you can create certain energy which travels through the track, impacting the entire clan. Even now, this is happening to some extent, where medical science is coming up with medication that is specific to certain kinds of DNA makeup.

Similarly, it is possible to do spiritually beneficial things to the entire clan, across generations, by just doing it in one place. For example, when kulas were maintained, everyone in the kula did not need to go to the temple. If one person went and prayed, or one big ritual was done, everyone could benefit, whether they were physically present in that space or not, because all of them were connected and the energy moved through that connection.

For thousands of years, people maintained the genetic track in their own way, never mixing it up, never doing anything that would disturb the track, so that the progeny was well maintained. They had whole systems of how to marry, intermarry, and not marry among their own clan. All these things created a very strong runanubandha, which ensured the survival and well-being of that clan. Today, kula is understood as caste and we just react to atrocities that have been committed in that name. We think everything must be dismantled.

In any case, it is all broken and gone now. Today, the genetic material of people is all mixed up. Society has changed. Today, your son may fall in love with the girl next door and she could be from any caste, religion, or race. So it will not work the same way. Today, your choices have become more important than maintaining those kinds of things. So those things have become irrelevant. You cannot revive that but there was a deep science with immense benefits in it. It worked phenomenally for some societies that kept it. When things were maintained like that, not visiting temples at a certain time was a very relevant thing. It was a wonderful understanding of life, a fabulous understanding of genetics and how it functions.

When the kula system was still relevant, if there was a death in the kula, all the members of the kula who were related to the dead person in a certain way were asked not to go to the temple for forty days after the death. This makes sense only for the Kula Devata temple. This is because they wanted to avoid the possibility that the deity would confuse the person with the dead person because of the close resemblance of the genetic material with that person. The deity may recognize your energy and the dead person's as the same and it could disturb your system; it could cause destabilization of your body. In extreme cases, it could even cause death. So when that energy is hanging around you, you don't go to your Kula Devata, but you can go to a Shiva temple or a Kalabhairava temple.

Memorials, Samadhis, and Pyramids

Building memorials for people who are dear to us or those who were of certain significance or prominence, after their death, is common in all cultures of the world. The famous Taj Mahal of India, for example, is a memorial built by a king in memory of one of his wives. This is also one way of handling one's grief. These memorials also have social and political significance where they help in building our identities. However, beyond these reasons, is there any need or existential significance to it? That depends upon many factors.

Once it happened: A five-year-old boy accompanied his mother to the cemetery. He had never been to a cemetery in his life. While his mother was paying her respects at one particular grave, the boy went about everywhere reading all the inscriptions on the tombstones. He then came back to his mother and asked her, "Mom, where do they bury all the horrible people?" Every tombstone declared this was the most wonderful person, so he wanted to know where the horrible ones were buried! Generally, people want to have good memories of people who have died, so their memorials also say good things about them. But Hindus created another kind of memorial called samadhis. There is some spiritual significance to such samadhis, and people go to a samadhi not just to remember the dead or pay their respects but also to be in its presence and meditate.

In India, if someone died in a certain way, people recognized that there was a benefit in preserving that place and wanted to make the energies they left behind available to people. For example, there is Vijji's samadhi at the Yoga Center. If you simply sit there, you will see that the samadhi has its own aura and energy about itself because of the way in which she left her body. It is like a solvent. It is a kind of dissolving energy. Generally, for certain people, I tell them not to sit there for too long because it is a very body-taking kind of energy. It can slowly dissolve you. It was set up with the intention that there is one corner in the Yoga Center that nurtures a very different type of energy altogether. It is mild and subtle. It is also very beautiful and pleasant. If you simply sit there without aspiring for anything or relating to anything or trying to imagine things, it can give you a bodiless kind of feeling. For one who is doing sadhana, it is good to be in such spaces. That space is fundamentally of the Anahata Chakra. A lot of people go there probably out of curiosity, but if you look at people who go there regularly, they are a certain type of people. They are Anahata-oriented people who are naturally drawn to that. They prefer to sit in the samadhi rather than in the Dhyanalinga simply because they are of a certain type.

There are many places like that in India. One such place is Kumara Parvatha, near the Kukke Subramanya temple in the Western Ghats, Karnataka. It is believed that Shiva's younger son, Kartikeya, or Subramanya, as he is known outside Tamil Nadu, left his body on top of this mountain. He was a fierce warrior yogi who unleashed destruction wherever he perceived injustice. It is said that one day he realized the futility of his deeds and decided to put an end to it. He washed his bloodied sword one last time in the river at the foothills of Kumara Parvatha and climbed the hill. He never came down—they say he shed his body at the top of the mountain. It is said that he was such an accomplished yogi that he shed his body in the standing position. His energies are very much intact there even today.

About twenty years ago, we went there with a group of residents from the Yoga Center. Halfway up the mountain, there is a house that belongs to two brothers who live there. People going up the mountain usually camp there on their way up and down. Once we reached that place, I knew I would not be able to make it to the top.

The energies there were so intense that I knew my body would not be able to withstand this sort of energy during that phase of my life. That entire night, I could not lie down and sleep. Every time I tried to sit or lie down, my body would just spring up. I was in a tent and my body would stand erect, dismantling the tent itself. So I ended up standing the whole night.

Another such experience happened when I was in a small village in Tamil Nadu called Velayuthampalayam. I was conducting a program there and stayed in a home opposite a small hill. In Tamil Nadu, there is bound to be a temple on top of every hill. Very few hilltops are unoccupied. So there was a temple on top of this hill too and every day I would see people going up and coming down. I went to this village a few times, but I never went up that hill. Then they told me there was a cave up there and some Jain monks had stayed there some 2,400 years ago and that a local king had beds carved for them on the rock. I thought about this—2,400 years ago meant they could be direct disciples of Mahavir* or just after that. So now I was interested.

One day, I went up the hill. It was like a bird's nest, precariously positioned on top of the hill, amid some big boulders. The place was not well kept, it was being used for all kinds of things. There were empty alcohol bottles and things like that. The walls were all defaced by those ugly love proclamations you commonly find in India: "PKT loves SKP" and rubbish like that. In a corner, I saw the carved beds on the rock. There were small two-inch protrusions for pillows too. I just sat on one of these beds and my body was literally jumping up and down. I said, "This is a loaded place. Clean it up, we will come and sleep here in the night." That night, about nine of us went up with mattresses to sleep in that cave. No one slept for a moment because the energy was bursting there in strange ways. And

---

* The founder of the Jain religion, a contemporary of Gautama the Buddha.

I could clearly see that the person who used to lie on the bed that I happened to sleep upon had no leg below his left knee. What had happened, we don't know, but there was no left leg. They must have been that kind of intense people that their energies were distinctly bouncing there, even after more than two thousand years.

There are many more such places in India. Some are maintained with some reverence, but most are anonymous and unkempt. If you want to experience such an energy on a much larger scale, more multidimensional, you must go up to the Seventh Hill of the Velliangiri Mountains. Sadhguru Sri Brahma left his body there through all the seven chakras. So the place is explosive in terms of energy even today. It is something one must experience. It is a tremendous dimension and possibility.

However, for people who led an ordinary life and died, if you want to remember and honor them, that is up to you. But you must know it is a lot of real estate. You are making an investment of your emotion. It may not have any existential significance. Take the Taj Mahal, for example. At least Shah Jahan built something beautiful. Is it reverberating with the energy of his wife Mumtaz? Nothing like that. It is a beautiful piece of craft that he built. It is a jewel. No one goes there to grieve for her. People just go there to enjoy the craft. Her name may be written somewhere, but existentially the monument has nothing to do with him or her right now. It has something to do with the people who worked on it, though.

Ancient Egyptians took this whole memorial business to another level altogether. The pyramids of Egypt are perhaps physically the largest and most spectacular attempt ever at connecting the here with the hereafter. A tremendous amount of thought, engineering, and effort have gone into building them. In terms of physicality, perhaps no other human effort to ensure the well-being of the dead is so desperate. So what would be the spiritual value of these pyramids? How far do they go in ensuring the well-being of the departed? Is this effort worthy of emulation in the present times?

Egyptians started building pyramids because they were very death-oriented. It comes from their obsession with pleasure. Death and pleasure are very directly connected. People always think life and pleasure are connected. No, death and pleasure are very directly connected. Pyramids are just one aspect of what they built. They built some very fabulous temples also, but the pyramids have become very popular because of some modern death-oriented people who wrote books on them.

The basic quality of the pyramid is preservation. Some people are promoting the pyramid as a meditative process. A pyramid has nothing to do with meditation. Sitting inside a pyramid and meditating is just ignorance. If you are doing it for health purposes, it is okay. It definitely supports health, but if people think that sitting inside a pyramid and meditating will take them to higher levels of consciousness, it is a very wrong notion. With the pyramid, you can create health, organic unity, and maybe you can increase your lifespan to some extent, but it is not a spiritual process. It does not help the dead in any way, except assisting in the preservation of the physical.

Pyramids work because of their geometry. Even if you make a paper pyramid whose angles are exactly 51.5 degrees on all four sides and on the top, it will work. You can place a vegetable inside it and you will see that what would normally rot in about three days will still not have rotted even after three weeks. It would have shrunk, shriveled up, but not rotted. This is because if you create a pyramidal form, Vyana Vayu gets trapped there naturally. Vyana Vayu is in charge of the preservative function of the body. So something can be preserved for a long time, if you can hold it. This is how mummies were preserved for thousands of years.

In India, preserving the dead body is the last thing we want to do. The rule is if someone dies, within four to six hours after death you must cremate the body. Traditionally, they said, once death has occurred—by the next dusk or dawn, whichever occurs first—the body must be cremated. Destroying the body immediately is very good for both the dead and the living. Preserving the body is only a torture for the person who has departed.

PART III

LIFE AFTER DEATH

THE DARK ONE

When I first heard the sounds of
Darkness and silence meeting within me
The little mind argues for light
The virtue, the power, the beauty
Light a brief happening could hold me not
All encompassing darkness drew me in
Darkness the infinite eternity
Dwarfs the happened, the happening,
  and yet to happen
Choosing the eternal
Darkness I became
The dark one that I am
The Divine and the devil are but a small part
The divine I dispense with ease
If you meet the devil you better cease

CHAPTER 10

The Life of a Ghost

In a way, everyone is a ghost. Whether you are a ghost with the body or without a body is the only question.

WHAT ARE GHOSTS?

Ghosts are a part of the folklore of every culture in the world. Perhaps no child in the world grows up without hearing a big dose of ghost stories—about their lives, deeds, and idiosyncrasies. So what are these ghosts? How did they come into existence? What is the basis of their existence? Why are they even around? This lack of understanding is because, right now, you understand only embodiment as life. Not because you are opinionated but simply because that is your experience of life. But life extends beyond the body as well. That is why you have what are generally known as ghosts.

It once happened: There was a very shy man. He got admitted to a hospital for a medical checkup. A very pretty nurse attended to him. So she checked his blood pressure, did a blood test, urine test, enema, and everything. She went out for some time and, in the meantime, before he could get up from the bed, his bowels revolted against all the atrocities committed upon them, and things happened on the bed. He could not control himself. Being a very shy man, he was too embarrassed. He did not want the pretty nurse to see this mess. When he heard the footsteps of the nurse coming in, he just grabbed all the sheets on the bed and threw them from the fifth-floor window.

Down below, a man was returning home from a party. It is such an unfair world, you know, a man is expected to walk straight on a round planet while the damn thing is spinning! With great difficulty, he was walking sideways and the sheets fell on him and covered him. He screamed and fought these sheets. It took him a few minutes to get them off. By then, the security came rushing and asked, "What was all the commotion about?" He was dazed and, looking down at the sheets, said, "It looks like I have beaten the shit out of a ghost."

What are ghosts, actually? All beings are a combination of time, memory, and energy. Of the three, time is not in your hands, but how you live your life will determine how much memory and energy you gather or dissipate. Let us say, with lots of activity and a certain focus you use up a lot of memory—the Prarabdha Karma part of it—very quickly. Now, if you are unable to open the warehouse of Sanchita Karma, then you may have an untimely death, because the energy is still intense, but you have run out of memory. Once you run out of memory, you can either die or become vegetative. But generally, you will die, because if memory collapses, there are many things which cannot function. However, if your energy runs out and memory is still there, then too you will die, but you will continue to exist as what we call a ghost.

A ghost has a manifestation but because there is not enough energy to keep the physical body integrated and keep it going, the body is gone. But its memory body is still strong, strong enough to be felt by other people. In a way, you can say, everyone is a ghost. Whether you are a ghost with a body or without a body—whether you are an embodied ghost or disembodied ghost—is the only question. And all beings, embodied or disembodied, are playing out their lives only as per their karmic structures. The only difference is that when you are embodied, there is more possibility of using your will. That is all.

What you call ghosts are those beings who left their body, usually in an unnatural way. They had strong Prarabdha Karma left unfinished, but they died because of either an accident, a disease, a suicide, or murder. Somehow, the body broke so much that it could not sustain life anymore. Such beings will have a denser presence and their tendencies are very strong. They are active in a certain way so you can feel them or even see them more easily. Existence in the form of a ghost or the life of a ghost—if you want to call it that—is considered undesirable because it can unnecessarily extend for a long time. Let us say, this person who has died had some amount of unfinished Prarabdha Karma when they died. If they were in the physical body, maybe their Prarabdha Karma would have lasted for another twenty years. Now that there is no physical body, the dissolution of karma is only by tendency, not by conscious action. As a result, the lifespan may be two hundred or two thousand years instead of twenty years.

A ghost generally cannot have conscious intention because the intellect is gone. But they can function by tendency. Let us say, when the person was alive, his tendency was pinching people. Even after his body is gone, he will still want to pinch. It does not matter who, he will just want to pinch. Let us say, there was someone who giggled all his life. His ghost will also giggle. This action happens by tendency, not by conscious intention. If you happen to see ghosts, because of your own inhibitions and limitations, you may get really paranoid. Mostly, it is your psychological response. It has nothing to do with that being. Suppose you see a person floating and not walking around you, you will go through all kinds of weird emotions. This is not necessary and has nothing to do with these beings. Unfortunately, they get a lot of bad press for all this.

The English word "ghost" is a crude and generic term that bundles all disembodied beings in the same category. But they are very varied in terms of where they came from, what they are capable of, and where they are going. There are some who lost their bodies before they ran down their Prarabdha Karma and are hanging around. Then there are yogis without bodies who are wandering, always looking for a possibility for their dissolution. Then there are celestial beings who are on a vacation. Some others are of a completely different dimension and have no relevance to your life. Then there are certain forces which people generally refer to as Divine Forces, which can take on almost any form they wish. So there are actually a variety of things and you cannot bundle them all together.

Just to be able to classify these things, to be able to recognize one from the other, is a serious amount of work. Traditionally, different levels of bodiless existence are referred to as *bhoota, preta, pisachi, chaudi, yaksha*s, *kinnara, gandharva, deva,* and so on. They are at different evolutionary levels, or we can say they are on different types of vacations. Someone is in the first class, someone is in the second class, someone is in another class, while someone else is in a bad condition, which you call hell. Essentially, they are all on some type of vacation, but their vacation will end sometime, and they will take on another physical body. No one remains a bhoota or a preta or a yaksha or a gandharva or even a deva forever. He or she enjoys or suffers it for a certain time and then takes on a physical form again.

For simplicity, we can loosely call those beings who are aware and have refused to take a body and are looking for ways of dissolution as celestial beings. They still have some choice and discretion because they lived and died in a certain sense of awareness. The others are disembodied beings just functioning by compulsion, the same way you are. These are the ones you are most likely to come in contact with. Again, to make it simple, we can just classify them simply as intense, mild, and meek types.

Those who are intense have a more active presence and people may feel it. They may even have a form which at least in other people's experience is nearly physical. Mild types are not like that, but they could cause certain things to happen to people. If you interact head-on with an intense one, spooky things will definitely happen. Their tendencies will be very strong so they will behave in a certain way. It will be a very strong reaction. Some may be intense and calm, but generally they will be compulsive in some way.

If you meet the mild ones, unknowingly people will go through some disturbances, like maybe someone will run a temperature or someone will be disturbed for no reason at all. It is not like a ghost is sitting on your head—that energy could have disturbed your system because they are everywhere in some way. Many of them may not be intense enough to maintain an individual form but they are there. Meek ones have almost no impact on your system unless you are super susceptible, which some people are. This is the reason why all these klesha nashanas are done—to clear out all such influences.

The problem here is to decipher what is just a psychological phenomenon and what is real. It is a serious challenge because anyone can believe they saw a ghost or a ghost possessed them. To completely deny it would be stupid. Though these beings are incapable of having intent, they may do something compulsively. And there is a tendency to seek their own Genetic Memory. They may not feel comfortable somewhere else. They want to seek their own Genetic Memory. So they may hang around places where these memories are. But are they out to harm you? Not at all. These beings have no tendency to interact with human beings, as such. They don't have a discriminatory intellect to choose, "I want to interact with this person or that person." That is from your own psychological processes.

I think this entire problem is because people have been projecting that these ghosts are waiting and they will pounce on you or harm you in some way. This is all made up by people wanting to profit from it—you can call them commercial ghosts. It is because of all these movies that have been made where the person who died is waiting on a cloud, wanting to talk to you or hear what you say. All these things have deeply influenced the human psyche in such a way that they cannot draw a line between what is reality and what is made up in their mind. People's psychological realities are so true for them that they think that is a truth by itself. These things have given much currency to all those ghost stories that you hear.

Native Americans maintain a strict code about places where they rest the dead. Once they create a place for the dead where they leave the bodies for the birds or whatever, no one enters that place. One reason is for your own safety. Another reason is you don't want to disturb them. You want them to be comfortable and work their time out. This is also the reason why, traditionally, the crematoriums and burial grounds are usually outside human habitations—the dead should be given some space. This is a very wise thing to do.

Now, people ask, are all the disembodied beings human forms or are there any non-human disembodied beings too? Well, there is no such thing as non-human disembodied beings. For example, does a grasshopper go about hopping without a body? Not really. There are some exceptions to this—cobras are one. We already saw that cobras and cows are capable of having a subtle body.* It is not

---

* Refer to the section "The Scope of Kalabhairava Karma" in chapter 8.

completely logically correct to say this, but it is like saying that just as with human beings there are human ghosts, there are also some snake ghosts which can also possess a human being.

In Hindu culture, it is common knowledge that there is something called *Naga Dosha*.* Naga Dosha happens when a disembodied cobra has touched you somehow. Once again, we must understand that a disembodied being has no intention of its own. It is incapable of intentions, but it has tendencies. So when you come in contact with it, it can impact you. When people have Naga Dosha, it can particularly affect certain layers of your skin. Usually, in such people, the skin breaks into rashes. It looks like psoriasis but is not exactly psoriasis. The skin begins to peel away in scales. It can also create a very strange sense of stillness and movement, which if not handled properly can lead to psychological distress. Otherwise, it can cause people to have serious hearing impediments. I have seen people who have recovered totally from those things by just doing *Naga Pooja* and things like that.

When a disembodied cobra impacts someone, the period of impact is not very long because its own structural integrity is in question. It will dismantle itself because it does not have the necessary integrity to hold itself for too long. The duration is usually between twenty-seven days and fifty-four days. But Naga Dosha, the ailment caused by the impact, can last long. This is if the impact has affected you negatively. It can also impact you positively. If it impacts you positively, you will see that the strength of your spine, how it functions, and your perception will be enhanced. It is because the disembodied cobra lingers about for some time after its death. In India, if people find a dead cobra, they perform a complete funeral for the naga.

---

* A certain kind of negative energy influence.

Speaking of cobras and their impact, I have experienced both positive and negative ones. Once it killed me,* but at once it made my life in so many ways. After the consecration of the Dhyanalinga, my health situation was quite bad. We did many energy processes to recover, and a few people really dedicated their lives to making me well again, but certain parts of my body—especially the right side, just next to my navel—were like a vacuum, creating problems. Tumors had started forming there. They used to form one day, and disappear after a few days. Doctors said my red blood cell count was excessively high because my liver function was starting to fail. We could have fixed it, but I needed time—at least a month or two for myself—but because of my schedule, I never got it. So this condition kept getting worse. Off and on, we did small patch-up jobs here and there, but we never really paid proper attention to the system.

One night, in December 2001, I was lying down in my bedroom in the Isha Yoga Center. It was about four forty-five A.M. and when I opened my eyes, I saw a huge, disembodied cobra next to me. It was larger than normal proportions. Its hood was raised. I have always kept a little brass cobra next to my bed; they were the ones who said good morning to me every day, and now there was a big one with a giant hood right there. I was looking at it and then it came toward me and bit me, next to the navel. I closed my eyes. It remained there for some time and then it left, not to be seen again.

The bite caused wounds to my belly—four fang marks, with blood oozing out. I even showed it to some people. However, from that day, the space or the vacuum was gone; this encounter with the mystical or celestial cobra took it away from me.

Recently, I had to undergo an MRI. The doctor who examined the MRI mentioned more than a few times that he had never seen

---

* See the section "My Past Lifetimes" in chapter 11.

anything like this—that I had the spine of a thirty-year old. The spine over time usually starts to collapse or telescope and shows signs of aging. Two years prior to this, at sixty-five years of age, as part of the Save Soil movement seeking to mobilize action toward revitalizing the health of our planet's soil, I rode a motorcycle for eighteen thousand miles from London to southern India in one hundred days through twenty-seven nations and all kinds of terrain with numerous events all along the way. Everyone including seasoned motorcycle riders said this would break my back, there is no way a person's back can hold up for so long, riding such a long distance. Not only did I complete the journey without any problems, but just two days after finishing, I traveled back to the United States and continued with my engagements. This is a testament to the Yogic system, which places a lot of significance on keeping up the health of the spine. The spine is fundamental to how a human being experiences life, because all experiences of life are transmitted through it, and as it degenerates over time, one's sensitivity to life starts going down unless one performs the necessary sadhana to keep it vibrant. This is also the significance of why Adiyogi is depicted with a cobra around his neck.

Ghost Troubles

Though most claims about ghost hearing and seeing and the ill effects that they can cause are largely psychological projections of individual people, there is a reality beyond the physical body.

Most disembodied beings are incapable of holding any intentions of their own. So they cannot harm a person. However, you may get harmed because of them. They cannot kill you by direct action, but it is mostly by possessing someone or by just creating certain fearful situations that they can be fatal. When one is possessed by such beings, usually death will happen soon, because they will create a situation where the person will walk into a well or walk off a mountain, or something like that. This being will possess everything, your intelligence, emotions, and your body. One part of you may still be struggling but they can just walk off the mountain and fall straight down. It is not their body, it does not hurt them, but you die in the process. It is like when someone else drives your car; they don't care. They bang it through everything and go.

It is not that they can do this to anyone they wish. There needs to be some sense of vulnerability in that person. If a person is well established, all these things will not have any power over them. If a person is a meditator, if some quality of meditativeness has arisen in them, then they cannot be possessed by anything. It is not possible, but these beings may create terror in you by just appearing in very distorted forms. Let us say, you walk outside and you see a distorted being. It need not do anything. If it just stands there, it is enough. If someone is standing there, carrying his own head in his hands, it is enough to freak you out, isn't it? If you are very balanced, you may just look at him and go. Then there is nothing he can do. A headless person should be the easiest to manage! But if you are the kind to get frightened, then, by appearing here and there, it can kill a person psychologically. Just fear or terror can kill.

Disembodied beings cannot even see you as a physical being. They see you as an energy form. You may have heard that someone was possessed or tormented by some other being. Maybe you have even witnessed situations like that. This usually happens only if there is some kind of relationship to the energy. They could be of the same blood and the same karmic substance. In some way, those beings are drawn to this particular person who carries that kind of thing. Let us say, someone died in your family halfway through their Prarabdha Karma. If you happen to be wearing their clothes, unknowingly they will come at you. It is not that they are seeking you. It is just that these clothes carry, in some way, a part of their body and energy, so they tend to gravitate in that direction.

This is why, traditionally, it was said that when a person dies, you should never wear their rings. If someone with strong Prarabdha Karma has died and you wear their rings on your ring finger, it becomes very easy for that being to enter you. You become very accessible. They are not trying to torment you. They are not trying to do anything. They have no such intentions. They will just function according to their tendencies, which will be a torture for you in some way. Otherwise, the situation of some disembodied being coming and tormenting you or even becoming visible to you does not arise.

If you have raised yourself to that level of awareness where you can feel these beings, you will have no problem with them. So there is no need for you to do anything to protect yourself, unless you are involved in some kind of work which involves these beings and you are trying to draw them and do certain things with them. Only then, the question of protecting yourself arises. Otherwise, you don't have to bother about it. If you become meditative, there is nothing that they can do to you. In fact, they become good company. If you are not, you can wear the Rudraksha* or a Linga Bhairavi pendant on your body. These are some simple things that can protect you.

One of the things not to do is to wear metal rings on your thumb. Unknowingly, these days, particularly all these New Age people have started to wear rings on their thumbs. This is a recent phenomenon. I don't know how they got inspired to do it, or if it is just by chance and they are just fixing things upon wherever they can fix anything. Nowhere, in no culture, did people wear rings on their thumbs. If

---

* Sacred beads worn by spiritual seekers in India.

you wear a ring on the thumb, you will attract certain forces which you may not be able to handle. These forces that will be drawn toward you need not necessarily be pleasant. They are beyond your understanding and capability to handle, so they could easily bring illness, accidents, or just a severe disturbance to one's life. So no metal should be worn on the thumb. Never ever. Only those actively engaged in sorcery or black arts wear metal on their thumbs.

Ghost Solutions

Disembodied beings can be trapped. A tantrik, or one who is well-accomplished in the occult sciences, can do this. It is like how even a great sage like Sadhguru Sri Brahma was put behind bars during the British era by an immature social system. Similarly, on a different level, you can trap these beings too. If I have a being with me who does not have a body and who does not need transport to go from here to there, can you imagine how many things I can get done through them? But I will never use them in any way. My only interest is in their emancipation; my involvement with them is only on that level. But there are people who use them. They will put the disembodied being into some person out of whom they want to extract something. Now that person will do whatever they want.

Trapping anything has its limitations also. You cannot keep something trapped forever. At least when the occult person dies, the being is going to be released. But for most people who are into such occult practices, their power does not last until their death; it goes before that. At some point, they lose their hold on it. When that happens, these things depart by themselves. Generally, these things will not hover around where that kind of a person is. They can easily sense it. An unaware or ignorant being may get easily trapped, but those who are a little aware will not get trapped so easily. They know what's what. They can feel the energy around them and are very cautious.

It is a very negative karma to trap and use such beings, because these beings are, in a way, very helpless creatures. It is as treacherous as molesting a child. Moreover, it can backfire on you at any moment. But, usually, such people have their own protection systems. They take care of themselves in a certain way and do it. This is not something that a spiritual person will ever do. But there are people who find a lot of pleasure in terrorizing someone. It can become a means to wealth for them. However, usually people who use such beings die a very horrible death; it catches up with them over time.

Do disembodied beings need help? Can they be dissolved? Yes. The difference between embodied beings and disembodied beings is just this: When you are embodied, you have more discretion. As you become more aware, you gain more discretion. When your awareness diminishes, you have less discretion. Once you are embodied and are here as a human being, you can either evolve or regress. Both are possible for you. That is the beauty of having an intellect which can discriminate and choose. As a human being, if you don't make use of your awareness and discretion, if you waste human life, your goose is cooked! However, these disembodied beings can exist only in the level of awareness in which they left. They cannot gain or lose awareness. They are in a kind of a limbo. It is a stagnant state—like a lightbulb, it has a certain lifespan, after which it will burn out. The bulb cannot choose how long to burn or when to go out. It burns for so many hours and then it goes out. These beings are just like that. They can neither evolve nor regress. What you have, you just experience, that is all. So even the disembodied beings who are a little aware can do with some help to progress.

The only reason why they are able to retain their form as a separate entity from the rest of the Existence is because there is a karmic structure. The physical body has been shed, but the karmic body is still intact. Only because the karmic body is intact is there a form and an individuality about it. They too have individual likes, dislikes, compulsions, and desires. But those disembodied beings that we call celestial beings longed for something higher and they got there. But they too can do with some help. It is like this: Someone longed to be a rich person and they became rich. But only the rich person knows his struggles, his problems. The poor man on the street never understands that a man who is driving a Mercedes could also be struggling, but the rich person has his own problems and he knows his riches are not getting him anywhere. They are not adding to his happiness. Now it is easier for him to understand the need to turn inward. It is a similar case with these celestial beings.

Now, in terms of dissolving that being, what we do is just break the karma. How do you break someone's karma? Karma is stored on the level of your mind, physical body, sensations, and energy. Once someone has shed their physical body, sensations don't exist. The mind is there, but it has lost its logical nature. So, fundamentally, for a disembodied being, the karma is in the energy body. In ancient times, courtesans used to wear elaborate jewelry. With that, they played an elaborate game with the men who came to them. Their whole body would be covered with jewelry. The man would come to this woman, full of desire, but he would be unable to get this jewelry off. It would take hours to get it off. Whichever way he would try, it would not come off. But the woman would know the trick. There was just one pin, and when she had teased him sufficiently she would just pull that pin and all the jewelry would just fall off.

Both the mental and energy bodies are like this. All your karma is held by certain pins. These pins are in certain points of your body. In a way, we can say they are chakras. Not necessarily only the seven chakras; there are other points too. So all we do is pull those plugs and the karmic body just collapses. All kinds of jokers are talking about activating chakras and doing irresponsible things with them. That is very dangerous. If you meddle with these things unknowingly, it can be disastrous. The chakras are like pins. If I just pull them, I can release you right now, but you will not retain your physical body. You will be liberated, but you will be dead as far as the world is concerned.

The same can be done for disembodied beings also. All beings seek dissolution, whether they are aware of it or not. Out of their limitations, fears, and misunderstandings, they may think they are not seeking it, but every being seeks dissolution. Always. If your body would not fall on our hands, it would be so easy to dissolve you. That is why a Guru always waits until your body becomes ripe enough. When the moment of death comes naturally, he will interfere and do what he has to do. Maybe he will make you leave a few days earlier, but he will pull the pin and dissolve you completely.

Dissolving Frozen Beings

There have been many disembodied beings that I have come across and interacted with. One peculiar situation was with a Native American being. Native Americans are always portrayed as very proud, fit, and strong people. They were good warriors, had great pride in their culture, and were very straight. He would fight a battle with you today, and tomorrow, if you so much as called him a brother, he would be willing to give his life for you. That is how they were. For them, killing and dying in battle was an honor. They never knew that someone could come and usurp their land or take it away. They just did not understand. They saw the Earth as a live force that sustained them. This is one of the few cultures in the world that did not look up when you said "God." They looked to the Earth as the force that created and nurtured them.

If you know American history, just south of Tennessee there is this trail called the "Trail of Tears," because in the mid-nineteenth century whole tribal nations were forcibly moved westward to free up land for European settlers. So entire tribes walked. Their weapons were taken away, because with weapons they could be dangerous. Without weapons, they could not hunt for food, so they starved and walked. The old and feeble died. The Native American way was such that if they buried their dead somewhere, they had to take care of that place. Now, because they were traveling, they could not bury their dead. So they carried their dead. The bodies rotted and fell apart, and they cried and cried and they walked on. By the time they reached their destinations, nearly 70 percent of them were dead. So this is called the Trail of Tears.

These were very earthy people—they have a certain Earth sense. For them, their religion, their occult, their practices, were all about the Earth. They have a very deep connection with the Earth. When these people suffer, they leave puddles of suffering all over the place, and it stays. A few years ago, when I happened to be walking in a certain part of the Appalachian Mountains in Tennessee, I saw a man standing still, frozen in a certain position of despair and shame. I saw that he was just standing there in the full regalia of the ancient native tribes, completely frozen—frozen in time. Whenever I see someone in extreme movement or when they are intensely still, I put myself into it because both of these situations are possibilities for me to do something. People in extreme movement, they are a possibility. People who are utterly still, they too are a possibility. I cannot keep myself away from these two kinds of people. The in-between, medium movement does not mean much.

So then I saw that for more than two hundred years, this man was standing there frozen. I saw that the situation behind this was that this person had the responsibility and the privilege of protecting his elder brother, who was a certain kind of a leader or chief of the community. He was like a right-hand man, protecting him in every way. Now, in that tradition, a "brother" need not necessarily mean that he was born from the same father or mother. You can take up brothers in the same way that you take up friends. This man held this elder brother in great esteem and he deemed it a great privilege to walk by his side and protect him.

A situation happened where he had set up a meeting for the chief with some military people, the white men. Somehow, this chief was deceived and killed by the white men. This man felt so responsible that he just stood there in absolute despair, failure, distress, and shame. Such extreme emotions were within him that he had been just standing there for a few centuries. When I saw him, he was still standing right there. Not in a physical body—obviously, the earth fell back to the Earth—but the rest of him stood there, just as he had been in that moment. So I thought it was time he moved on. Too much time in shame, too much time in defeat, is not good. I helped him to move on from that situation.

This is a poem I wrote just after that incident.

AMERICA

The brooding darkness of these woods
Fed upon the native blood
In the twisted tangle of the fallen wood
The spirit of the fallen Indian stood
O brothers your identity a mistake
Those who oceans crossed did make
The greed for gold and land
Laid waste the spirit of wisdom and grace
The children of those, who by murder did take
Are taintless of their forefathers' mistake
But those who lived, fed upon the milk of courage and pride

> *Stand as spirits of defeat and shame*
> *O the murdered and the murderous*
> *Embrace me, let me set your spirits to rest*

Probably that moment—the encounter with this being—is the most painful moment of my life. And it was then that I started noticing how there is such a deep sense of pain in many parts of that region, which will play out in human lives whether we are conscious of it or not. If a rock can suffer, a human being for sure will not be spared. Untold suffering will simply happen without any reason. When there are puddles of pain like this imprinted in the Earth upon which you live, you will never know what true wellbeing is in your life. You may build a big house, you may carry a shotgun and shoot whatever you like,* but you will not know a moment of rest in your life. When the Earth that you walk upon is in such a state, if you don't know how to take care of the material which makes you, you will never know even one moment of wellbeing in your life.

There was another situation that lingered for a long time. During the Dhyanalinga consecration, there was a disembodied woman who used to frequent the roof of my house. Before the consecration, we had done many things with such beings and dissolved them, but this particular one hung around for more than a year and a half, maybe two. After the consecration, my body was in a certain state of instability and I did not want to deal with her. Such beings have no sense of judgment. They just have a longing. It is like how someone who is in a deep state of desire has no judgment about life. Someone wants to drink, someone wants to rape, that is all. It is not because they are good or bad that they do it. They have no judgment about life, they have only longings. According to their

---

* Referring to the gun culture in those areas.

karma, they have certain *vasana*s, or tendencies, and they simply go by that.

There are other kinds of creatures, which have gone totally out of shape. They have not been able to retain their human form. They have become subtle. But this was a woman who had retained a heightened sense of femininity in her form. No woman in the world would be like that. She was extremely beautiful and in a much larger proportion than normal. She also created an illusion of wearing beautiful dresses and presenting herself well. Her vasana was femininity, which was always in counter to masculinity. So if you tried to meddle with her, naturally she would come as a woman. She would not know any other way to approach. This could have led to so many unnecessary situations, but she would not do anything on her own. If I had invited her into the shrine in the house to dissolve her, in a moment it would have been over.

However, as I have mentioned earlier, in those days my body was in a state of fragility and instability after the consecration, so I did not want to risk it with her. In the night, she would be walking in the inner corridor of my house, her anklets making the sound: *jing, jing, jing, jing.* It was not just me who heard her. Whoever stayed in the house would hear her walking throughout the night. If you opened the door and came into the corridor, she would be sitting up on the roof with a forlorn look on her face. She sat up there for almost two years. She would not enter the shrine. She did not dare to, but she kept walking and waiting. I did not do anything with her. I just left her there. There was a bit of concern because my daughter was eight years old then and even she heard the anklet sounds. These kinds of disembodied beings can harm female children, so I had to take precautionary measures for the girl's room. However, the woman never showed any signs of interest or violence at any time—just forlornness.

I did not try to ward her off because she was so forlorn and longing, seeking something. Once my body became more stable, I decided to dissolve her. Since her body had become so subtle, it was much easier to pull her pins than those of embodied human beings. I wanted her to leave in a very conducive atmosphere and did not want her to get into a state of fear or disturbance. So I just brought her inside and asked her to bow down to the shrine. When she did, I just pulled the plug and dissolved her. It was finished. She is no more.

Dissolving people in their disembodied state is a much easier thing to do if the necessary conditions are in place. For example, if all the women on the planet decided that for the next year there shall be no conception on the planet, then all those beings whose time has matured and who need a womb would be floating around in a limbo. Their unconscious desire would be to find a womb, but there would be none available—this would be an ideal situation for me to crack them before they find one more cycle. When they have just died and are floating around, you cannot fix them because they are too unconscious. But when their Prarabdha Karma is compelling them to find a womb, and none of the women are cooperating, it is an ideal situation for dissolving them.

There are so many young women with us who have not gotten pregnant and they will not get pregnant, because they have chosen to live such a life of intense involvement that their biological urges have become insignificant. But if all the women on the planet decide not to get pregnant for the next year, that would mean there would be at least 130 million beings waiting for a womb.

It is easy to do this with those who have bodies also, but until the final moment comes people will not give up their personality. It once happened: Matilda and Agatha were sisters. For thirty-seven years they had not spoken to each other because of a feud. Then one day Matilda became seriously ill. So she wrote a note to her sister. It started, *Agatha*—not *Dear Agatha*, because she was still angry—*Now that I am dying, I forgive you for all the nasty things you have done to me. Matilda.* Then she thought for some time and added: *PS: In case I recover, everything stands the way it is right now.* When death knocks on your door, your life will be focused and naturally you turn inward, because the outward is of no use anymore. When people are approaching death, their personalities drop and the pretensions that they carry on with the external will become unimportant.

NIRMANAKAYA

In spiritual circles there have always been talks about yogis who lived on the planet long ago but now make rare appearances by materializing and dematerializing their bodies at will. These days there is a lot of interest in people being able to materialize and dematerialize at will because there is too much talk about Babaji[*] everywhere. The popular stories making the rounds about him in India are that there is one man who lives forever and appears at will, again and again. It is not so. It has become fanciful for people to talk about such things because people like legends. They don't like the living because with legends you have the freedom to twist and turn them or blow them out of proportion or whatever. If you exaggerate something about me, for example, I will knock you on your head and tell you that it isn't so.

Some confusion regarding this is because there are yogis who are *nirmanakaya*s. *Nirman* means "to create," *kaya* means "a body." It is very rare that this would happen, but there have been some beings who have done that. These yogis are of the highest caliber and are able to materialize their body at will. Essentially, they build a conscious energy body, which is all made by them but is not for serving

---

[*] Mahavatar Babaji was a legendary Indian spiritual guru, believed to have lived in the second century AD.

the physiological purposes of the physical body. You know, at least 20 percent of your energy body is serving physiological functions. So these yogis create a large energy body which has no physiological association but is just stationed in the physiology. So he has two energy bodies—one that he was born with and another to transmit what he wants to transmit, which is of another dimension. He cannot transmit without the second one. Both are the same as far as other people's perception is concerned. Without this kind of an arrangement, with just regular physiology, it is impossible to run a program like Samyama, for example. It cannot withstand the sheer intensity and complexity of what is being done there. It will die right there.

Now, even after the physical body is dead, the subtle body is preserved and he makes it visible now and then. It need not necessarily be full flesh and bone, it just becomes visible. That is all. Usually, these are yogis who have taken on this role where they will reappear once in so many years. That does not mean they are living somewhere. They keep the subtler aspect of the body intact, but the physical body is gone. They re-create it now and then. They are not reborn, nor is this forever.

When you are born through a womb, you too are creating a body. Your own energy is doing it. You take nutrients from your mother, but you create the body. It is not the mother who is creating it. After you are born, you are still creating this body, aren't you? You are creating it in the same way—taking nutrients through food, through the air that you breathe, the water that you drink. Before you are born, that mechanism is not established yet. So you use the mother's mechanisms of eating, drinking, and breathing to structure the body, but it is your own energies which are doing it. Now, one can acquire the capability to create a body without the help of a mother's womb. You can create it by yourself. It need not be a small body. The small body is created because only that can fit in a mother's womb. But when you sit and create it, you can create an average-sized body or one that is twenty feet tall. Generally, people choose to create their youthful form.

So, these nirmanakayas are in subtle states and use elaborate processes. They have chosen to be in that state. They live in a very minimal way. They choose to be in that state, either out of their compassion or because they have been ordained by their Masters, who told them, "Don't worry about your mukti, just do this." Once in a while, they may create a gross body to come back and do certain things. They can do only a minimal amount of work, because each time they create their bodies they have a certain span and a limitation on activity. Most of the time, it is just an appearance that they can manage. The period of time in which they do this may be very long in normal human terms. It could be a couple of thousand years to even ten thousand years, but even that has a certain span to it. Eventually, they will dissolve completely.

Most of the time, they do this because they want to protect their lineage. They want to appear, so that minute corrections can be made in their lineage. They cannot do much with the general population. Now, for example, Isha is a certain type of Yoga; it is a lineage. Because people can go off track over time, some distortions will creep in. Now, I will not do such things, so you don't have to fear that I may come back again. I will not. But let us say, we want to make sure that every hundred years corrections happen. So every hundred years I could reappear and make some corrections and go back. There is a very short period for which you can appear and do such things.

You must know, not everyone who creates a nirmanakaya uses it the same way with the world. Not everyone uses it to make it appear and disappear in the world. It is like you have a great car, but how you use it is up to you. You may want to go to the office in it or race it or just drive it for fun—it is left to you. It is your vehicle.

Even if you did not want to do anything with it, you could still own one. Maybe there are collectors who just keep the car parked in their garage! It is similar for nirmanakayas. It is very rare that these things happen, but there have been some beings who have done things like that. Without them, I would not be so knowledgeable. But the phenomenon has been too exaggerated and presented in many distorted ways.

Downloading Beings

About thirty-five thousand years ago, there was a yogi called Sunira. This yogi floated a certain being. The idea was to create an ideal being who can transform the whole world in one shot. This being has been around for quite some time. Many other yogis have put their inputs into this being. Even Gautama the Buddha talks about this, and he also has put his inputs into this. Krishna himself did something about this being. Gautama predicted that somewhere between twenty-five hundred and three thousand years from his time, this being will mature and find a body in the world and he will be the ultimate teacher in the Creation.

We were not going for anything like that. It is just that there are so many exalted beings who are constantly after us to do something for them. For a time, we even accommodated a few of them in our own body. At one point, when we were in certain types of sadhana and certain states, without our permission some of these beings got into us and stayed with us for a period of time. We carried them for quite some time, and physically it was not easy, because they were so desperate to find expression in some way. At that time, there were periods when it was absolutely confusing for people who lived around us. There were many times when this would just drive Vijji to insanity because we would be just sitting in a chair and when she looked elsewhere and turned back, we would have become totally someone else. She would be terrified—terrified and petrified! We allowed those things for a certain time because we were working on the consecration of the Dhyanalinga.

So for some time we thought about downloading a few of these beings. These are beings who are highly evolved and are reluctant to take on a new body. They have that much choice—they cannot be compulsively drawn into a womb. They have become aware enough where it is a question of choice, so they are looking for a suitable vehicle through which they can fulfill the final phase of their lives. So if you make your body available—that is, only if you have done sufficient work and preparation and are absolutely willing—they can be downloaded into your body. It will need lots of preparation and sadhana to make people receptive enough for something like that. They must be strong enough but not too strong. They must be vulnerable enough but not too vulnerable. It is a different level of sadhana altogether.

If one has to put that being in the same body as another being, that person also must be of the same quality. Otherwise, they will be bad company for them! They are choosy—so choosy that they find no worthwhile womb in the world to get into. When they are that choosy, you are going to have a hard time with them, aren't you? Living with such a person is difficult. So what happens to you, where do you go? You don't go anywhere. You cease to exist. Would you call this a takeover? No, this is obliteration. I could use a more positive word—mukti. This is called Moksha. Call it Nirvana, if you want to use negative terminology.

If such things are done, the existing being has to work to a certain point of willingness, where the life process could be untied completely and one can be unplugged so that this being is over for good. Now, if the physical body is still intact, if it is kept in a certain space and if the other being has been wooed close enough, they could be put into it. It is a complex process, and one will not be successful every time with something like that. It is much more complex than people coming out of spaceships and doing some fix job and going back inside. I would say this is much more complex because keeping the body in a live condition but evacuating a person can be very difficult. Just getting people out of a rented home—getting a tenant out of the house is so difficult. So getting a person out of their body when the body is still fit and well is not that simple at all. It takes a lot of wooing. You can woo a man out of many things, but trying to woo him out of his body is the most difficult thing to do. But with the necessary preparation, it can be done. We are talking about getting a life to evacuate its physical structure without damaging it, so that it is still in good form to stage life.

I think we live in a society which is too logical and too immature for other aspects of life. So we are trying to do what makes the most sense to them—planting trees, running hospitals, schools. People are even beginning to call me a "tree planter"! This downloading is not just for entertainment. It will be a phenomenal boon to society. But after having been here for this long, if we could not produce sufficient beings here of such a level of evolution, then we have to import them from somewhere. I hope such a need will not come to us; we are doing good work. The work here is very intense and there are lots of dynamic and static volcano-like people with us. When all this is there, I am hoping we should not have any need for importing beings. So let us work with the people who have already slipped out of the womb. All of you are here! It does not matter how you came, let us see what we can do with you.

CHAPTER 11

The Riddle of Reincarnation

> Right now, most people are not even able to handle what is happening in this life, so why do they want to dig into their previous lives? They don't know how to handle the thoughts, emotions, and relationships of this life. How will they handle the thoughts, emotions, and relationships of many lives?

Taking on a New Body

Immediately after conception, the physical body slowly starts developing within a woman's womb. But it is only like a nest. In Nature, there are some birds who build the nests, but some other birds come and lay their eggs in them and make a life there. This is like that. Two people came together and started creating a body. Someone else who is ripe for that and is looking for a body comes and occupies it. Before that, the fetus was not a being, not because of the smallness of the body but because it was not occupied. It was just a bundle of cells. After this, the other life occupies the womb and this bundle of cells becomes a being. Maybe not yet a full person, but in many ways a person.

Generally, the physical body in the womb is ready to be occupied after forty days. Most of the time, I would say 99.9 percent of the time, life enters the womb and takes on a physical body between forty to forty-eight days after conception. Sometimes, in rare cases, it may take a little longer. Certain beings who have become conscious beyond a certain point wait for the body to grow a little more in the womb. But they will not let any other life enter that womb either. When such things happen, it is very easy to know. I will not go into the details, because then people will start looking at every pregnant woman and check to see if she has an aware child or an unaware child!

During pregnancy, there are many signs which clearly indicate whether life has entered the womb or not. A mother can easily feel this if we train her a little bit. If life has not entered the womb after forty-eight days of conception, then something a little extraordinary is going to happen with that child, for sure. There is no question about it. You must have heard that someone saw Gautama's mother and said, "You are going to deliver a phenomenal being." Such things can be foretold simply because someone may notice that life has not entered the womb after forty-eight days of conception but a little later than that. That is the sign of a phenomenal being arriving. It is because of certain qualities that it guards the womb but does not enter it. It will wait for the body to develop a little more and only then enter.

This sort of situation can leave a mother in a certain state of distress or a fundamental level of discomfort. This is not a physical lack of comfort but a sort of existential anxiety. Between forty-five and sixty-five days into the pregnancy, if you notice tears welling up for no particular reason beyond normal maternal emotions or see flashes of bright-blue color off and on or dream of snakes in a very benign way, this means a sage or a sorcerer or a great conqueror is on the way. When such signs are noticed, various processes to transform the yet-to-be-born are done. A sage or sorcerer or conqueror means a certain level of competence or capability. The difference is only one of intent. Toward what purpose one will use their competence makes all the difference. This is why many efforts are made to establish an all-inclusive intent the moment pregnancy has occurred, as it is definitely our responsibility as to what sort of life we bring into the world and what level of consciousness we release when that life departs this world.

Only after this, somewhere between eighty-four and ninety days, the engagement with the body for this life truly begins. Till then the life is just foraging; it checks if this womb is the right place for it. This is not a conscious choice. It is an unconscious choice. Tendency-wise, it is checking out the womb to see if it matches it. Traditionally, we call these tendencies vasanas. Depending upon your vasana, you look for an appropriate body. During this time, depending on how conscious the being is, there is a little bit of choice as to what kind of body he or she chooses.

When I say "choice," it is not like you go into a shop and buy this shirt or that. There is a karmic choice. There is a natural tendency for the person to go in a certain direction, toward a certain womb, toward a certain body. Even when you are within the physical body, you have a natural tendency to seek out certain people, because that is how your karmas are. Similarly, when you don't have a physical body, you do the same. It is much more unconscious, but still the karmic substance that you carry with you seeks out a certain type of body.

It is just like this: If we let a whole group of people into a hall for the first time, everyone settles down in their own place. The choice is not entirely random. It is based on your karma to a large extent. You may have the karma of back pain; then you will settle down near the wall. You may have the karma of always hiding and looking. You want to be there in the situation, but you don't want to be visible. So you will find a big person and sit behind him. Your karma may be that you always want to be in the front row, so you just come and sit there. It may be unconscious, but that is how you do it. It is your karma that makes you settle down in a place. Similarly, there are millions of wombs and millions of beings looking for a body. They will settle down according to their attributes and tendencies.

Once it has found that body, it is the vibrancy of the prana of that being which enhances the quality of the physical body. From this point onward, it is not just the mother who is making the baby. This is why there are millions of instances where probably the mother is weak, undernourished, on the street, and yet she delivers a very healthy baby. But there may be someone else who is in a family where everything is taken care of and everyone is very well-fed, but the mother may give birth to a very fragile child. This is the pranic substance, the pranic vibrancy of the being acting upon that particular body. Accordingly, the new life takes a new physical body.

The chakras also start developing gradually in the womb. Somewhere around the twelfth week, only one chakra is formed, which is the Muladhara Chakra. Within the first twenty-eight to thirty weeks, depending upon the developmental quality of the fetus, the first five chakras up to Vishuddhi Chakra are fully established. The other two—Agna Chakra and Sahasrara Chakra—do not establish to the same extent in every human being. I would say, in nearly 30 to 35 percent of newborn infants, the Agna Chakra may not be developed. If you observe the way their eyeballs move, you will know whether an infant's Agna Chakra is established or not. This is why the moment a child is born, the first thing they do in this culture after washing the baby is to put a little bit of *vibhuti* between the eyebrows. In Tamil Nadu, they make a large coin-sized spot by applying the resin of a particular tree in between the eyebrows. As it dries, this resin draws the skin around it and creates a strong sensation toward the spot in the middle of the eyebrows. This is just in case the Agna Chakra is not yet developed; we want the child to start focusing in that direction.

Traditionally, by just looking at the eyeball movement, people could say if the infant would become a sage. A sage need not necessarily mean someone who will go and sit in the jungle or a cave. A sage or a seer is someone who sees things that others do not see. It could also be a visionary business person or a visionary leader—someone who sees things more clearly than others. This does not mean that those whose Agna Chakra is not developed at birth cannot develop it in their lifetime—they can if they work on it. But they will need to do a little more work than others.

The Sahasrara Chakra generally is not developed for most at the time of birth. That slowly evolves thereafter. As mentioned before, on the top of the head there is a spot known as brahmarandhra. *Randhra* is a Sanskrit word; it means a passage, like a small hole or a tunnel. This is the space in the body through which life descends into the fetus. When a child is born, there is a tender spot where the bone does not form until the child grows to a certain age. This is because the life process has the awareness to keep its options open about whether this body is capable of sustaining it or not. So it keeps that trapdoor open for a certain period, so that just in case it finds the body unsuitable for its existence, it can leave. It does not want to leave from any other passage in the body; it wants to leave the way it came, just as a good guest always arrives through the front door and goes out of the front door. Even when you leave one day, if you leave consciously through whichever part of the body, it is fine. But if you can leave through the brahmarandhra, it is the best way to leave.

THE ARITHMETIC OF REINCARNATION

One of the first questions people have about reincarnation is that if the world population is increasing, are more animals becoming human? Is this the reason that animal populations in the world have declined in the recent past? Is the population of the world—animal and human put together—a fixed number? These questions come from the ignorance of believing and thinking of Existence numerically. When you talk about life energy, it is not in terms of numbers. You cannot think in terms of, "Okay, only one person died, but how are ten people born today?" It is not in terms of numbers like that. Numbers are only for bodies. Life does not happen in numbers. When you talk about the unbounded, there is no such arithmetic.

When you are talking of life, you are probably thinking there is a being. But what if there is no being? That is why Gautama went on saying you are *anatma*. This was total sacrilege for the Hindus. He said this because if it is atma, there could be any number of them. But if it is anatma, how many can there be? How many non-beings can you create? How many "emptinesses" can you create? The question now sounds absurd. You always think in terms of numbers because it comes from the dimension of your experience, which is very limited.

In reality, if you go on producing bodies, they will get occupied anyway. Life will happen. So where will the karma come from for them? Where is the karmic substance for them? There is plenty of this substance in the Existence. In reality, if you want, this person who is sitting here right now as one person can take on a million bodies with the same karmic content that he or she has now. It is possible. There are many situations where yogis have taken up two bodies. With the same karmic substance, they took on two bodies. So the question about numbers is not a relevant question. It is a logical, mathematical, arithmetic question. But life does not happen like that.

Life is just one. Numbers are only in your mind. There is no such thing in Existence. Let us say, there is a pond full of water and you dip your bucket and take out water in it. Can you say that I have taken this particular water? It is just some water. Once again if you dip the bucket into the pond, you will get some more water. But there is no such thing as this water or that water. It is similar with life. The fundamental life force is not in terms of numbers. Just one is enough. One can populate the whole population. What we are referring to as the being is beyond the physical. Once there is no physical, there is no boundary. For that which has no boundary, there is no one or two or ten or million. So that is not the way to think at all.

Science has been successful in cloning plant life for several decades now. It has, in recent years, been able to clone animals like sheep and dogs. Of late, multiple streams of research are afoot to clone the human being as well and the widespread belief is that it is just a matter of time before they succeed. How does cloning relate to the theory of karma? Where will the software for the cloned life come from?

You must understand that by cloning, all that you are doing is just producing a human body. If it is hospitable enough, if all the ingredients are there, life will occupy it. It does not matter how you produced it. But when there are so many women who are perfectly able to bear children, I don't see why billions of dollars are being wasted to do it in a laboratory. When there is a pleasurable way of creating children, you don't have to make it so obscene and ugly with all those test tubes and other things from which the baby comes out. Above all, a woman does not just give body to the child; she molds the child when it is in her womb. Depending on how she is during the pregnancy, a whole lot of things develop for the child when it is still in the womb. Elaborate care used to be taken in this country about this, once a woman conceived. Every step of what she should do, what she should not do, how she should do it, whose face she should see, whose face she should not see—all this was regulated because everything has an influence upon the unborn child. This is because she is not only giving it a body but also molding the consciousness of the person who is to be born. You must understand that you are manufacturing the next generation of people. How the world will be tomorrow is determined right now in your body. It is a tremendous responsibility. It needs to be handled that way.

Now, just because with technology we know how to do a few fanciful things with the outside world, we don't have to do everything we can do. This is very juvenile. This is the source of destruction on this planet. As a race, we humans have not matured mentally. We must be able to make a decision as to what to do and what not to do based on what is needed, not on what we can do.

Now, is it possible that a woman can prepare herself for the possibility of a being with a higher consciousness coming to her as a child? Definitely. But if a woman has such aspirations, it is best that she works upon herself well before the pregnancy happens, because during the pregnancy, usually, her situation becomes such that she is unable to attend to these subtleties. So, at that time, her being able to maintain a certain level of consciousness could be rare, but not impossible. There are certain other things that can be done, but she may not be able to do them by herself. If she seeks assistance from the right kind of source, it could be done for her. But in general, what she can do by herself is to become generally meditative. If she brings that quality into her before such a situation arises in her body, then the results will be good. To be meditative, to be very loving, could ensure a pleasant being. This is not necessarily so because there are various other aspects. But by and large, this will ensure a pleasant being.

Now, if you are thinking of producing an ideal being, yes, there are ways to do this. You can do things so that the best possible being will inhabit the small crucible of life that has begun to happen in your womb. For this, you have to go beyond the karmic substance or the karmic software that you carry within you and attract something that is of a different nature from who you are.

This would take a completely different kind of work. Generally, the mother will not be able to do it by herself and will need help from someone else who can set up the situation for her.

At one time, we thought we would roll out a whole set of processes that such people could undergo at the Dhyanalinga. Even otherwise, from the day of conception, if she remains in that kind of atmosphere every day, definitely she would attract a certain type of being. But that would make the Dhyanalinga purpose-specific. Otherwise, being in a consecrated atmosphere like that would attract a certain type of being.

If we do something more, we could also bring down those kinds of beings who are unwilling to come down and be reborn but are not fit enough to dissolve completely. These are beings who have transcended certain limitations in the disembodied state, where they are aware enough not to be driven by tendencies, yet are not free enough to burst the bubble and go. They have not attained their Ultimate Liberation but they have reached a certain point of freedom. Such beings can be brought down. There have also been situations where beings who don't belong to this realm have been brought down into human wombs. There are many conditions for this; if all those things are fulfilled, we can definitely ensure that certain kinds of beings are attracted.

Past-Life Recollection in Children

There have been many recorded instances of children having clearly recollected their past lives. The descriptions and details provided by these children have even been verified by researchers in the past few decades. But the phenomenon is even more widespread than what these studies suggest. I would say at least 70 to 80 percent of the children below three to six months of age remember their past life because the memory screens between lifetimes are not set up yet. Life is yet to decide how much to take on; it is still fluid. In that stage, it is the survival instinct which draws the child toward the mother. Otherwise, the child does not care a hoot who is who. If you observe them, you will see they will go with whoever is nice to them. It looks like he or she loves the mother. No, they do not care a hoot for anyone because their personality has not been established yet. Only the survival instinct is keeping them oriented toward the mother's breast. They know that they have to go there.

During this time, the memories of many lifetimes are playing within them in so many ways. Slowly, it consolidates. Breastfeeding is an important part of this. With breastfeeding, Nature is trying to establish the child's memory cycle that this is where your life is. If a scientific study is conducted, it is possible that they find a correlation between breastfeeding and past-life recollections in these infants. The screens may not be set up as rigidly for a child who is not breastfed as it is set up for a breastfed child. The screens may be a little more porous, and that could translate into unexplained levels of confusion in all matters of life.

In this culture, among royalty, particularly, they believed that when a child was born to a king, if he had to become a good king, he must be breastfed by three women. When the queen got pregnant, they would identify two other women who were in the same stage of pregnancy. When the prince was born, they would also ask those ladies to come and live in the palace. They would rotate the breastfeeding of the prince among the three of them. One reason was to ensure that he got the best nourishment, another was to confuse him of his origins. A king should not have any attachment, even toward his mother or father, because, otherwise, he will not make a good king. So they always said a king's son must be breastfed by three women.

People often ask me if a person will be born the same gender as in their previous life. It is not necessary. I have a very immediate experience of this in many different ways with quite a few people. There are people around me who are of a different gender now than what they were in an earlier life. What gender or form you take is determined by the type of longing that you create. This is determined by your tendencies. If someone's karmic tendency is extremely feminine, they will tend to become masculine in the body. If someone's tendency is extremely masculine, they will tend to become feminine in the body, because the meeting of the dualities has to happen. If the karmic tendencies are highly masculine, too masculine, and if it happens to find a masculine body, this will be a skewed person.

Exploring Past Lives

In the spiritual communities, these past-life connections are a big-time hallucination. I am sure even at the Yoga Center many people go about talking like this, "I was with Sadhguru in his past life and the life before that and before that," and so on. I keep saying that those who are here after their past life with me are failed candidates so that they do not carry that as a badge. You were there then and you missed the opportunity and wasted my life and effort; now you are again here to trouble me! This is not a good state to be in.

So will this knowledge of past lives not help me resolve the difficulties in my present relationships? Now, the only way you relate to anything from the past is through thoughts, emotions, experiences, and relationships. Whether it is in another body or this body, it does not matter—this is the way you remember. Let us say, you and I are constantly bickering about something right now. We can look back and see how in my past life you were bothering me, so now I am trying to bother you. Let us say, we found this out. What will we do? Probably we will extend the bickering to another life! Really! Suppose it sheds light on all the horrible things you did to me in my last life, will I become free from it, or will I become more resolved about bothering you in this life?

People say life is also complicated. What is it that is complicated? Life by itself is not complicated. Only if you want to push the world in a certain direction could it be a little complicated. But if you are not trying to push the world in any way, if you are just fine with whatever you are eating and drinking, where is it complicated? It is only your memory which complicates everything. Just see, there are people who are so stressed, distressed, and freaked out and everything. But let us say, they get Alzheimer's disease. Now you will see suddenly they become so simple and sweet. Life is just happening by itself.

Now, if three lifetimes or ten lifetimes of memory descend upon you, most probably the firmament of your mind will not be able to hold, it will crack up and collapse. Even with me, the level of memory that came to me almost threw me off completely. It is that hard to handle. It is not within the capacity of the mind to absorb that kind of experiential memory. If I did not have the necessary mental fortitude, it would have broken me. So unless you have prepared for it in a certain way, you handling it is out of the question. This is why we say sadhana, sadhana, and sadhana. Sadhana is not to download memories but to be able to hold the memory of this life at least in such a way that you can pick what you want and the rest of the time it does not touch you. Data is useful only when you are able to pick what you want. If it is all the time blowing in your face, how is it useful?

Right now, most people are not even able to handle what is happening in this life and the memories of this life, so why do they want to dig into their previous lives? Let us say, you realized that your neighbor's dog was your husband in your previous life, then I don't know whether you will go and kiss him or throw stones at him! Both ways, it is dangerous because he does not remember.

Moreover, by throwing stones at him, you will get into trouble with your neighbor. If you kiss him, you will get into trouble with the dog. So, both ways, it is not safe for you. If the past opens up, so many emotions of love, hate, resentment, and affection may happen.

When you are in a condition where you suffer even what happened ten years ago, if you remember everything that happened in the past ten lifetimes, it will drive you nuts! Why only the past ten lifetimes; if you remember everything just from this lifetime—your thoughts, emotions, experiences, what someone said when you were ten, what your friend did, what your teacher did—if all this plays in your head right now, you cannot live a normal life. If all the love, hate, resentment, affection from those lives pour into your present life, you will go insane.

Moreover, of these four things I just mentioned—love, hate, resentment, affection—you are counting two things—love and affection—as positive. Actually, all of them are negative, because all of them are happening compulsively. If I have a deep sense of resentment toward you—"I hate you, I hate you, I hate you"—you understand this is not good. But if I unnecessarily have affection toward you—"I love you, I love you, I love you"—this also is not good. Suppose we are just two people walking on the street. You don't know me, I don't know you, but I have enormous affection for you; would you like it? If I have a lot of resentment for you, you wouldn't care. "Okay, man, you burn with your resentment. What is my problem?" But if I have too much affection for you, you will not like it.

So it is not the question of affection or resentment. This love or hate is compulsive and that is the problem. This compulsive sense of love, affection, resentment, and hatred are all equally bothersome and equally entangling in nature. You should learn to respond consciously, to bring yourself to a level where your response is unbridled and seamless. You should be such that in any direction you can respond. You have no such thing as, "to this I can respond, to that I cannot respond." You can respond to anything. Until it becomes like that, the past is a problem and the future is a problem. Both should not open up. If they open up, it will only become troublesome. What you find in the past may look like some kind of explanation for what is happening right now. But it will only entangle you deeper in terms of moving toward mukti or your Liberation.

Let us understand this. This mukti that we are talking of is not an invention of the Hindus. Mukti is the aspiration of this creature. This creature wants to become the Creation. This is mukti. Instead of being a creature of the Creation, it wants to become Creation itself. It wants to merge. This is not a Hindu idea or an Indian idea. This is the way life is. We want life to progress with a very minimal number of impediments; in that context, both compulsive love and compulsive hate are problems.

There is another way to look at it. Instead of calling it past lives and present life, look at it as different compartments of memory. That is all they are. Only because it is in your memory is it coming out. It is not hanging out there in the sky. It is all there in the system. Suppose these compartments are breached and suddenly your Evolutionary Memory opened up—it would create havoc in your life. No need to go that far. Suppose you woke up in the morning and, let us say, the memory of the last three lifetimes opened up in you and it all became one. Right now, what happened ten years ago is in one compartment, what happened yesterday is in another compartment. So you have a short-term memory, long-term memory, and all this stuff. In normal life, what happened a lifetime ago is screened. Suppose the screen broke, and what happened a lifetime ago feels like it happened yesterday. Now, let us say, in your last life you were something else. Let us say, you were a woman then and now you are a man. Then when you wake up in the morning, you go to the wrong bathroom, to start with! Trouble, isn't it? Many things like this will open up and it will lead to huge levels of confusion and struggle within the human being because it is too much to handle.

What is the purpose of all this pursuit of past lives? The question is whether you want to find the cause of it, or you want to find a solution. All my lamentations are because you are looking for solutions in past lives when we are teaching you a simple process called Inner Engineering. The solution is in this. If you pay enough attention to it, it handles all of it. Let this one thing sink into you—just seeing that I am 100 percent, absolutely, absolutely responsible—it will handle your past, present, and future. Once your ability to respond is seamless, you will know how to respond to any situation, whatever may be the cause. In fact, both the past and the future will open up in your experience. Now, if you are in such a seamless state of response, even if the past opens up, even if ten lifetimes open up, it is no problem. Even if the future opens up, it is no problem. But if you are in a selective state of response or a discriminatory state of response, then if the past opens up, it will cause one kind of problem, and if the future opens up, another kind of problem.

I know a lot of absolutely bizarre things are going on in the world about exploring one's past lives. They are just ridiculous psychological exercises. If you really want to see something of the past, you must be able to raise yourself into very heightened levels of awareness where it will cut through the memory lines. Whatever you call "past life" is just unconscious layers of the mind in terms of memory. If you bring yourself to heightened levels of awareness, these unconscious layers of the mind, which are ruling you from within, could be broken down, could be dissolved.

We were doing something like this in Samyama. Let us say, you are sitting and meditating: After some time you are fully conscious but suddenly you find your body is beginning to slither around like a snake. You know it is happening, you want to stop it, but the body is just slithering like a snake. When you come out of meditation, you are perfectly normal. You sit for meditation, once again the body crawls. Then maybe it hops around like a bird, maybe it goes around like a dog or a tiger or something—it may take many forms. These days we have put a nail on its head largely; only once in a while someone breaks through and goes into such firewall breach. These things happen because we open up the Evolutionary Memory. It was all working out in the form of the body. Some of the people became conscious of this memory and we had to do things to take it from them. Suppose someone became conscious that they were a chimpanzee somewhere or a fox or a hyena; if this memory comes unknowingly, you will wake up in the morning and start making all kinds of noises! Can you deal with that?

Why this is happening is because, in the unconscious layers of the mind, there are so many dimensions which you are unable to access, but which are influencing everything that you do. So if you go through a process where, with heightened levels of awareness, you bring unconscious layers of the mind into conscious states—not in terms of memory but in terms of energy and experience—you can work these things out and leave yourself completely free in a big way within yourself. In that context, it is relevant, but remembering something memory-wise is not of any consequence. It will only complicate and mess up your life.

You will have the capability to handle it only if your ability to respond is non-discriminatory and seamless. If your response is selective, then you will only multiply the karma. Suppose you realize that ten lifetimes ago I was very dear to you, then you will respond to me in one way. Suppose you realize that lifetimes ago I was your enemy, you will start responding differently to me. You cannot just take it away, because your ability to respond is limited. Once your ability to respond is limited, your memory is a bother and the more you open up, the more troublesome it gets. Now, if you have no such things and you will respond as is necessary right now, then even if you remember that ten lifetimes ago you knew me, it will not matter, because you will be the same way anyway. Otherwise, you will only multiply your karma if the past opens up for you.

Baby Hitler

Sometimes people also ask me, "Hitler was such a horrible man, he was responsible for the horrors of World War II and the death of millions of people, what would he be reborn as? Would he be reborn as an animal? What would Gandhi be reborn as? Would he be someone rich, famous, and popular?" They want to use this reference to know how reincarnation works.

First of all, whoever said everyone has to reincarnate? Moreover, you may think you know a lot about their lives, but how the world knows them is not necessarily how they were within themselves. How they were within themselves existentially is what counts. Life does not care whether you were adored as a saint or despised as a tyrant. So what happens after is also not dependent on that.

In your society, a tyrant may be evil and a saint may be great, but existentially it could be the reverse. I am not saying it is so, but it is possible. It could be the reverse because we don't know how tortured they were within themselves. It is very much possible that a man who tortured everyone else lived well within himself, and a man who tried to do good to everyone tortured himself. But it shows how different life could be existentially from what you or the society perceives. Reincarnation does not depend upon that.

Now, is it possible that someone who is a human could be reborn as an animal? People have certain urges and desires. It is desire that becomes the karma. It is the volition, attitude toward life. Fundamentally, you can say it is desire. Right now, let us say, you have certain desires which are not fulfilled. Let us say, your desire was to collect a billion dollars. But you have neither the brains to earn it nor the courage or capability to rob a bank to get it. You are not made like that. So if you get ten dollars you will save five. You will starve yourself, you will go through all kinds of difficulties to save, save, and save. With this process of collecting, let us say, by the time you die, you have saved only a few million.

Now, there is a big urge within you to collect more, but you die before that with the same lust of wanting to collect. Your karma does not know what you want to collect, whether it is money or stones. What rubbish it wants to collect, it does not matter. It only knows it has to collect. It does not have the discriminatory power. It is almost like your genes. It is a subtler gene, not a physical gene. It knows only that you like to collect. So the next time, this gene may decide, "Oh! All my Master wants is to collect. Which will be the right form for me to collect? Maybe I will become an ant or maybe I will become a bee." You may become that, we don't know. You collect the honey, someone else eats it.

If a particular quality is very dominant in you, your karma will seek whatever kind of body and physical situation is best for you to fulfill that quality. Suppose your whole thing is to eat—you want to eat, eat, and eat. Suppose you die without eating, unfulfilled, thinking of food even on your deathbed. The next time, you may come back as someone's pet pig and be really well-fed. People think it is a punishment to come back as a pig. This is not a punishment for you. Nature is not thinking in terms of punishment or reward. Depending on your tendencies, whatever is unfulfilled within you, you get the kind of body that is best suited to fulfill those tendencies. It need not necessarily be an animal form; it may choose that kind of human form in that kind of situation and in that kind of surroundings where it can be fulfilled. But it could be any which way.

This is like a game of snakes and ladders. You go step-by-step, sometimes jumping, sometimes leaping, sometimes falling back. You climb one ladder, but as long as the snakes are there, it can swallow you and bring you back to square one. You climb up for a few days and again go back down. It just goes on. When you are on an active spiritual path, we give you a device with which you can strip off all the snakes. If you just take the responsibility, there will be no more snakes on your board. Then you cannot build any more karma; it is over.

The moment you focus your whole attention on yourself, you will see you are the source of everything that is happening here. The moment this awareness comes into you, you cannot build any more karma; it is finished. Now you have to handle only what is stored up. It is very simple. Otherwise, you will go on emptying from one side and filling from the other side. There is no end to it. So to maintain focus on your goal and create that longing which is beyond all these limitations is the best way to ensure that Nature does not know what to do with you.

When Nature does not know what to do with you, it is good for you because you can work your things out very effortlessly. When Nature knows what to do with you, you will get put in this chamber or that chamber—the male chamber or the female chamber or the pig chamber or the cockroach chamber or some other chamber. A body is just a chamber. So if you maintain that longing which is not for this or that, Nature will not know what to do with you. It cannot push you this way or that way. It cannot make a decision on you. It gives you an advantage. That is the significance of equanimity.

Couples for Lifetimes

A husband and wife spend most of their lives together. They probably share more things between them than in any other relationship. For most people, the relationship between the husband and the wife is one of the deepest human relationships. So if anything lasts beyond death and is carried over to the next phase of life, then people expect this one relationship to be the best qualified to do so. This is also, to some extent, the basis of the adage that marriages are made in heaven. But in reality, is this true? Do husband and wife come together in the next lifetime too?

These days, in the West, people are constantly on the lookout for who their soulmate is. They keep searching even after getting married several times! But in India, people want to know if they were married to their spouse in their previous life also. But what they are really asking is, "How did I ever marry you!" If such a question comes to you, then you must look at yourself as to what is happening with you. After many years of marriage if you are still wondering, "How did I ever marry you?" you really need to look not at previous lives but at the life that you are now living. I think this was promoted hugely by the Indian cinema of the 1970s and 1980s with all those songs about *"janam janam ka sathi"* (companion of many lifetimes) and all that. This is not so much a problem of today's generation. In today's movies, they are all thinking of relationships, their expiry date, and all that. If your pursuit of truth is guided by commercial cinema, then these things happen to you.

This belief or hope may have come about because somewhere, someone said that husband and wife come together for seven lifetimes. If I say this is true, probably most people will not want to get married at all! But it is not right to deny this possibility entirely.

Couples coming together again is possible if they were married in a certain way. If the person who was conducting the marriage married them in such a powerful way that they tied those two lives together in a union to lead to an ultimate union, then it is possible. But this is extremely rare.

Today, people want to know this because they want some special reason to hold on to. If the only way you can hold on to someone is by believing that you have been stuck together for many lifetimes, it is a horrible way to live. Don't create such horrors in your life. I am with you now because I want to be with you—this is a beautiful way to be with someone. Moreover, if you have been together for three lifetimes, maybe it is time to part! People keep putting me through these works all the time. They ask, "Sadhguru, was I with you in the last lifetime?" Whatever makes you think that if I had seen you in the last lifetime, I would ever come in front of you once again?

What happened yesterday is of no consequence, but now you are trying to create a consequence for what might have happened. This memory is crippling you. It is not allowing you to use your mind as an instrument of penetration, as an instrument to open up dimensions of life. If that is the only way you can relate to your husband or wife, what a pathetic way to relate to people! You should find value in the human being who is sitting in front of you for what he or she is now, not for what they were somewhere else.

One accomplishment of modern society is that we don't value you for who your father was; we value you for who you are. What you have made out of yourself now is important, not who your father was. This is the big shift we have made from a feudalistic way of living to modern-day societies. If you came to India fifty to a hundred years ago, no one would look at your face and ask who you were. They would only ask who your father was. That has significantly changed. A little chaotic we are, but it is still quite a significant step.

Now, asking what were you in your previous life is worse than asking who your father is. What you are right now, what you have made out of your life right now, is the most significant thing. So don't waste your time and life digging into the past. Unless needed for spiritual reasons or to perform a task that would not be possible without the involvement of certain people with past associations, this dimension should not be opened up at all. Most people are unable to handle the memories, thoughts, and emotions of one lifetime. So opening many will not bring well-being.

THE ONLY ENDURING RELATIONSHIP

In spiritual lore, it is often said that if you have a Guru in your life, then if you are born again, you will become the disciple of the same Guru. So, in general, if other relationships do not continue across lifetimes, how is this an exception to the rule?

First of all, you need to understand what a relationship is and why there are human relationships. Now, you may have formed various types of relationships in your life for different purposes. Some are for your emotional needs, some for physical needs, some for financial needs, some for social needs, some for psychological needs, some for comfort, etc. In so many ways, you have formed relationships. Whatever kind of relationship you form, whether it is emotional, psychological, social, financial, or physical, fundamentally it is concerned with the body. When the relationship is based in the body, when the body drops, the relationship just evaporates. That is the end of it.

Only if a relationship transcends the physical limitations is there then a possibility of this relationship extending beyond the limitations of the physical body. Such a relationship can extend beyond lifetimes or extend across lifetimes. Only when you in some way transcend the physical limitations can it extend across lifetimes. When I say "physical," I am referring to the mental structure also as physical and the emotional structure also as physical. There have been husbands, wives, and lovers who have come together again for lifetimes because their love was so strong that it transcended the foundation of a need-based relationship. There could be a few examples of other relationships going beyond the physical limitations, but all these are very rare. Generally, it is only the Master-disciple relationship which gets carried for lifetimes. All the other relationships come together for the convenience of the physical; once it is over, it just breaks apart.

Even if the disciple has no idea of the Master's being, the Master's business is only with the disciple's being. This relationship is always energy-based. It is not emotion-based, it is not mind-based, nor is it body-based. An energy-based relationship does not even realize whether the bodies have changed or not over lifetimes. It continues until the energy reaches dissolution. For the energy, there is no rebirth. It is only the body which is reborn. The energy just continues as one flow and accordingly carries the relationship.

There are many people here with us at Isha who were connected with us in the past. But not all of them are connected in the Master-disciple manner. Some are connected in some karmic way from close to four hundred years ago too. It is not only those who supported us but even those who persecuted us, who tormented us, who are also somehow mostly in Coimbatore today. All of them are not our meditators, but they are with us. It is like that. That is the way life functions.

Now, why do all these people end up in one place? Do you know why the breeze is blowing in a particular direction and not the other way? The whole momentum of the wind in the world is just this: It moves from high-pressure and high-density spots to low-pressure and low-density spots. During the day, when the land gets heated up, the density becomes low. Wherever the density is low, the wind rushes in there. Then it cools or sometimes even rains and then that becomes high-density and the wind moves backward. In Nature, wherever there is emptiness, everything rushes there.

This is so with karma also. When someone's karmic bag is empty, all those other bags of karma which have been one way or the other connected to that for so many lifetimes tend to move toward that direction, knowingly or unknowingly—mostly unknowingly—because for all of them there is a possibility now. When one bag empties, every bag that is connected has the opportunity to become empty. But unless there is some spiritual significance to these things, we do not pay attention to the past connections.

Most of those coming toward me are doing so because of their past karma from another lifetime, not by conscious choice. Many times, their present mindset and arrangements of life that they have made are in confrontation with their helpless longing to be here. Many, after they fulfill their karmic role, are bewildered as to why they are here. Those who have earned something of the beyond here in this life will continue; those who are here because of their old stock of food may, unfortunately, have to go. My commitment is only to fulfill the spiritual obligation but I cannot always fulfill the emotional and social aspects of these enduring relationships.

Life Beyond a Thousand Moons

People who die after the age of eighty-four years or, in other words, those who have witnessed more than 1,008 full moons, will die a death that is very different from other kinds of deaths. Even if such a person has lived a stupid life, even if they never looked up to the sky when they were alive, such a person will not be reborn. Once we were visiting one of our neighbors in the United States. We had gone unannounced, so when we entered the gate, the neighbor came out with a shotgun to see who had come. He was a very elderly man, and it was a little strange to see him come out with a shotgun. So I asked him, "Why do you bring a shotgun to check who has come? Do you have a lot of enemies?" He just shrugged and said, "No, all the buggers are dead." So if you just live long enough, you can even score over your enemies! This is like that.

When one crosses 1,008 full moons of time, which amounts to nearly eighty-two years of age, something wonderful starts happening within a person. Somewhere between eighty-two and eighty-six years of age, suddenly, a certain loosening happens within people who live that long. You will notice that many of them suddenly become very sweet. Their grumpiness is gone, they are not complaining, they are quite fine because the karmic grip on their life will loosen up. This process reaches a substantial level of maturity when one crosses eighty-four years of age. Organically, eighty-four years of age is related to the basic integrity of the elemental and pranic organization of the physical structure. Crossing these milestones, healthfully and consciously, always leads to an unusual sense of wisdom and balance in an individual, which is essentially the consequence of obliterating the illusion of life and death.

The physicality of our birth is a conspiracy hatched between the moon and the Earth. Our very birth is rooted in the menstrual cycles of our mother, and that cycle is linked to the lunar cycles. The sun then provides the basic energy and ambient atmosphere that is needed to hatch life. The cycles of the feminine and the cycles of the moon have come to such a concurrence in the human system that we cannot aspire for further physical evolution. So this has naturally resulted in evolution in terms of consciousness or attempts to evolve in ways other than physical.

Of the many things that we do as life upon this planet, there are three most vital aspects—one is that of self-transformation that one transcends all identities, the second is to ensure the quality of the yet-to-be-born, and the third is to evolve or find an absolute release for the life that has departed. In fulfilling these three most vital aspects, the cycles of the moon have a significant role. If we utilize the full moon and new moon situations with some understanding, we need not be swimming against the current.

Even during our life cycle, the moon's cycles play a significant role in many aspects of our physical and psychological status, but the impact of the moon cycles is really huge in conception. A couple who are conscious will make efforts to conceive twelve to sixteen days ahead of the full moon so that the being that enters the womb can do so on the next full moon day. There are many more aspects to factor in. If one is willing to approach facilitating the life process as a sacred duty, not just as a consequence of one's passions and longing and the fulfillment of pleasure, we can go into a lot more details about timing and the nature of conception.

It also has a similar impact on the process of death. When the body has seen 1,008 full moons, the energy body comes to a certain level of instability. When I say "instability," I am talking in a positive way. It is not able to retain that structure very clearly. The bubble's walls are thinning because it has gone through its full cycle. So when the person dies, he or she cannot seek another womb because they do not have the necessary karmic fire in them. So they hang around. Now, it is very easy to liberate them. Even if it takes a body, it will definitely be a much larger bubble than the way it was. But it is possible it will just hang around for a while and burst. This is true for a whole lot of them. But some may hang around and take a body as a much bigger bubble, a more significant life. If people hang on till they are eighty-four years old, regardless of how they lived their lives, it is possible—I am not saying it is guaranteed—it is possible that they attain Mahasamadhi. The possibility is much higher now, simply because the fools endured long enough!

Many times, people lose the natural advantage of crossing 1,008 full moons because, by then, they become completely unconscious in terms of memory or access to the Karmic Memory bank. If you are beyond eighty-four, but you have lost connection with the substance that makes you, you will become like a ghost or the living dead, because it is the karmic mass that is making you this kind of a person. The Prarabdha Karma,* or the one bowl of memory that was taken out for this life, is over, but you don't know how to dip into the bucket, or the Sanchita Karma, and take another bowl for you to keep going. If you knew how to take another bowl and another bowl of karma or if you could open up the entire bucket and use it, then you can live for two hundred years, there is no problem. Now when you have exhausted everything, you will attain mukti, and you will go. But if you are unable to take out the next bowl and you still keep the body going, then you will become ghostlike. This is why the pursuit of immortality and longevity through unnatural means is fraught with too many dangers.

BIRTH: ALWAYS A BEGINNING

If Enlightened people are reborn, are they born Enlightened? Does Enlightenment also get carried on to the next birth? And specifically, in my case, people ask: If I had two Enlightened lives behind me, why did the experience on Chamundi Hills have to wait until I was twenty-five years of age?

We already saw that for most people their moment of Enlightenment and their moment of leaving the body is the same. When

---

* See the section "What Makes Us Tick" in chapter 2.

their energies reach a certain pitch, they leave the body. That moment of leaving the body is also Enlightenment for them. So unless they have a certain mastery over the mechanics of the body, and they manage to retain their body because they have some specific work to do, the question of coming back does not arise. If your objective is just Liberation, then Enlightenment and leaving the body will always be together. If you have other objectives of wanting to do something else with what freedom you have found within yourself, then there is something more to be done.

It is just like this: Let us say, you release a prisoner from the prison; he is liberated. He goes away. He never again wants to get back to the prison. But there are some who are ambitious enough or stupid enough to want to not only become free from the prison but also run the prison. He is a prisoner, but now he wants to become a prison officer. Only when you have this kind of a problem do you retain your body. Otherwise, the normal prisoner's aspiration is to somehow get out. He will not seek employment in the prison. It takes an idiot like me to do that!

So will a person who is Enlightened be born Enlightened? If you take a mango sapling, it has all the qualities of a mango tree—it is capable of producing mangoes. But it does not spring out mangoes the moment it sprouts out of the ground. It takes its time. Nature allows this time for the mango sapling to grow to a certain sturdiness, strength, maturity, balance, and capability to hold its ground. Only then it flowers and fruits. The moment two leaves sprout, if the mangoes appear, the tree could die. So it will wait for it to come up to a certain height and sturdiness, only then will the mangoes come out.

Similarly, an Enlightened being has certain qualities which are enshrined in him or her, which cannot be taken away. But when he is born, he is born like anyone. The qualities are still there, inherent in him. It will wait for a certain time and space where it can find expression. This is the intelligence of Nature. It knows exactly when it should flower to find maximum fruit. If it flowers too early, it will not find its full fruit. So it will wait. Depending on what type of work he intends to take up, accordingly he will develop.

We have seen this in India for a long time: Many *bala yogis** become Enlightened by the age of six or seven. Most of them never cross the age of twenty-five or thirty. Before that, they will go because they cannot sustain the body at that intensity of existence. So if Nature gives sufficient space that the mind, body, and emotions develop and mature in a certain way before the dimension becomes alive in that person, they can hold it much better.

This is true of me also. Although there was an experience of living an Enlightened life for two lifetimes, I still had to wait until the age of twenty-five before the reminder hit me. This is because the very reason why this body was taken this time was fundamentally for the consecration of the Dhyanalinga. For this, it is not just Enlightenment—you need a perfect body in many ways. When I say "perfect," I am not referring to athletic perfection, but a perfect body in terms of management of your energies and what you can do with it. This is not possible in a child. When I look back at those twenty-five years, the way activity happened in my life, the kind of activity that happened, it all occurred in perfect progression for my purpose. Everything happened in such a way that everything that was necessary for the development of this body and this mind and stabilizing my emotions naturally happened as a process of living.

For example, at the age of twelve, though I was someone who was wild, playing, climbing trees, trekking, and doing things like this, the best Yoga teacher that was available in southern India came to me and somehow inspired me to learn Yogic practices.†

---

* Child yogis who are adept from a very young age.
† Referring to my first encounter with Malladihalli Swamiji, who started me on Hatha Yoga at the age of eleven years.

And without a single word or thought, I just took it on. Some twelve years later, big things happened to me. So this process of when it should happen is Nature's intelligence. You never question Nature's intelligence, because your intelligence is too small to question the intelligence of Nature. Whatever happens naturally is always right, there is no question about it. It is just that your short-term goals and objectives may not be in tune with what is happening, so you struggle with it. But in the real sense, it cannot be wrong. It always moves in the right direction because Nature does not decide things with thoughts and emotion. It just decides things as per your tendencies. This is not a thought. With thought, you can always make a mistake, but with tendencies there can be no mistake.

See, today you may think something is the right thing to do. But tomorrow if you just start thinking in the opposite direction, at the end of that day you can clearly come to a conclusion that this is not the best thing to do. This is the nature of thought. With thought, you can always make a mistake because it functions with very limited data. And most of the thoughts are just a mistake. But Nature operates out of tendencies. A mango tree does not think how to produce a mango. Its tendency is like that. It just moves in that direction and just does what it has to do and everything happens at the right moment.

In my youth, I was not a person who was drawn toward spirituality. But at that time in my life, simply, accidentally, here and there, I just began to meet people on the spiritual path. At that time, just like that, things fell into place because the tendencies were slowly coming to the surface and the necessary support to manifest that also came. So for an Enlightened being who is reborn it depends on what type of work that person has as an objective for his life. Accordingly, at the right time, things will happen. Enlightenment is about going beyond individuality and becoming available to Universality.

My Past Lifetimes

There are any number of my lifetimes which are there in my memory but I don't pay attention to any of that. I have a piece of life in Zambia, for example, but I pay attention only to that which has been spiritually significant in some way. The rest of it is of no consequence. There are many things around me today which are a legacy of my past. But I have carried only those things which are of spiritual significance. Who my mother was, who my father was, who my brothers were, who my sisters were, who my children were in all those past lives, I can pursue them very easily—but I will not. I have not even paid any attention to them. Only those who were with me in spirit—not in flesh or blood—do I nurture. Those who were with me in flesh and blood, I leave to the Earth, because it is to the Earth that they belong. In that sense, I consider only my last four lifetimes significant.

BILVA

In the early 1600s, there lived a young man in a small village (the present-day city of Raigarh) in the central Indian state of Chhattisgarh. His name was Bilva. He was a tribesman who lived a wild and intense life. There is a certain tradition in India where some people called the *budubuduku*s just walk through the streets, usually very early in the morning, when it is still dark. They wake you up with their drumbeats. Intuitively, if they see something, they will tell you. They may say, for example, that death will occur in such and such house in two weeks' time, or someone will fall ill somewhere, and so on. Generally, people paid attention to these spontaneous utterances because they were known to come true. If nothing came to them that day, they would simply sing songs in praise of Shiva. After this, they would go and sit in a temple for some time, where people would go and make some offerings to them.

This was a tradition within the Shaiva culture, where this particular tribe of people is also involved in snake charming. Snakes and Shiva are deeply connected. Bilva belonged to a tribe like that. Bilva was deeply in love with what he was doing. These were people who lived totally, loving life for what it is. They were not the kind to accumulate anything. They had no sense of money, property, or possessions. They simply lived and Shiva was the most important aspect of their lives.

Bilva loved snakes. Mind you, snakes are generally poisonous creatures. If you are the kind who loves poisonous creatures, you have to be a different kind of person. To kiss a snake, you must be very courageous. He was a person for whom love meant everything; the rest was secondary. Being alive itself was secondary. That is the kind of person he was. He was someone who could not fit into the social structure and was looked upon as a rebel. For one of the many rebellious acts he did—not respecting the prevalent caste distinction—he was put to death at a very young age by a cobra's bite, while he was tied to a tree.

At that time, you could not really call him a spiritual person; he was a devotee of Shiva. But during those last few moments of his life, he watched his breath. There was nothing else he could do and breath watching just happened. The cobra's venom entered his body and his breathing became very labored. Death was just a few minutes away. During this time, he watched his breath. It was more of a consequence than a conscious awareness. Bitten by a cobra and left to die, he was lying face down, almost dead. Yet he managed to be aware of those last few minutes of life. This was more out of Grace rather than any sadhana. From those few minutes of breath watching, a new spiritual process began which changed that person's future in so many ways.

SHIVAYOGI

In his next two lifetimes, he was a very intense seeker of the Ultimate Nature. Shiva was his way. Both the times he was known as Shivayogi. In the first life of sadhana, he died at the age of thirty-seven. He had no disease, just hunger and the intensity of his sadhana did him in. He did not die Enlightened, but he died in full dignity. He died not screaming, yelling, or crying, but just trying to do sadhana, to be meditative and die. The second time over, he fared better. He lived to fifty-five years of age. He went through heartbreaking sadhana, but still final Realization had not happened. At this point, he was bestowed the Ultimate Grace.

Usually, I don't talk about my Guru. He was called Sri Palani Swami and was a being beyond proportions. That was not his real name, but he was so called because he had attained a certain samadhi state near the town of Palani in Tamil Nadu. He remained in this state for about two and a half years. After that, he wandered all over the country, enlightening many people. He came to Shivayogi, in the second lifetime, and bestowed his Grace upon him, a forlorn sadhaka.

When this Shivayogi saw him, he recognized that this was the Guru. Until then, he would not accept any human being as his Guru. For him, Shiva was the only Guru. He wanted Shiva to come and initiate him, but when he saw Sri Palani Swami he recognized that this being was at the very peak of consciousness and he offered himself. But somewhere there was still a little resistance because he could not offer himself to another man. He would only offer himself totally to Shiva. So the Guru, out of compassion, took the form of Shiva himself. Shivayogi surrendered. Sri Palani Swami did not even touch him with his hand or foot; he just took his staff and tapped on Shivayogi's Agna Chakra, or forehead. At that moment, Shivayogi attained his Ultimate Nature.

This contact with the Guru lasted only a few hours. After that, they never met again, but they were constantly in touch. Sri Palani Swami attained Mahasamadhi in the Velliangiri Mountains. Somehow, he identified Shivayogi as a person suitable for establishing the Dhyanalinga and entrusted this work to him. Not in speech, not in words, but wordlessly he communicated the immense technology needed to consecrate the Dhyanalinga. So Shivayogi began working toward establishing the Dhyanalinga. He was not able to fulfill his Guru's vision in that lifetime because of limited resources and lack of support. So the rest of his time in that lifetime he spent mostly with his eyes closed.

SADHGURU SRI BRAHMA

To continue the work of creating the Dhyanalinga, Shivayogi came back as Sadhguru Sri Brahma. He started the work toward this in Tamil Nadu. He traveled extensively in the state and established several small institutions but his work on the Dhyanalinga was centered around Coimbatore. Here he faced a lot of social resistance from people. Because the Dhyanalinga is the highest manifestation of the Divine, it includes all aspects and manifestations of life. So consecrating it involved men and women in very intense processes. If a man and woman sit together, people can think of only one thing. So a lot of resistance came up and he was literally hounded out of the place. He became very angry that he could not fulfill his Guru's will and left Coimbatore in great fury, as if on fire.

Those were the worst times in Sadhguru Sri Brahma's life. But in many ways, the best came out at that time. After lifetimes of sadhana and then fired by a phenomenal Grace of the Guru, he was quite sure that what he set out to do would happen. But he burned with fury when it was robbed from him by very ordinary and mediocre people, whom he had underestimated. He realized that the power of ignorance is never to be underestimated. It is very powerful and the world is ruled by it most of the time. You think your knowledge, your fire, your Enlightenment will do things, but the Enlightened are always an individual; the ignorant are in masses. There is a huge power to that.

He did not do the cold calculations necessary to work in the world, not because he was incapable of it. He did not do it simply because he thought his fire and his knowing would carry. But that is not how the world always works. The material aspect of the world, the human beings of different kinds, need to be handled as it is fit. Otherwise, it will not work. And this is a wonderful lesson for everyone—a lesson I have not forgotten even for a moment in my life—even if you carry the Divine Light within you, there will still be darkness behind you. So unless you have created a lot of small lights behind you, you need to constantly turn back and check what is happening.

Sadhguru Sri Brahma was alone. There were people here and there that he had lit up, but he did not like anyone following him, so he was alone. Because he was alone, behind him there was darkness, and it followed him and did not allow him to fulfill the purpose of his life. This is a good lesson for anyone: Even such a magnificent human being as Sadhguru Sri Brahma, who could do things which are not considered human or humanly possible, could not fulfill what he came for. And it does not matter how many things you do; if you cannot fulfill the purpose that you have stood up for, that is considered failure. Sadhguru Sri Brahma failed and he did not like it; he did not like it one bit. So knowing the only emotion that he knew—he got angry. He was always angry—not about anything or anyone, but anger was his vehicle for intense existence.

In that anger, he started to walk in no particular direction. Seeing his fierceness, no one was able to go near him, except for one disciple by the name of Vibhuti who followed him. Sadhguru Sri Brahma walked without stopping to eat, sleep, or even sit for three or four days. During this time, the disciple would follow him, try to gauge in which direction the Master was going, cook food and run to reach his Master and place the food in front of him, step aside and wait in the hope that he would eat.

Where would he walk? He eventually began walking in the direction where the scent of Grace for him was. So he walked toward the town of Kadapa, in the state of Andhra Pradesh. Initially, when he set out, he did not even think about where he was going. He was just walking blindly to cool his head a bit. But invariably he went in that direction because there is this temple in Kadapa[*] where Sri Palani Swami himself had spent a lot of time. Probably it had been re-consecrated by him. So Sadhguru Sri Brahma went in that direction.

When he finally reached the temple in Kadapa, his anger had still not subsided. Even after four or five months, he was still angry. No one could go near Sadhguru Sri Brahma and his disciple. It is not that they did anything or harmed anyone, but they were so fierce—fiercer than wild animals—even if they were only sitting, no one wanted to go near them. Within a few days, all the priests in the temple left, because they could not stay there because of the intensity of that being. Sadhguru Sri Brahma knew that he did not have much time. He knew that because of certain karmic limitations he would have to leave his body within the next two years.

When his head got a little cooler and when he was able to put down the shame and resentment of failure a little bit, he settled down to make some very cold calculations. From being a fiery, exu-

---

[*] Someshwara temple, Devuni Kadapa, in the state of Andhra Pradesh.

berant, don't-care-a-devil kind of yogi, he came down to being a cold calculation, a highly pragmatic, controlled fire. He sat with his disciple and plotted how to make the Dhyanalinga happen in the next life. Many things were decided there—who should be involved in the consecration process, where they should be born, in which womb, how, and at what time. He plotted every aspect that would be needed and determined solutions for many issues that could impede it. Sadhguru Sri Brahma even decided what kind of a person he should be born as, how his physical body and state of mind should be. Everything was created right there. The fundamental blueprint for the Dhyanalinga was made in that Kadapa temple.

Sadhguru Sri Brahma then came back to Coimbatore for the last time. He was heading up the Velliangiri Mountains, which also contained his Guru's samadhi. There were many people gathered at the foothills that day. To them, he declared, "This one will be back." He ascended the mountain for the last time. Now, Sadhguru Sri Brahma was supercharged with failure and, having been unable to fulfill his Guru's will, he executed an extremely rare feat—of exiting through the seven chakras all at once. He was one of the very few Masters who had mastery over all seven chakras and was referred to as Chakreshwara.

He was only forty-two years old at the time. He did this phenomenally rare thing as a preparation for the consecration of the Dhyanalinga. Though he knew his failure was that of mismanagement of social situations, he was ascertaining for himself that it was not a lapse of his own ability. Exiting the body through all seven chakras meant this person had complete mastery over all one hundred and fourteen chakras. It is because of that mastery that now we can have people blowing up everywhere with intense experiences like explosions. He chose the peaks of the Velliangiri Mountains for this incredible feat, because his Guru's samadhi was in these mountains—it was the lap of his Master. Thus, he assured himself that the next time around there would be no failure or mishit.

Even today, the place where he attained samadhi and shed his body exists. It is very vibrant; it pulsates with energy. People who go there can feel it and experience it. The quality of this place at the top of the Seventh Hill—just at the edge of the mountain where chilly, wild winds blow constantly—says everything about this man. That is where he felt most comfortable. It is a very powerful spot. If you are a meditator, if you are a little sensitive, when you go there you will go crazy. It is like that because he left with a certain purpose. He has a certain purpose to fulfill, so he left in a particular way. It is not just about Liberation and dissolution. He used his energies and even his death for the future establishment or manifestation of how he wanted to be.

Before Sadhguru Sri Brahma shed the body, he made one more futile attempt to achieve the work he had started. A certain yogi in central India had left his body at the age of twenty-six. He was a bala yogi who had attained Self-Realization at the age of eleven. This yogi spent about three and a half years in samadhi. When he came out, he was eager to share his experience, but he found only five or six disciples to impart it to. Even they were not sincere enough. So he got angry and he left his body.

Sadhguru Sri Brahma immediately took hold of this bala yogi's body and tried to fulfill his purpose through it. He did this because he had no patience to be born again and go through the process of life all over again. For a few months, Sadhguru Sri Brahma was in two different physical bodies at the same time. In this attempt to create the Dhyanalinga, he gathered a few disciples around him and tried working with them with tremendous intensity, because the time span available was very limited. When people did not meet his expectations, he chose to shelve the effort and depart with a declaration, "This one will be back."

Will I Come Back?

People ask me, "Many spiritual Masters in the Buddhist tradition have come back again and again for the sake of their followers. You yourself took two more births after Enlightenment to fulfill your Guru's dream. So will you be coming back again, just for one last time, in case we do not make it this time?"

Let me confirm this for you once again: I am not coming back for sure, because my expiry date is long over. Some people who are a little more perceptive clearly see that I don't even exist. This actually happened: Every year we take a large group of Isha meditators to the Himalayas, and Tapovan is one of the places they visit. One year, for some reason, I stayed back at Gomukh. I did not accompany them to Tapovan. In Tapovan there is a lady called Bengali Maa. She has been living there for many years. She asked our meditators, "Who are you people? Where are you coming from?" They said, "We are Isha meditators and we have come with our Guru." She said, "Can I see his picture?" So they pulled out a picture of me and showed it to her. She looked at it and said, "Oh, he is wonderful but he is gone, long time ago." They said, "No, no, he has come with us, he is walking with us." She said, "No way! He is gone."

So these people came back to Gomukh. They thought that during the time they went up I had gone. They were a little terrified when they saw me, and then they told me what happened. I thought I had covered myself pretty well, but if she was able to see it, obviously it was not well enough. I am real or I have made myself more real than most people are. But from the account books of humanity I am gone a long time ago. This gives me much freedom, though. But stretching it one more time is not a proper thing to do. Even this time it happened only because I got tangled up with the project of the consecration of the Dhyanalinga. Otherwise, this one would not be.

As it is, all the basic infrastructure that is needed for life to continue has been dismantled, but I am still on. This is not good. Existentially, it is not considered good. Once the basic infrastructure that is necessary to keep this life going is gone, that person has no business here; they should be gone. In my longing for Liberation, I dismantled all the infrastructure. Then, because I ended up with an impossible project, I tried to continue on and on. Now that is also done, and no one knows why the hell I am continuing anymore. Just to see some more full moons, maybe! Not really, because I remember too many of them and the damn moon is not changing.

Once you have deciphered the fundamentals of how it happens, even if a totally new Creation happens tomorrow, it would still not be interesting enough to go there. It is like this: Let us say, there is a super hotel which has a million rooms. If you go there as a customer, they give you a key card which opens only your room. You are entering just one room, so you are very excited when you enter it. Now, if the hotel manager tells you there is another room with a better view and asks if you would like to take it, you say, "Yes, yes. I am excited." But there is a cleaning person there—she has one simple key which opens every room. But she is not excited about the new room with the view because she has seen plenty of rooms. She has seen all the superficial small decor changes from room to room and all that.

I am sure even she has not opened all the million rooms, but because she has seen so many and she even cleans them every day she is not excited about entering one more new room. This is so with Self-Realization also. Once you have this key, you can open any number of rooms. Have you opened everything? No. If you have the time and the inclination, it is possible to open every room, but one room is not so different from another. Similarly, if you enter a new Universe, everything may look different but it is not so different. The fundamentals are all the same. So when you have seen enough, you start dismantling the fundamental infrastructure that is necessary to sustain life.

There is a certain span a life can run. Even now, without the support that I take from a few people around me, I would not be able to keep my body intact. I am doing fine, but without a little bit of support around me it would not be possible to maintain the integrity of my body at all, because it is well past its expiry date. Besides, technology-wise, me coming back is crude technology. We are establishing a slightly better way of doing things. Moreover, it is very wrong to think that if this person is not there, what will happen? This happened when Kamaraj[*] was the chief minister of Tamil Nadu. You should know that most of the infrastructure that you see in the state was all done during his time. We are still enjoying what he did.

Once Kamaraj was touring the state when he was the chief minister. He was somewhere near Madurai. It was some village and they had just transferred a police sub-inspector from there. That officer had been there for a few years and he had bonded well with the people and done many things for them. So he was a very popular sub-inspector and the people were very agitated by his transfer. In India, it is very rare that people love a policeman. But this policeman had earned the people's love and they all protested. So when the chief minister came visiting they said, "We don't want this sub-inspector to be transferred." Kamaraj replied, "It is wonderful that there is such a wonderful sub-inspector here. But I want you to know, we are capable of producing many more wonderful sub-inspectors. You will see the next one will be even better." Even a political leader had such wisdom. Fortunately, we had wonderful people in the country, but unfortunately, they never had enough power in their hands to do anything. So don't get into this mode,

---

[*] Kumaraswami Kamaraj (1903–75), a popular politician from southern India.

"Please come back, Sadhguru! Come back, Sadhguru!" No. It is not necessary. The next generation we produce should be far better than us.

Whenever I leave—whenever that is—for eighty years after that, my presence will be stronger, much stronger than the way it is right now. This is to ensure that all of you are dead before I go! Yes. This is because once you start people on a certain process there is a certain responsibility that you finish it. So I want to ensure that everyone who was in some way touched by me is cleaned up from the planet before I leave completely. Because they taught you all those tricks in Inner Engineering with which you may live 160 years, I am keeping it for eighty years after the body is gone—just in case you survive to become 160! That is why these eighty years. Eighty years is almost like another lifetime, but there will be no physical presence. For physical presence, we will establish enough systems, but the presence will be much, much stronger than the way it is right now because the burden of carrying a physical body will not be there.

So am I going to be a disembodied being? Obviously, if my body is buried or burned, I will be disembodied, if you want to call it that. But the body exists on many different layers. What you pick up from the planet you have to put back. The rest of the body—to put it in modern terminology—is more like a software. The software still stays on a minimal platform. Right now, it is on a solid, physical platform. If this platform goes away, it will stay on a very minimal platform. It will not take another physical platform. This will be far more efficient than being on a physical platform because of various things.

So why not stay forever? There is no such thing as forever, long or short. If it is needed, one can hang on and do that kind of thing. But it is not needed because we have set up a more sophisticated arrangement for that purpose. We will come out with many more spiritual processes which can be transmitted to the masses without much preparation. It will still be a very potent method, not some frivolous thing. Right now, I thought it is not relevant to do that because I am still around; I can do these mass transmission processes more intricately. I adjust this very intricate process to a particular mass that is there in front of me and make things happen. It is still very much possible for us to do it that way, but mass processes will slowly roll out of this after some time because that will be long-term insurance. Above all, there is the Dhyanalinga. So there is really no need to hang on forever.

Why do you care? You will be dead and gone anyway.

CHAPTER 12

Final Round

We can make this life the last one for you but we cannot make this the most wonderful one. That only you have to do. For that, you must do sadhana. You must promise me that.

ONE-DROP SPIRITUALITY

When I was twenty-five, suddenly this big spiritual experience burst upon me.* After that, I thought I would teach the whole world how to live ecstatically—truly in ecstasy. I thought, "This is it, what is the problem in teaching it? Everyone can get it." But now as age is catching up and my hair is turning gray, I have matured. Now I am thinking, If we are not able to teach them to live well, at least let us see if we can teach them how to die well. I am very concerned about this because I see most people on the planet die badly. Those who learn how to live well, wonderful for them. But at least if other people learn how to die well, it would be great.

Teaching people how to live well takes a little more work; we may not be able to do it for everyone. But at least they must die well. This is important because the period of life in a disembodied state is much, much bigger than that in an embodied state. When a

---

* My experience of Enlightenment at Chamundi Hills in 1982.

being is disembodied, whether their experience of life becomes heavenly or hellish largely depends on how they die. Not entirely, but largely.* So even if we cannot teach the whole population a way where they can live beautifully every moment of their life, if we can at least teach them to manage the last moment of their life sensibly, then this will see them through disembodiment very beautifully.

People may believe they are living well, but they are not. They live in good homes, drive good cars, wear good clothes, but they think they are living well because they look at other people who don't have the same things and feel happy about it. This is not living well. This is a sick life. They feel happy by comparing themselves with someone who is not doing as well as them. This is all the joy most people have in their life. So I don't call that living well.

For me, living well means you are able to sit here in such a way that nothing matters; whether you have something or not, even whether there is food to eat or not, it does not matter to you. You are just fine. It is not that you are incapable of earning your food and other things, but that does not decide who you are right now. What kind of garment you are wearing does not decide who you are right now. What kind of house you are living in does not decide who you are right now. How someone else treats you does not decide who you are right now. What someone says to you does not decide who you are right now. How you are looked up to or looked down upon does not decide who you are right now. If you are like this, you are living well for sure. Wherever you sit, your experience of life will be beautiful.

I have been particularly concerned about this because in the recent past I have seen some people who were dear to me going in a very bad way. These were not people who had failed, but people who believed that they had lived very well. Everything that they

---

*See the section "Does Death Need Preparation?" in chapter 6.

wanted in life happened for them. They got educated, got a job, got married, had children, their children grew up, they got married and settled abroad and had grandchildren. For most people, this is their dream life. Their lives worked out according to their dreams, and when they came to the final phase of their lives, the last mile of their lives, they were completely out of sorts. They were completely broken people and died in a bad way. About 90 percent of even those who believe that they are successful and are living well also die badly because modern societies are neither aware nor have they taken care of this important aspect of how to die well.

So I felt we should hand down at least a simple spiritual process which can be imparted in a few minutes so that people can handle at least one moment of their life sensibly, wonderfully. My dream is still that people should live blissfully—it is possible. But, you know, many of them have given up, many of them are die-hard miserable people. Do what you want, they are determined; they want to invest in their miseries. So now I am beginning to think, "Okay, if we cannot teach everyone how to live blissfully, at least they must be able to die well." It is a horrible compromise, but, you know, there are eight billion people. You can never get eight billion people for seven days, three hours a day, to sit, learn, and do these practices in their life. It is not going to happen. We still hope that people will go for it. But in case they are die-hard miserable people at least let them have the dignity of dying well—not dying confused, not dying bewildered, not dying miserably. At least this must happen.

I thought I would never do this in my life, but you know, I am getting practical. I am coming to terms with this reality because between possibility and reality there is a distance that not everyone is willing to walk. And unless someone is willing there is no way you are going to do this. You can coax them, you can cajole them, you can, you know, push them around a bit; beyond that, you cannot do much. If you go beyond that, they will leave. I have no illusions about that. Almost anyone, if you push people beyond a certain point, they will all leave, I know that.

If we had them in an airtight can, then I would not give up that possibility of making them live well, but we don't have the whole world's population in a can. Even at the Isha Yoga Center, it is not so. At the most, we can have a handful of people in the airtight can, whom we can push all the way. But I am sure we can teach everyone how to die well because it does not take so much time. It is simple, it is easy, and I am finding ways where, whether they are willing or not, we can teach them. We can put something into them which will come into play when that moment approaches.

The spiritual process is about helping people die well, not only helping people live well. Helping people die well does not mean assisting them in dying, as euthanasia supporters advocate. Helping people die means helping people manage the moment of passing from physicality to beyond, from being embodied to being disembodied, in utmost awareness and grace. If one wants to exercise this choice by oneself, a certain amount of preparation is needed. There are many methods to cultivate this awareness in life so that when the moment of death comes it will carry you through in grace. But otherwise we can create that moment for every human being if that human being is willing to cooperate and willing to pay some attention to themselves now.

This is how most of the initiations were done in the past. A yogi would sit in one place and initiate people like this. What happened? Nothing. Someone may argue, "Nothing happened in my life." It does not matter. When that moment of passing approached, it would come into play. It is not that we have not also done this. We have, but not actively so. Now we want to do it actively on a massive scale so that there will be something in everyone's life. If it does not play up right now, at least when that moment approaches it will play up, for sure.

Many times, people who are very old and ailing ask me to visit them. Or sometimes there are people who find that their parents have reached a very ripe age and are suffering, who send me a picture of them. If I see there is enough maturity in them and they are asking me not to make them well but to release them, or if their Prarabdha Karma is nearly finished, then, if I visit that person, or if I look at the person's picture, within seven to eight days they will be gone, because without software that life is anyway on the very edge.

However, it works both ways too because sometimes it is good to stretch someone's life and sometimes it is good to curtail their life. It is like this: Let us say, you are traveling in a boat. Once you reach the other bank, you must get off the boat. If you still don't get off the boat for some reason, then drifting will happen unnecessarily. So both may have to be done. Sometimes you stretch their life because this person has not reached where they should reach but has run out of steam, and sometimes they have reached it but still have steam, so you have to release them. Both are needed in life.

Is it possible that they will be liberated? Someone being liberated for good is possible only when someone has run the full course of prarabdha. Now when everything is over, they are in a certain space where there is a karmic break. There are many people who die of old age; they may have lived as utter fools, but in the final few days, suddenly there is a new sense of wisdom within them, a new sense of awareness about them because their karma allotment has finished.* Just the minor things are left and the next quota of karma has not come in yet, so that is a blessed period. Even for a person who lived an ignorant life, you will see that suddenly they know, "In the next three days I will die." Such people can be dissolved very easily because they have come to that blessed state where there is no karmic burden. There is a stock somewhere else, but here is a little

---

* See chapter 3: "The Quality of Death."

space of no karma. We can help them die consciously rather than in an unconscious state. If there is a conducive atmosphere, dissolution is possible. They can be liberated. But when they die of disease before the Prarabdha Karma is complete, if one tries to dissolve them it is not going to work. Nor will I do such a thing. All we can do for them is help them die with awareness; then they will have a little enhanced life somewhere else.

Is it possible to do this even if this person does not know me? See, when I am talking on this level, I am not talking about myself as a person, as some bundle of habits and patterns and things. As a person, you may know me or not, but at this level there is no one who does not know me, because here, that which I call "myself" is you also. In that dimension, there is no individual person. So it does not make any difference whether as a person you know me or not. I have often said that I have initiated more people that I have not met than those I have met. This is also like that.

ONCE YOU MADE A MISTAKE OF . . .

The moment of death is a tremendous possibility for someone to intervene. I could help you die well, but I could help you live well too! It is better you live well, not just aim toward dying well. If you are planning on coming back a hundred times over, you can live a stupid life. But if you want this to be your last life, especially then you should learn to live well. The last lap must be the best lap, mustn't that be right?

When things have come to a head, when the situation has matured to such an extent that it has become life and death and nothing else matters, then it is just one moment's work for me. But how long you are going to take to get there is up to you. You could make it happen this evening or you could wait for a few lifetimes. Once you have come to me, I will not give you the option of a few lifetimes. But you can wait until the end of your life. If you keep postponing it till then, when death comes knocking, you will be hopeless. When death comes knocking, all of a sudden you will find that this body does not mean anything. All your qualifications will not mean anything. Your husband, wife, and children will not mean anything. Your fancy clothes will not mean anything. You will be hopeless. Like a vulture, I will wait for that moment, because, then, you will become willing. But if you are intelligent, if you have any sense in you, you will create that willingness right now.

If you do not create that willingness within you, you will resist what needs to happen. When you have a discretionary mind, if you come here with walls of resistance we will try to wear it down. It may not be completely gone, but we will wear it down. This is a long and tedious process. One who is dead does not have a discretionary mind, so it is very easy to influence him, compared to you. It is like this: You are a hardcore ghost with a body. A ghost without a body is easy to handle in comparison because he has no discretionary mind. He will receive whatever you say. The only thing is that you cannot speak in English with him because he will have lost his ears along with his body! So you need to speak to him in a different language, but he is willing to listen. He is absolutely willing because he has no discretionary mind. He cannot set up a resistance. So we say something sweet to him and he will become sweet immediately and we can do what needs to be done with him. But if you are willing, you need not wait till then.

Those who have given themselves totally to me, even for a single moment, they do not have to worry about their Liberation. Liberation is assured. To live gracefully or not, that is not assured. That is something that you have to earn, but Liberation is assured. So how does this work? One common word which has always been prevalent in the spiritual arena of the East is the word "maya." We don't use it, but it is a fantastic word. It says exactly what we want to say, but it has been so horribly abused over time that we generally refuse to use it. Maya means that the way you are existing right now, your perception and understanding of life, is illusory. The most essential part of this illusion is your idea of you as a being or an individual. It is illusory. Now, if I asked you, "Are you connected to the Earth?" you say, "Yes." It is not true. It is true, but not true in your experience. It is true, not because you are plugged into the Earth, but because you are a piece of the Earth. But because of your inability to drop the illusory idea that you are only connected to the Earth and not a piece of the Earth itself—you exist as an individual.

At the Isha Yoga Center, the reason why all the brahmacharis have their heads shaved, all wearing the same clothes, is because if they turn around they should not know whether this is them or that is them. But even in the little things, like the way they apply the vibhuti on their foreheads, they want to do it in their own style, even though everything else is the same. In the process of living in the world, everyone is constantly trying to strengthen their fences, strengthen their boundaries. *Brahmacharya* means you are on the path of the Divine. What is the way of the Divine? The way of the Divine is that there is no individuality. It is a universal process. So if you sit here even for a moment without strengthening your boundaries, it would be fantastic. You cannot do that with a tree. But you could easily do that with me, for various reasons. Nothing is wrong with a tree, but because neither the tree nor you are conscious, and two unconscious entities cannot come together, they will always remain two separate bubbles of their own, even though the atmospheric transfer between the two is happening.

So this illusion that you are a separate entity is a big problem. The idea of sitting with a Guru is that you sit without boundaries. If you simply sit, it will happen. So I said if you sit with me for even one moment, if you can be with me totally, then it is done. It could have happened in the form of an initiation or it could have just happened because of a look. It can happen even when they have never ever seen me but they just heard about me. There are many people like that. They have not even seen me physically. By just seeing a picture, they opened up. Any number of people have experienced this.

The whole process of being with something means just this, that you did not fix your boundaries for a moment. If you can do it for a day—that you did not fix any boundaries, you are simply here—we will worship you because that which does not have boundaries is Divine. So not a whole day; if you have experienced this state without boundaries for even one moment, there will be no more rebirth for you.

I avoid saying certain things because I am afraid that you may turn lazy tomorrow morning. But if you have for one moment—not for hours and days, just for one moment—if you have really been with me, this is your last life. But with this assurance I don't want you to turn lazy. Your last life should also be the most wonderful one. We can make this life the last one for you, but we cannot make this the most wonderful one. That only you have to do. For that, you must do sadhana. You must promise me that.

Once we were trekking to Mount Kailash. During the day we were trekking and in the evenings there were satsangs.* This was a small group of people, so the atmosphere was quite informal and we were talking about many things—life, the afterlife, alien life, and all that. So an American meditator asked, "Sadhguru, it has been great for us to be your disciples. How does it feel for you to be our Guru?" Only an American can ask this! I said, "See, it is fantastic to be a yogi, I wouldn't be any other way. But being a Guru is frustrating because what can be done in a moment, people make it a lifetime." If you give yourself to me for a moment, I can ensure that you

---

* Spiritual gatherings in the presence of a Guru.

are really dead. If someone shoots you with a gun, you will pop up again somewhere. But if you give me permission I will shoot you in such a way that a gun is not needed, but you can never pop up in another womb again. Just one moment—not lifetimes!

Once you made the mistake of sitting with me, in some ways you are already fixed, unless you really want to fall off and want to really go against it within yourself. Otherwise, in many ways, you are sorted. I don't want to interfere with your life. But your death I usually hold it in my hands. This is contrary to the general thought that we will go somewhere after death, which is essentially perpetuity of life—a human fallacy that life doesn't end, but we go into a different ambience of existence, either a good one called heaven or a bad one called hell, but a perpetuity either way. Life is not perpetual, it is cyclical. Breaking the compulsive cycles of life is called Liberation, from the ambit of compulsive revolutions to evolve beyond the limitations of a cyclical life. This is what it is ultimately about—Conscious Evolution, not Revolution.

GLOSSARY

Adiyogi. The first yogi, one of the many epithets of Shiva.

Aghoris. One of the ascetic sects of Shaivites. Their practices are often severe and grisly and contradictory to that of orthodox Hinduism.

Agna Chakra. The center of knowledge and Enlightenment, the Agna is one of the seven major energy centers of the human body. Physically located between the eyebrows, it is also known as the "third eye."

aiyyo. Cries of desperation in southern Indian languages.

aakash. Refers to the sky or ether. One of the five elements of Nature.

Akaal Mrutyu. Untimely death.

Amma. Mother. A reverential way of addressing a woman.

Anahata Chakra. The heart center, one of the seven energy centers of the body.

Ananda. Bliss, unconditional joy.

Anandamaya Kosha. The innermost body or the bliss body.

anatma. Literally, "the soulless one."

Annamaya Kosha. Food-formed sheath, or the physical body, made up of the five gross elements, or bhootas—earth, wind, water, fire, ether—which are restored again into their initial states after death.

antyeshti. The final ritual to be done for the deceased.

Apana Prana/Vayu. One of the five pranas in the human body.

Arjuna. A hero of the great epic Mahabharata to whom Krishna imparted the Divine message of the Bhagavad Gita.

Atharvana Veda. The last of the four Vedas that expounds the technology of using physical energy to one's advantage.

atma. Individual being, the supreme soul, or Brahman.

aum. The primordial sound made by chanting the sounds A-U-M.

Avighna Yantra. A spiritual energy form to remove obstacles, available at the Isha Yoga Center.

Babaji. Mahavatar Babaji, Indian saint and yogi, believed to have lived in the second century AD.

bala yogi. Child yogi. Refers to someone who attains Enlightenment at an early age and usually does not retain the body for long after that.

Bhagavad Gita. Literally, "Song of God." A sacred Hindu text, is a dialogue between Krishna and his disciple Arjuna, occurring in the Mahabharata. Krishna expounds on the ways to Truth and the nature of Existence.

Bhishma. The grand old patriarch of the Mahabharata.

bhoota. A ghoul or ghost. Also refers to the five primary elements of Nature—earth, wind, fire, water, and ether.

Bhrumadhya Sadhana. A Yogic practice where the eyeballs are focused between the eyebrows.

brahmachari. *Brahman* means Divine and *charya* means path, so, one who is on the path of the Divine. Usually refers to one who has formally been initiated into monkhood through a certain energy process.

Brahmacharya. The path of the Divine. A life of celibacy and scholarship on the path of spirituality moving toward the highest modifications of the senses. One of the stages of life as per the Varnashrama Dharma.

buddhi. The faculty of discrimination, analysis, logical and rational thought; the intellect.

budubuduku. A traditional gypsy soothsayer.

Chakreshwara. One who has attained mastery over all the chakras.

Chamundi Hills. A hillock in Mysore, where Sadhguru had a deep spiritual experience.

chandala. Someone who deals with the disposal of corpses. Also a Hindu lower caste, traditionally considered to be "untouchable."

Chaudi. A kind of disembodied being.

deva. A Sanskrit term referring to a divine or celestial being.

Dhritarashtra. The Kaurava king under whose rule the Mahabharata war took place.

dhyana/dhyanam. Sanskrit for "meditation."

Dhyanalinga. A powerful energy form at the Isha Yoga Center in India, it was consecrated by Sadhguru exclusively for the purpose of meditation.

dosha. Defect or blemish. Specifically refers to defects in the physical, mental, or energy bodies.

Gandhari. A prominent character in the Mahabharata. She was a princess of Gandhara and the wife of Dhritarashtra, the blind king of Hastinapura, and the mother of a hundred sons—the Kauravas.

gandharva. A class of celestial beings who are usually gifted with extraordinary talents such as music and dance.

ghat. The bank of a river where people usually come to bathe, wash, and swim.

Gita. Literally, "song." Here it refers to the seven holy books, of which the Bhagavad Gita is the most famous one.

gnana/gnanam/gyan. Knowledge, perception, discrimination.

Gnana Yoga. Knowledge, perception, discrimination; one of the four kinds of Yogas.

Gomukh. Literally, "cow's mouth"; a place in the upper Himalayas, the location where the glacier forms the Ganga River. The glacial form has melted in a way that it resembles the face of a cow.

homa. A Hindu ritual in which oblations or offerings are made into fire.

jeevasamadhi. A Yogic practice where one ends one's life by burying oneself or immersing oneself in water.

Kalabhairava. One who has mastery over time; a fierce form of Shiva.

kapalabhati. A Yogic practice that involves forceful exhalation.

kavacha. A shield.

kinnara. A kind of a celestial being.

Klesha Nashana Kriya. A cleansing ritual performed at the Isha Yoga Center to cleanse the aura.

kriya. Literally, "act, rite"; refers to a certain class of Yogic practices, inward action as opposed to karma, external action.

kumbhaka sadhana. Breath retention during Yogic practice, especially in the practice of pranayama.

Kurukshetra. An extensive plain near Delhi, scene of the great war between the Kauravas and the Pandavas, as it took place in the Mahabharata.

Linga Bhairavi. A spiritual energy form for the well-being of the family, available at the Isha Yoga Center.

maha. An adjective or prefix meaning "great," "mighty," "powerful," "lofty," "noble."

Mahabharata. A historic Indian epic that took place almost five thousand years ago.

Mahamrutyunjaya Mantra. A sacred Sanskrit chant that is supposed to ward off death.

Mahasamadhi. The highest form of equanimity that entails the complete dissolution or neutralization of the personal in the universal, whereby all traits of individual nature are transcended. Also known as Nirvana and Mahaparinirvana in other Eastern spiritual traditions.

Manipura Chakra. One of the seven major chakras, located a little below the navel. All the energy pathways of the body meet at this chakra.

Manomaya Kosha. One of the five sheaths of the human body, related to the mental dimension.

maya. Delusion, the veil of illusion which conceals one's true nature or conceals reality. It is used in contrast with the absolute reality.

metti. Tamil word for toe ring worn by married women in India.

moksha: Liberation from the cycle of birth and death; freedom from all worldly bonds.

mrutyu. Sanskrit for "death."

Mrutyunjaya. Victory over death.

mukti. Release, Liberation, the final absolution of the Self from the chain of death and rebirth. The highest goal of all spiritual seekers.

Muladhara Chakra. Located at the perineum, the Muladhara is the foundation of the energy body.

Mumtaz. One of the wives of the medieval Indian emperor Shah Jahan, in whose memory the famous Taj Mahal was built.

naga. Literally, "serpent"; a symbol of the Kundalini coiled at the base of the spine; one of the secondary types of life forces (prana).

namaskaram. Traditional southern Indian greeting.

nirmanakaya. Literally, "one who has manufactured one's body"; refers to accomplished yogis who materialize and dematerialize at will.

nirvikalpa. Literally, "without qualities." A type of samadhi, or equanimity, beyond all qualities or attributes, where a person's contact with their body is minimal.

ojas. Subtle energy.

Palani. A southern Indian town that is famous for its Murugan temple.

Pancha Vayus. The five vital energies or pranas in the body (which include Apana Vayu, Prana Vayu, Samana Vayu, Udana Vayu, and Vyana Vayu).

Pandavas. The protagonists of the Mahabharata.

pisachi. A kind of disembodied being.

prana. The fundamental life force.

Pranamaya Kosha. One of the five sheaths of the human body.

Prana Vayu. One of the five pranas of the body.

Prarabdha Karma. The portion of karma that is allocated for a particular lifetime.

preta. A kind of ghost or being.

Rudraksha. Sacred beads; the seeds of a tree (*Elaeocarpus ganitrus roxb*) found mostly in the Himalayan region. According to the legend, a tear from Lord Shiva fell to the Earth and from it grew the Rudraksha tree. Known to have many medicinal and transcendental qualities, a Rudraksha mala, a string of sacred beads, is one of the few possessions of an Indian spiritual seeker.

runa. Literally, "debt"; in this context, it refers to the debt of relationship.

runanubandha. The bondage caused or the debt accrued due to the debt of relationships.

sadhaka. A spiritual seeker who has undertaken spiritual disciplines, usually under the guidance of a Master.

sadhana. Literally, "tool" or "device." Spiritual practices which are used as a means to Self-Realization.

Sahasrara Chakra. The chakra, or energy center, of the human system located at the fontanelle, or crown, of the head.

Sallekhana/Santara. An ancient Jain practice of progressively fasting to death.

samadhi. Deep state of equanimity, one of the eight limbs of Yoga. Greatly celebrated in the Indian spiritual tradition, the experience of samadhi is therapeutic and deeply transformative in nature.

Samat Prana/Samana Vayu. One of the five pranas of the body.

samskara. Ritual, in the general sense. Denotes rites such as the birth ceremony, tonsuring, marriage, and cremation. In Yoga, it stands for the indelible imprints left in the subconscious by daily experiences.

Samyama. A confluence of the states of dharana, dhyana, and samadhi. Here it refers to the eight-day meditation program conducted by Sadhguru, where one is transported into explosive states of meditativeness. This program offers the possibility of shedding lifetimes of karma and experiencing deep states of meditativeness and samadhi.

Sanchita Karma. The whole volume of karma of a person.

sanyasa. On the path of spirituality, a stage of life as per the Varnashrama Dharma. The withdrawal from the world in search of Self-Realization.

satsang. Literally, "in communion with Truth"; a congregation of seekers.

savikalpa. Literally, "with qualities." Used to refer to a type of samadhi, or equanimity, with qualities or attributes.

Shakti Chalana. A kind of Yogic practice taught at the Isha Yoga Center.

Shambhavi Mahamudra. A Yogic practice taught by Sadhguru.

sharira. Literally, "body."

Shivayogi. A name borne by Sadhguru in two of his previous lifetimes.

Shoonya. Literally, "emptiness." An effortless process of conscious non-doing, Shoonya meditation is an extremely powerful and unique form of meditation taught by Sadhguru in a "live form" at the Isha Yoga programs.

shraadha. Annual death ritual of the Hindus for one's ancestors.

Su-mrutyu. Timely death.

Swadhishthana Chakra. Literally, "abode of the Self"; one of the seven major chakras, situated just above the genitals.

Tantra. Literally, "technology"; in this context it refers to the technology of spiritual transformation. Commonly refers to a spiritual path in India.

tantrik. A practitioner of Tantra.

Tapovan. A place above Gomukh, on the banks of the Gangotri, the glacial origin of the Ganga River.

Taraka mantra. A secret and powerful mantra for Liberation that is whispered by Kalabhairava into the ears of those who die in Kashi.

Teerthakund. A consecrated body of water at the Isha Yoga Center.

Udana Vayu. One of the five pranas of the body.

Vamachara. Literally, "left-hand path"; a path of Tantra that involves socially unconventional methods for spiritual growth.

Vanaprastha Ashrama. One of the stages of life according to the Varnashrama Dharma. People usually live away from their families during this stage, mostly in the forests.

Varnashrama Dharma. The traditional Hindu system that outlines four stages of life (ashramas) and four social classes (varnas), providing guidelines for spiritual and social duties.

vasanas. Tendencies or inclinations; subliminal traits in a human being, the residue of desires and actions.

Veda. Refers to the oldest portion of the Hindu scriptures.

Velliangiri Mountains. The sacred mountain ranges in Tamil Nadu, in the foothills of which the Isha Yoga Center is located.

vibhuti. Sacred ash that is made by burning cow dung; this is usually consecrated with the energies of a powerful deity before it is used. It is often smeared over certain parts of the body, especially the forehead and over the chakras.

vignana. Science or special knowledge, in traditional terms.

Vignanamaya Kosha. One of the five sheaths of the human body.

vishesh. Special or extraordinary.

Vishuddhi Chakra. One of the seven major chakras, Vishuddhi is the center of power and vision. It is located at the pit of the throat.

Vyana Vayu. One of the five pranas of the body.

yaksha. Celestial disembodied beings who are believed to inhabit secluded places.

yamadoota. Agents of Yama, the Hindu God of death.

Yantra. Literally, a "tool" or a "device"; in this context it refers to an energy form, which can be designed and consecrated in different ways to bring prosperity and well-being to one's life.

yatana. Suffering.

yatra. Travel, journey, pilgrimage.

Yudhishthira. The eldest of the Pandava princes, known for his virtues.

ABOUT THE AUTHOR

Yogi, mystic, and visionary, **Sadhguru** is a spiritual master with a difference. Absolute clarity of perception places him in a unique space, not only in spiritual matters but in business, environmental, and international affairs, and opens a new door on all that he touches.

Ranked among the fifty most influential people in India, Sadhguru is internationally renowned as a speaker and opinion maker. He has been accorded the Padma Vibhushan, India's highest annual civilian award, conferred for exceptional and distinguished service.

Over the years, Sadhguru has launched large ecological initiatives addressing the urgent need to increase green cover, revitalize rivers, and restore soil health. These initiatives have been recognized globally as game-changers in establishing a blueprint for ecologically sustainable economic development. As part of the Conscious Planet initiative, he has launched the world's largest people's movement: Save Soil, which has so far reached more than 4.1 billion people.

Sadhguru has been a primary speaker at the United Nations General Assembly and several other UN forums. He has also been regularly invited to speak at establishments such as the World Economic Forum, the World Bank, the House of Lords, the University of Oxford, MIT, Google, and Microsoft, to name a few.

With a celebratory engagement with life on all levels, Sadhguru's areas of active involvement encompass fields as diverse as architecture and visual design, poetry and painting, aviation and driving, and sports and music. He is the designer of several unique buildings and consecrated spaces at the Isha Yoga Center, which have received wide attention for their combination of intense sacred power and strikingly innovative aesthetics.

More than three decades ago, Sadhguru established the Isha Foundation, a nonprofit human-service organization, with human well-being as its core commitment. Isha is supported by more than seventeen million volunteers in more than three hundred centers worldwide.

app.sadhguru.org
isha.sadhguru.org
Facebook.com/sadhguru
X: @SadhguruJV
Youtube.com/sadhguru

Isha Foundation

Recognizing the possibility of each person to empower another, Isha Foundation has created a massive movement that is dedicated to address all aspects of human well-being, without subscribing to any particular ideology, religion, or race.

Isha is involved in several path-breaking outreach initiatives: Action for Rural Rejuvenation (ARR) enhances the quality of rural life through healthcare and disease prevention, community revitalization, women's empowerment, the creation of sustainable livelihoods, and Yoga programs. Isha Vidhya empowers rural children with quality education. Project GreenHands (PGH) initiates mass tree planting and creates a culture of care for the environment to keep this planet livable for future generations. Rally for Rivers and Cauvery Calling are campaigns to revitalize the rivers of India, which are in a serious level of depletion, and addresses one of the gravest crises facing our generation.

Isha's unique approach in cultivating human potential has gained worldwide recognition and reflects Isha Foundation's special consultative status with the Economic and Social Council (ECOSOC) of the United Nations.

ABOUT THE AUTHOR

The foundation is headquartered at the Isha Yoga Center, at the base of the Velliangiri Mountains in southern India, and at the Isha Institute of Inner-sciences on the spectacular Cumberland Plateau in central Tennessee, USA.

isha.sadhguru.org
ishaoutreach.org
Facebook.com/ishafoundation
X: @ishafoundation
Youtube.com/ishafoundation

ISHA INSTITUTE OF INNER-SCIENCES

The Isha Institute of Inner-sciences is a breathtaking mountain retreat created to build a foundation of complete well-being. The center offers the essence of Yogic science in its purest form, through classical yoga and meditation classes within powerfully energized spaces such as the Adi Yogi: The Abode of Yoga. Guests journey from around the globe to visit this unique destination to relax, reflect, and reconnect with nature in a tranquil oasis nestled in Tennessee's spectacular Upper Cumberland.

Located one and a half hours from Nashville and only forty-five minutes from Chattanooga, the Institute is open 365 days a year and welcomes visitors from all walks of life.

Learn more at ishausa.org.

ISHA YOGA CENTER

Isha Yoga Center, founded under the aegis of Isha Foundation, is located in the foothills of the Velliangiri Mountains. Envisioned and created by Sadhguru as a powerful *sthana* (a center for inner growth), this popular destination attracts people from all parts of the world. It is unique in its offering of all aspects of Yoga—gnana (knowledge), karma (action), kriya (energy), and bhakti (devotion)—and revives the *Guru-shishya paramparya* (the traditional method of knowledge transfer from Master to disciple).

Isha Yoga Center provides a supportive environment for people to shift to healthier lifestyles, improve interpersonal relationships, seek a higher level of self-fulfillment, and realize their full potential.

The center is located nineteen miles west of Coimbatore, a major industrial city in southern India which is well connected by air, rail, and road. All major national airlines operate regular flights into Coimbatore from Chennai, Delhi, Mumbai, and Bengaluru. Train services are available from all major cities in India. Regular bus and taxi services are also available from Coimbatore to the Center.

Visitors are advised to contact the Yoga Center for availability and reservation of accommodation well in advance, because it is generally heavily booked.

Learn more at isha.sadhguru.org/center/isha-yoga-center-coimbatore.

Dhyanalinga

The Dhyanalinga is a powerful and unique energy form created by Sadhguru from the essence of Yogic sciences. Situated at the Isha Yoga Center, it is the first of its kind to be completed in more than two thousand years. The Dhyanalinga is a meditative space that does not subscribe to any particular faith or belief system; nor does it require any ritual, prayer, or worship.

The Dhyanalinga was consecrated by Sadhguru after three years of an intense process of *prana pratishtha*. Housed within an architecturally striking pillarless dome structure, the Dhyanalinga's energies allow even those unaware of meditation to experience a deep state of meditativeness, revealing the essential nature of life.

A special feature of the Dhyanalinga complex is the Teerthakunds, consecrated subterranean water bodies, energized by *rasalinga*s. A dip in these vibrant pools significantly enhances one's spiritual receptivity and is a good preparation to receive the Grace of the Dhyanalinga. The waters of the Teerthakunds also rejuvenate the body and bring health and well-being.

The Dhyanalinga draws many thousands of people every week, who converge to experience a deep sense of inner peace.

Learn more at dhyanalinga.org.

Linga Bhairavi

Consecrated by Sadhguru, Linga Bhairavi is an exuberant expression of the Divine Feminine—fierce and compassionate at once. Representing the creative and nurturing aspects of the Universe, the Devi allows devotees to go through life effortlessly; all physical aspects of their lives—health, success, and prosperity—will find nourishment. A variety of rituals and offerings are available for one to connect with the Devi's outpouring of Grace.

Learn more at lingabhairavi.org.

Inner Engineering

Inner Engineering, designed by Sadhguru, is offered as an intensive program for personal growth. The program and its environment establish the possibility to explore the higher dimensions of life and offer tools to re-engineer oneself through the inner science of Yoga. Once given the tools to rejuvenate, people can optimize all aspects of health, inner growth, and success. For those seeking professional and personal excellence, this program offers keys to meaningful and fulfilling relationships at work, home, community, and, most important, within oneself.

Inner Engineering can be thought of as a synthesis of holistic sciences to help participants establish an inner foundation and vision for all dimensions of life and find the necessary balance between the challenges of a hectic career and the inner longing for peace and well-being.

The approach is a modern antidote to stress and presents simple but powerful processes from the Yogic science to purify the system and increase health and inner well-being. Program components include guided meditations and transmission of the sacred Shambhavi Mahamudra. When practiced on a regular basis, these tools have the potential to enhance one's experience of life on many levels.

Learn more at isha.sadhguru.org/IEO.

Isha Kriya

Isha Kriya™ is a simple yet potent practice created by Sadhguru, which is drawn from the wisdom of Indian spirituality. The word "kriya" literally means "internal action," while "Isha" refers to that which is the source of creation. The purpose of Isha Kriya is to help an individual get in touch with the source of one's existence, in order to create life according to one's wish and vision.

Provided as a free guided meditation online and within the "Sadhguru" app on iOS and Android, Isha Kriya offers the possibility of experiencing the boundless energy within.

Daily practice of Isha Kriya brings health, dynamism, peace, and well-being. It offers tools to cope with the hectic pace of modern life.

Learn more at ishakriya.com or app.sadhguru.org.

ABOUT THE TYPE

This book was set in Centaur, a typeface designed by the American typographer Bruce Rogers in 1929. Rogers adapted Centaur from a fifteenth-century type of Nicholas Jenson (c. 1420–80) and modified it in 1948 for a cutting by the Monotype Corporation.